MANCHESTER MEDIEVAL LITERATURE AND CULTURE

IN STRANGE COUNTRIES

Manchester University Press

MANCHESTER MEDIEVAL LITERATURE AND CULTURE

The Manchester Medieval Literature and Culture series publishes new research, informed by current critical methodologies, on the literary cultures of medieval Britain (including Anglo-Norman, Anglo-Latin and Celtic writings), including post-medieval engagements with and representations of the Middle Ages (medievalism). 'Literature' is viewed in a broad and inclusive sense, embracing imaginative, historical, political, scientific, dramatic and religious writings. The series offers monographs and essay collections, as well as editions and translations of texts.

Titles Available in the Series

Language and imagination in the Gawain-*poems*
J. J. Anderson

Water and fire: The myth of the Flood in Anglo-Saxon England
Daniel Anlezark

The Parlement of Foulys (by Geoffrey Chaucer)
D. S. Brewer (ed.)

Sanctity and pornography in medieval culture: On the verge
Bill Burgwinkle and Cary Howie

Greenery: Ecocritical readings of late medieval English literature
Gillian Rudd

Forthcoming Titles

A knight's legacy: Mandeville and Mandevillian Lore in Early Modern England
Ladan Niayesh (ed.)

In strange countries

Middle English Literature and its Afterlife

Essays in Memory of J. J. Anderson

EDITED BY DAVID MATTHEWS

Manchester University Press

MANCHESTER AND NEW YORK

distributed exclusively in the USA by Palgrave Macmillan

Copyright © Manchester University Press 2011

While copyright in the volume as a whole is vested in Manchester University
Press, copyright in individual chapters belongs to their respective authors, and no
chapter may be reproduced wholly or in part without the express permission in
writing of both author and publisher.

Published by Manchester University Press
Oxford Road, Manchester M13 9NR, UK
and Room 400, 175 Fifth Avenue, New York, NY 10010, USA
www.manchesteruniversitypress.co.uk

Distributed the United States exclusively by
Palgrave Macmillan, 175 Fifth Avenue, New York,
NY 10010, USA

Distributed in Canada exclusively by
UBC Press, University of British Columbia, 2029 West Mall,
Vancouver, BC, Canada V6T 1Z2

British Library Cataloguing-in-Publication Data
A catalogue record for this book is available from the British Library

Library of Congress Cataloging-in-Publication Data applied for

ISBN   978 0 7190 8450 8 hardback

First published 2011

The publisher has no responsibility for the persistence or accuracy of URLs for
any external or third-party internet websites referred to in this book, and does
not guarantee that any content on such websites is, or will remain, accurate or
appropriate.

Typeset
by Servis Filmsetting Ltd, Stockport, Cheshire
Printed in Great Britain
by the MPG Books Group

Contents

List of illustrations

List of contributors

Dr Rosamund Allen was formerly Reader in Middle English Literature at Queen Mary, University of London.

Dr Anke Bernau is Lecturer in Middle English Literature at the University of Manchester.

Professor Ralph Elliott is Emeritus Fellow in the Research School of Humanities, Australian National University.

Professor Alexandra Johnston is Emeritus Professor, University of Toronto, and founder and director of the Records of Early English Drama project.

Professor Stephen Knight is Distinguished Research Professor at Cardiff University.

Dr David Matthews is Senior Lecturer in Middle English Literature and Culture at the University of Manchester.

Professor Peter Meredith is Emeritus Professor of Medieval Drama at the University of Leeds.

Professor Susan Powell is Professor in Medieval Texts and Culture at the University of Salford.

Dr Gillian Rudd is Senior Lecturer in English at the University of Liverpool.

Alan Shelston was formerly Senior Lecturer in English at the University of Manchester.

Dr Kalpen Trivedi teaches in the Department of English at the University of Georgia and is also Director of UGA's Oxford Study-Abroad Programs.

Carole Weinberg was formerly Senior Lecturer in Medieval English at the University of Manchester.

Preface

The Manchester Medieval Literature and Culture series was founded in 2005 by J. J. Anderson and Gail Ashton, then both teaching Middle English literature at the University of Manchester. The series initially bore the title 'Manchester Medieval Literature'; when we inherited it in 2007, we broadened the brief slightly, adding the 'Culture' term. As successors to John and Gail in the teaching of Middle English at Manchester, we were of course delighted to continue the series they began. But at the same time, this inheritance came with sadness, because it will always bring to mind John's untimely death in May 2007. When we began work on the series later in the same year, it was a simple matter to resolve, as our first publishing decision, that a volume should be published to mark John's work, his contribution to medieval studies, and his nearly forty years of teaching Middle English in Manchester. It is an honour to present that book and to thank all those who have made it possible.

We are grateful to all the contributors, who have remained patient through the evolutions this volume has undergone. Our thanks go to them all, but especially to Peter Meredith and Alan Shelston, who have helped with many aspects of the book's preparation. There are several other scholars who, for various reasons, were not able to contribute, and others still who graciously stepped aside when the volume threatened to grow unfeasibly large: we are very happy to acknowledge Chris Abbott, Gail Ashton, Ruth Evans, Chris McCully, Brian Merrilees, Raluca Radulescu, Diane Speed, Louise Sylvester, Meg Twycross and Ron Waldron. Matthew Frost and Kim Walker have helped us shepherd the volume through to its final form, and we are grateful for all their work on the Manchester Medieval Literature and Culture series. Alison Kelly edited the book meticulously. Finally, we thank Joy

Anderson for entrusting us with the project: we hope it does justice to John's memory.

David Matthews
Anke Bernau
Manchester, March 2010

Abbreviations

BL	British Library
BN	Bibliothèque Nationale de France
CUL	Cambridge University Library
EETS	Early English Text Society
o.s.	old series
REED	Records of Early English Drama
s.s.	supplementary series

Introduction

David Matthews and Anke Bernau

In the late fourteenth-century romance *Sir Gawain and the Green Knight*, the knight embarks on a quest which, even as it fulfils romance norms, veers away from the norm in an unexpected way. Instead of unfolding in a vague wilderness or a generic forest, Gawain's quest for the Green Chapel and its custodian the Green Knight famously takes on geographic specificity as the knight rides along the coast of North Wales, approaching the northwest of England. In most romances at the equivalent point, knights errant simply wander, troubled about little more than the character of the hostile knight who might be found in the next clearing. But Gawain – while batting aside wolves, dragons and wild men – has much on his mind: he has an arrangement to be kept just after Christmas, and worries about where he will hear mass on the feast day. It is at this point that the poet tells us of the winter landscape against which Gawain battles, far more memorably than in any of his duels against mythical creatures. About these, the poet laconically says, 'Hit were to tore for to telle of the tenthe dole' [it would be too hard to tell a tenth of it]. It is at this point too that Gawain's progress is described in a pair of wonderful lines: 'Mony klyf he overclambe in contrayes straunge, / Fer floten fremedly fro his frendes he rydes'. 'Many cliffs he climbed over in strange countries; far removed from his friends', as John Anderson translates the next line, 'he rides as a stranger'.[1]

Most romances simply accept that knights wander in foreign lands; this poet actually connects it to Gawain's state of mind. The adverb *fremedly* cannot be rendered in modern English with the economy of the original: John Anderson is forced to gloss 'as a stranger', but *strangerly*, if it were a word, might do. The word might modify, as John takes it to do, the verb *rydes*, so that Gawain's is a form of *strangerly* motion, an alienated travel. But the alliteration also links the word to the preceding participle, *floten*, so that this condition of strangerly wandering far from friends becomes a kind of floating; Gawain has floated away from his friends and what he knows, so that this quest, despite its geographic precision, does finally partake of the usual vagueness of knight errancy. The *poet* might know the terrain well, but Gawain himself is, after all, drifting.

By invoking these strange lands in which Gawain goes, *fremedly*, the poet sets up a strangeness or otherness *within* the otherness that is the world of romance. That otherness is usually something we as readers experience, but it is not always found equally remarkable by the characters of romance. A later romancer, Thomas Malory, constantly reminds us of the marvels and wonders encountered in Arthur's days. When people became aware of the sword in the stone, for example, they 'merveilled'.[2] Nevertheless, despite a constant stress on wonders and marvels in this telling, knights remain fairly phlegmatic in the face of them. For them, the appearance of grotesque creatures, or enemies in green, black, or red, seems to be not particularly surprising. In *Sir Gawain and the Green Knight*, however, the hero registers strangeness. In fact he never does grasp the essentials of quest, of errancy. In an unknightly fashion he is obsessed with street directions, always asking those he meets where he might locate the Green Chapel, only to find that 'al nykked hym wyth nay, that never in her lyve / Thay seye never no segge that was of suche hwes / of grene' [they all said to him no, that never in their lives had they seen such a man, of such green hues] (706–8). Gawain is like a character experiencing a romance for the first time – much as Arthur's courtiers themselves, at the outset of the narrative, seemed to have little idea of how to respond to the Green Knight.

We introduce this book with these passages because they represent for us one of the qualities of Middle English literature: its strangeness, and a preoccupation with strangeness which occasionally, as in *Sir Gawain*, becomes self-conscious. We both grew up far from Britain and hence our first encounters with *Sir Gawain* were doubly estranging. It is difficult to convey, for example, the powerful impact of a first reading of the poem in Australia in the 1970s (in Brian Stone's Penguin Classics translation, first published in 1959). It was, of course, simply strange, unlike anything else. It has taken years to work out the ways in which this was not simply a product of temporal distance – what Paul Zumthor calls 'l'éloignement du moyen âge, la distance irrécupérable qui nous en sépare'.[3] It is, in addition, something encoded in the poem itself.

Given the poem's dialect, it is not fanciful to imagine that such strangeness would also have been apparent to any southern reader in the late fourteenth century. Gawain, in this regard, is a figure for that reader, adrift in a landscape he never fully comprehends. This may be among the reasons that the poem had no impact in its own time.

John Anderson, too, encountered the poems of British Library MS Cotton Nero A.x on the other side of the world, as far from its circumstances of production as could be imagined, in New Zealand in the 1960s. Unlike us – even though we have taught and often read the poems – John made them a lifelong concern. His collaborative edition, with A. C. Cawley, of *Sir Gawain* and the other three poems of the manuscript, was originally published in 1976 in the Everyman's Library series. It reappeared, under John's sole editorship, in 1996, with glosses extensively augmented, making this the best version of the poems, short of translation, in which to experience the poet's original words. Appropriately, the Anderson edition always fulfilled the original ambition of Everyman's Library, by keeping a classic available and in print and reaching beyond the purely scholarly audience. In updating his editions, John was enacting the truth about these poems – *Sir Gawain* and *Pearl* above all – that they are poems one always returns to: in teaching, in reading and in research. This return is both intellectual and affective. John's last, major work is the product of precisely such engagement, constant return to the poems: *Language and imagination in the* Gawain-*poems* (2005) represented decades of reflection on the poems and their unknown author.[4] He read them closely in a way that, perhaps, only someone who had edited and re-edited them could do.

John's work ranged, nevertheless, far beyond the poems of this manuscript. He had a deep interest in drama in Middle English and in his later years at the University of Manchester he taught a course on Arthurian literature, medieval and modern, to excellent effect. While it seemed appropriate, consequently, that this volume commemorating him should also be diverse, we like to think that he, too, might have begun by returning to Gawain when looking back over a career, and might have felt, with us, that powerful sense that he had 'floten fremedly'.

But not, it must be added, 'Fer . . . fro his frendes'. One of the joyful things about working on this volume has been talking with scholars we have never met, who knew John and have contributed as his *frendes*, in a spirit of what is elsewhere in the poem called 'fraunchyse and felawschyp' [liberality and fellowship] (652). There is in this volume a substantial amount of work on the *Gawain*-poet. Gillian Rudd, whose ecocritical reading of Middle English literature, *Greenery*, was one of the early publications of the Manchester Medieval Literature and Culture series, turns her attention back to the *Gawain*-poet in her essay here, 'The Green Knight's balancing act'.[5] Rudd begins with the well-known observation that the Green Knight is a kind of nature figure. But as she suggests, the Knight is 'both an obvious and an uneasy figure or figuration of nature'. Beginning with an observation about the Green Knight's horsemanship as he enters Arthur's hall with both hands full and hence no reins in use, she suggests that 'the knight on his charger, stationary in the king's hall, is a tableau of balance apt for midwinter as one year turns into the next'. The holly and the axe he carries suggest balance; so too does the description of him as 'half etayn in erde'. Rudd teases out the implications of this last phrase, before going on to scrutinise afresh the tendency of readers to assume a static balance in the portrait of the Green Knight, and arguing for another sense of balance, that which implies restless movement, as one principle constantly outweighs another, before being outweighed in its turn. Balance, she suggests in her subtle re-reading, 'becomes something to be striven for constantly, rather than a pose that once achieved can be held'.

The *Gawain*-poet necessarily takes on his other guise as the *Pearl*-poet in Sue Powell's essay. Powell sets aside the typical preoccupation in discussions of *Pearl* with the relations between the Dreamer and the Maiden, in order to look instead at relations between the Pearl-maiden and Christ, the Pearl-maiden and the Virgin Mary, and Christ and Mary. Her reconsideration of the marriage of the Maiden to the Lamb ('crucial to her perception of herself and to the Dreamer's perception of her'), and her argument for connections between the Maiden and the Virgin, leads her to consideration of a short lyric found in a sermon in John Mirk's *Festial*. Paying tribute to John Anderson the editor, Powell presents a new edition of this lyric in an appendix to her essay.

Stephen Knight, Carole Weinberg and Rosamund Allen pursue the Arthurian theme. Knight charts the trajectories of the medieval figures Robin Hood and King Arthur. It begins as a perverse project; the two figures seem outwardly scarcely reconcilable, one an outlaw, the other a king, one contesting false authority, the other representing true authority, albeit in crisis. They come together in some of the less well-known nineteenth-century Arthurian texts, and a lightly disguised Robin is enlisted as tutor to the young Arthur in T. H. White's *The Sword in the Stone*. Knight points, however, to the late medieval tradition in which Arthur appears in his guise as do-nothing king, and sees a connection with Robin in his role as presiding 'Summer Lord' rather than active hero, or with Robin in the ballads in which he meets his match in fights. Hence, although in their origins they seem entirely different figures, as Knight finds in a range of materials, there are surprising links between the heroes as they evolve through texts and genres.

In these explorations, Knight ranges far beyond the Middle Ages, in the productive field of post-medieval Arthurian and Robin Hood materials. Likewise Rosamund Allen contrasts a medieval text with its later reinvention, looking at the treatment of violence in Laȝamon's *Brut* and Tennyson's *Idylls of the King*. While Tennyson was of course largely reliant on Malory as his source, he knew Laȝamon's work, in the monumental edition of 1847 published by Frederic Madden. Tennyson, describing how 'the savage beast within man, tamed under Arthur's early rule, re-emerges to precipitate the downfall of a society already made vulnerable by moral delinquency', has a problem: how 'to accommodate a hero renowned for winning battles' with an imperative to tame the beast of violence. 'How can a morally perfect leader be simultaneously a hero in bloody battle?' As a response, Tennyson distinguishes 'between the carnage which the legend proclaims as Arthur's achievement' and a 'man of peace'. As Allen argues, this 'matches very closely Laȝamon's own resolution of the way a man who values peace can present war'.

Carole Weinberg too focuses on Laȝamon's great, if under-read poem. While, as she notes, it is uniformly recognised as being directly based on Wace's *Roman de Brut*, Laȝamon's work is twice as long as its source. It was once argued that the English writer had access to a longer version of Wace's poem than that now extant. But as Weinberg suggests, it is possible to make the case for more independent artistry on Laȝamon's part. She builds her own argument by focusing on a single episode – the legendary foundation of Britain by the Trojan Brutus – and finds that Brutus is set up as a deliberate parallel to the later king, Arthur. Unlike his predecessors, while Laȝamon is capable of criticising individual British kings, he issues no blanket condemnations of the Britons. In a way quite different from that of Wace, or Geoffrey of Monmouth (whose work Laȝamon might have known), in his poem 'The over-arching design of God's will is played out at the human level by a secular historiography in which, at the personal and political level and over time, differing communities compete for dominion'.

Alexandra Johnston begins with Nicholas Love's translation of the *Meditationes Vitae Christi*, and Love's description of his intentions for his audience. Literature on the Passion, in its various forms, responds to 'Love's exhortation to experience the agony of the passion of Christ as he experienced it'. The way in which drama does this is unique, because of its public existence: 'the plays force the audience to be part of the Passion event'. Drawing in part on her direct experience of staging such works as the *N-Town Passion*, Johnston shows how the plays share many of the characteristics of meditation texts in making viewers 'þer present' at the Passion. She then examines in more detail the presentation of the Virgin in the Passion sequence of the *York Plays*, and the *N-Town Passion*, before concluding that were it not for their role as meditation texts, in line with the proposals of Nicholas Love, many of the plays would not have survived the Middle Ages.

Johnston's reading of the plays could be regarded as yet a further investigation into what is now well known as vernacular theology. Similarly preoccupied with what has been, in recent work on Middle English, one of its most fruitful areas, Kalpen Trivedi re-examines relations between orthodox and heterodox texts, looking at manuscripts of the late fourteenth-century *Pore Caitif*. This text has been regarded as orthodox, but infiltrated with Lollard sentiment in some of its manuscript appearances. Trivedi argues, by contrast, that the text came from within the early Lollard movement, or what he dubs the proto-Lollard movement. Re-examining the manuscripts, he notes that many of the copies which represent the supposed later infiltration of heterodoxy are in fact among the earliest manuscripts. 'What one observes', he argues, 'is a highly coherent early group of manuscripts with certain interpolations and omissions that may be *interpreted* as "Lollard" in sympathy'. Trivedi contends that the *Pore Caitif* was initially part of the early Wycliffite movement, produced possibly in Oxford circles, during the 1380s or even earlier. Those parts that have come to be regarded as interpolations were excised from the text's later recensions, as part of an effort to cleanse it of a Lollard appearance.

It is common to find, in recent medieval studies, a concern with so-called 'medievalism', or the Middle Ages after the Middle Ages. Peter Meredith's fascinating study, 'Reading a procession: Bishop Blase at Bradford', testifies to the extraordinary endurance of a medievalist practice long after any true medieval character has been lost. The martyred saint Bishop Blase was thought to have been the inventor of the woolcomb – an instrument with which he was tortured. The obscure saint was celebrated in various parts of the country in the eighteenth century, with a concentration in Yorkshire. Meredith has trawled through a rich archive of late eighteenth- and nineteenth-century material to put together a full account of Bradford's procession in honour of the saint in 1825 – the most fully described, but also the last to take place. He poses key questions about the procession: Was it 'a sop to the workforce' or 'a communal effort?' Was it 'a demonstration of worker coercion, or of worker–management solidarity? A 'calendar custom still in the hands of the people or . . . a "bread-and-circuses" reinvention?'

The volume concludes on a more personal note. Ralph Elliott, whose book *The Gawain Country* was published in 1984, recalls his early engagement with John and his ideas on *Sir Gawain and the Green Knight*.[6] Alan Shelston, a longtime colleague of John's, recalls his contribution to the teaching of English at the University of Manchester. From Gawain to Tennyson's Arthur, Laȝamon's Brutus to Bishop Blase, we are confident that for most readers of these essays – even those well versed in Middle English literature – there will be something that is unfamiliar, something that is strange. Relatively few readers will know of the Bishop Blase Procession. At the same time, readings of very familiar texts can still *estrange* them, as with Rudd's ecocritical reading of *Sir Gawain and the Green Knight*.

Late in 2006 we began a reading group in Middle English for students at the University of Manchester. John had retired from full-time teaching but was still working on a part-time basis at the university. He was still very active as a scholar, most particularly on the Manchester Medieval Literature and Culture series, which was inaugurated by *Language and imagination in the* Gawain-*poems*. In the reading group we commenced, classically enough, with Chaucer's *Troilus and Criseyde*. Before too long, however, we returned to *Sir Gawain and the Green Knight*, and began working through it line by line.

John was not a regular attender of the reading group. But we made sure to get him along to one of our sessions, where he was put on the spot about some of his own emendations. We had a conversation about what he might do differently if he were re-editing the poem. For many of the students it was the first time that they had seen editing 'in action' as it were, and glimpsed some of the complexities that manuscript texts present. The students saw that those editorial decisions so conveniently and apparently decisively packaged for them on the page in fact had their own histories, and were subject to reinterpretation and rewriting. Later that day, we hosted the poet Bernard O'Donoghue at an evening seminar where he talked about his new translation of *Sir Gawain*, which replaced Brian Stone's volume in the Penguin Classics series. The possibilities that day, for the teaching of Middle English at Manchester, seemed full and rich.

It is a great sadness that John has not been around to see these hopes fulfilled. The conversation we had about editing was almost our last. We did speak a few weeks later, in order to discuss the future of the Medieval Literature series. John hoped to continue with it, and have some involvement from us; instead, we have inherited the series, not at all on the terms we would have wished. It is an honour, though one we would happily have foregone; it is a pleasure to be able to make this present offering.

Notes

1 *Sir Gawain and the Green Knight*, lines 713–14 in J. J. Anderson, ed., *Sir Gawain and the Green Knight, Pearl, Cleanness, Patience* (London: Everyman, 1996).
2 Eugene Vinaver, ed., *Malory: Works* (London: Oxford University Press, 1966), p. 7.
3 Paul Zumthor, *Essai de poétique médiévale* (Paris: Seuil, 1972), p. 19.
4 John Anderson, *Language and imagination in the* Gawain-*poems* (Manchester: Manchester University Press, 2005).
5 Gillian Rudd, *Greenery: Ecocritical Readings of Late Medieval English Literature* (Manchester: Manchester University Press, 2007).
6 Ralph W. V. Elliott, *The Gawain Country* (Leeds: University of Leeds, 1984).

1

Robin Hood versus King Arthur

Stephen Knight

Robin and Arthur

Teaching and writing about Robin Hood and King Arthur seem mutually exclusive activities: Robin opposes false authority; Arthur represents true authority in crisis. Yet their origins and careers seem parallel, whether in medieval literature or recent medievalism. My own involvement with both was co-temporaneous. In the medieval options at the University of Sydney in the 1960s we naturally deferred to John Anderson on the *Gawain*-poet and, seeking other material, I worked on Malory and the ballads, in which Arthur and Robin were both intriguing and distinct.

There have been some rapprochements. In the ballad 'Rose the Red and White Lily', recorded in the late eighteenth century, the inventive Mrs Brown of Falkland created two brothers called Robin and Arthur, but while the former does become an outlaw, the latter only rises at court to the rank of nobleman, never king.[1] There is another near miss in Edgar Quinet's *Merlin l'Enchanteur* (1860) where on a visit to England, the mage judges Robin, like the other English, to be a mercantilist boor and excludes him from the project to restore Arthur's Franco-Breton glory. When both do appear, it tends to be in parallel: they are two of the British heroes in Clemence Dane's series of seven patriotic radio plays *The Saviours* (1942), in which Robin Hood is 'The May King' and Arthur is 'The Hope of Britain'. They are present in different though overlapping time-warps in Robert Holdstock's Buchanesque historic fantasy *Mythago Wood* (1984) and in much the same spirit, but more comically, Thomas Love Peacock has Robin join Arthur and others in the burlesque 1817 poem *The Round Table*. Unusually, T. H. White makes the two meet with some respect, including for each other, when Robin (here playfully surnamed Wood) helps educate the young Arthur in *The Sword in the Stone* (1938), to be the first book of *The Once and Future King* (1958) – but the point is that Arthur is learning in an unusual context.

Across the otherwise consistent separation of Robin and Arthur there can still be contacts of a kind: the outlaw can meet a king, if not King Arthur. In those classic and influential texts the *Gest of Robin Hood* of about 1500 and Walter Scott's *Ivanhoe* of Christmas 1819, Robin and a king respect each other's separate identity as commanders in alternative domains. In both cases Robin clarifies his own organic and communal values against those of feudal authority, and in both cases he escapes the world of royal power, in the *Gest* back to the forest for twenty-two years, in *Ivanhoe* to the cultural field of 'black-letter garlands'.[2] It is as if neither author wants to press home the possibility of a political conflict between the outlaw and the king; each withdraws to see them as unrelated opposites.

But not all outlaw–king encounters are so euphemised. Christopher Hill has written on the use of Robin Hood as a parliamentary symbol in the Civil War,[3] and that is strongly confirmed in *Robin Hood and His Crew of Souldiers*, a short play produced on the day of Charles II's coronation in Nottingham, where his father had first raised his standard. The only action is when Robin and his men humbly, and without any resistance, swear an unquestioning allegiance to royalty: Robin expresses a subservience to the king found nowhere else in the complex cycle of Robin Hood material that now covers five centuries and more genres.[4] But Robin Hood and the king are not often so much in conflict, especially in the context of Robin's gentrification. There are recurring contacts and overlaps, and there is even, especially in the modern period, a movement towards identity to elide the dynamic politics of the duo.

Outlaw versus king

Originally, Robin never seemed much like Arthur. Like a real outlaw, he has few supporters, lives close to nature, and operates through a highly limited scope of action. The difference is wide between that and the status of Arthur, the glorious leader of a huge and amazing retinue, capable of facing the most extraordinary threats, ranging from giants and huge beasts to the emperor of Rome and miscellaneous maddened kings. They are culturally as distant: where Arthur is always a figure of splendour and hyper-sophisticated chivalry, Robin enjoys birdsong, ale and venison, banter with his associates and a decent fight with a stranger.

Weapons used, means of transport, familial and social connections: these are prime ways of identifying the nature of a hero, past and indeed present. Arthur from the start has a range of named weapons and a horse to transport him. Robin Hood walks, and famously uses a longbow, the archetypal infantry weapon. Arthur is nobly born: a chief among princes in the early Welsh material but from the early twelfth century on, always a king and a son of a king, however bizarre his descent. Robin Hood has no genealogy until the processes of gentrification provided one. In the early ballads he is just there on the page, without past or family, and socially speaking he is a yeoman, a term which, multiple as its meanings can be from tied servant to ascendant landowner, essentially means of non-aristocratic family.[5] This Robin typifies Eric Hobsbawm's figure of the social bandit, a hero, real or mythical, representing the dissent of the dispossessed classes against supervening authority.[6]

Genre elaborates these differences. Arthur is generically more grandiose. First found among elaborated Welsh folklore important enough to be preserved in writing, he is parallel to pre-Christian Celtic gods and major figures of Britannic lore in the stylistically spectacular Welsh of *Culhwch ac Olwen*. He is elevated as a major war-leader and made the star of the British past by Geoffrey of Monmouth in highly persuasive twelfth-century-renaissance Latin rhetorical history – and so on into elegant courtly French verse romance and the finest German poetry of the Middle Ages, where he is the model of medieval monarchy.

In generic terms Robin's origins are distinctly homespun. The language and metre of the ballads and early songs is simple English, with at best a driving memorability, as in the popular multi-rhyming tag 'Robin Hood in greenwood stood'. The most widespread of the early references are not in fact literary: Robin Hood's Day was celebrated in late May and he was the central figure of village plays and games which harmonised natural and social life. As local hero, Robin evidently featured in simple plays where distant authority was defeated, like the scenes surviving in a Paston family manuscript, and it appears that a literary redaction of this conflict formed the basis for the Robin Hood ballads.[7] These are first recorded in the later fifteenth century but are spoken of a century earlier – the 'rhymes of Robin Hood' mentioned in *Piers Plowman* – and must be the basis for the popularity of the hero as being widely 'commendit gud' in Wyntoun's *Chronicle* of c.1420 or celebrated by 'the foolish people' in Bower's continuation of John of Fordun's *Scotichronicon* of c.1440. This kind of image and reception is a long way from the sonorous grandeur familiar in the case of Arthur, enshrined in English from Laȝamon to Malory.

Outlaw and king

For all this difference, the two traditions can approach each other. Robin fought with a sword more often than is now remembered (bow-and-arrow is not a close-combat weapon), he had about the same distant respect for religion that Arthur exhibits, and the same clashes with monasticism that the Welsh saints' lives report.[8] There are striking similarities between the heroes in terms of action, or rather inaction. Arthur is not a leading warrior knight: deep in the recesses of the French prose narratives, and Malory's transmission of them, it is not uncommon to find Arthur defeated in knightly jousts. True, in the earliest stories of Celtic provenance he can slay a witch who has defeated his champions and kill a giant who terrorises all others, and his courage as a leader in battle is recurrent, but Arthur throughout the romances does not do much; he is a great delegator of heroic action, named by the French a *roi fainéant*.

Robin Hood follows, in a simpler social and generic world, a similar pattern. At the Whitsuntide play-games, Robin's role was supervisory. He sat in his bower and watched the events; later in the day he presided over a 'Robin Hood ale', and it is not surprising that folklorists have seen him as in this context a version of 'The Summer Lord'.[9] The play of about 1475 found in the Paston papers shows Robin being imprisoned, and this is the initiating event of the earliest recorded ballad, 'Robin Hood and the Monk'. In the second, 'Robin Hood and the Potter', Robin at best achieves a draw in a fight with the brawny potter and the story then relates Robin's outwitting, rather than physical defeat, of the sheriff. Remarkably like Arthur's unstigmatised failures in jousting are the events of the most popular archetype of the outlaw broadside ballad, usually described as 'Robin Hood meets his match'. Strolling through the forest alone, Robin meets and fights some ordinary fellow – tinker, tanner, pinder, ranger, shepherd, and so on. Robin never wins: he calls a halt and makes friends with the former enemy who in many cases agrees to join his band. 'Robin Hood and Little John', though a fairly late ballad, has in film become the most famous of these episodes.

Like Arthur, Robin's forte is leadership not heroism. But as with the inactive but honorific Arthur, it is not clear just what his leadership skills are. He is at first offensive to Little John in 'Robin Hood and the Monk', and elsewhere there are traces of disagreement from his outlaws. He does outwit the sheriff on several occasions, but Robin's strategy in general seems, in the early materials, to be to rely on good fortune and support, sometimes summoned by his horn. The challenge to Robin's leadership in 'Robin Hood and the Monk' is itself paralleled in the initial dissent about Arthur's kingship, and in both cases the hero's authority is established through an affirmation of his right to rule and an active enactment of this right. There are clear relations between Robin and Arthur in terms of leadership and as clear a difference between them and the physically active heroes, notably Little John and Lancelot.

In terms of gender, the heroes' relationships have a good deal of overlap. Both Robin and Arthur operate in a homosocial world of male values and implicitly eroticised male friendship, and both traditions seem open to queer readings, though these have yet hardly been developed, especially in the case of Robin Hood.[10] Robin as a social bandit is without a female to relate to apart from the maternal role of his favourite religious figure, St Mary (thinking on her rescues him in 'Robin Hood and Guy of Gisborne'). This tutelary supervision by a quasi-maternal female may also be realised symbolically in the ambient forest and may return in the undersexualised form of Marian when, as a lord, Robin acquires a partner. They are never a romance, nor even a family; in Piers Egan's well-known novel *Robin Hood and Little John, or The Merry Men of Sherwood Forest* (1840) they are married and even have a baby, but the child dies and Marian spends most of the action with her relatives away from the forest.[11] In fact, having arrived as a gentrified appurtenance, Marian does very little in the plot – in part because Lord Robin does very little either: the rescues and robberies supervised by the bold yeoman are not part of lordly behaviour.

Guinevere's resemblance to Marian is marked: she also arrives as an appurtenance, queen to Arthur's king, and even the apparently agency-bestowing affair with Lancelot is a plot borrowed from the Tristan and Iseult story, not intrinsic to the Arthur material. In narrative terms both heroines are largely passive: very Marianesque is the fact that in Malory Guinevere is converted to Christian perfection only in reported form, while all the leading males enjoy moral agony on stage.

The possibility of plot-based convergence between the two figures is evident early. The first substantial Robin Hood text, the *Gest of Robin Hood*, which has continuing popularity in print throughout the sixteenth century, shows a clear move towards the world of nobility. In the opening sequence, unlike in the early ballads, Robin is represented as the definite leader of a band of men who take orders and advice from him; when he sends them off to find a guest so that he can enjoy his dinner, there is a clear link to the opening of many an Arthurian story. In support of this, the first story of the *Gest* shows Robin restoring the fortunes of an impoverished knight. The sequence is unique: unless later authors are directly copying the *Gest*, the story of the knight, unlike the others in the text, does not recur in the tradition. It is in fact a version of an Arthurian single-hero adventure: a knight comes to court; Arthur is generous; the knight goes off and achieves or re-achieves his high status; he returns in honour and takes a place in the world of the court. This generic raising of the outlaw story is presumably associated with the decision to print a substantial compilation, and an element of gentrification is signalled by the woodcut that heads the *Gest* in the National Library of Scotland version, showing a mounted man carrying a bow.

Most scholars are interested because the cut had already been used by Richard Pynson to illustrate Chaucer's Yeoman and is thriftily redeployed to illustrate Robin. A more critical analysis would note that Robin in fact never routinely rides a horse until the time of film: his social position is firmly non-chivalric, and this curiously persists even when he is gentrified – Anthony Munday's Robin is a pedestrian although an earl and in the hybrid ballad-romance 'Robin Hood and the Prince of Aragon' Robin, Will and John fight the prince's champions on foot.[12] I would argue that the *Gest* woodcut is in fact an illustration of the knight, returning to Robin's forest camp with his gift of bows and arrows for the outlaws after his successful reclaiming of his property from the abbey. But that, like the early privileging of the knight in the story, is only an opening idea or gesture. The initial convergence between outlaw and royalty is not developed through the *Gest*; in fact when Robin meets the king towards the end they are distinctly separate, men of parallel, potentially hostile and certainly not convergent worlds. Robin, like the story, ends with distance restored as he leaves the court for the forest, for the rest of his life.

Lord Robin and royalty

If the *Gest* only gestures at a rapprochement between outlaw and king, the full gentrification of the hero is also at first an incomplete

form of convergence. Sketched by the chroniclers John Major
in 1521 and Richard Grafton in 1568–9, canonised by Anthony
Munday in his 1598–9 plays *The Downfall of Robert, Earle of
Huntington* and *The Death of Robert, Earle of Huntington*, this
move in the tradition is a radical appropriation of the outlaw to
conservatism. As a displaced lord still loyal to the true king, Lord
Robert now resists bad authority, and so is fully in support of true
authority and traditional hierarchy. Munday located this gentrified
outlaw in the time of Prince John, and the story of Fulk Fitzwarin,
a real anti-John noble rebel, also an outlaw and forest-dweller, may
well have been the model for the displaced-lord narrative (probably through the lost English poem, which John Leland knew in
the mid sixteenth century[13]).

This gentrified Robin attracted little lasting attention at the
time. Although the Munday plays did well enough to be imitated
in a superior Italianate way by Shakespeare in *As You Like It*, the
highly popular seventeenth-century broadside ballads very rarely
mentioned a title for Robin or the lady that, as a lord, he now possessed. This lack of interest in the ennobled hero presumably arose
from the fact that in his gentry state he abandoned almost all the
exciting adventures of the yeoman bandit: there is only one rescue
in *The Downfall*, and Robin does not play his usual crucial part in
it. Ben Jonson's unfinished *The Sad Shepherd* (*c*.1632) contains
fine poetry and imagines Marian strongly as a forest huntress on
the model of Diana, but Robin has nothing to do – and the title
belongs to the pastoral plot which substantially displaces the
outlaw concept. Operettas with much feebler writing than Jonson's
appeared in the eighteenth century, and historians of the period
were, in their reified conservatism, keen to trace the family of Lord
Robin, but the gentrified move towards the genres in which the
Arthur myth so strongly lived – full-length tragedy, fine poetry,
pastoral imagery, chronicle and aristocratic biography – had at this
stage little real impact on meaning and function in the Robin Hood
tradition. Lord Robin may have been loyal to the king and restored
by him, but they had no closer contact or identity, and gentrifying
Robin Hood just makes him less of an outlaw.

So, in the earlier centuries of the traditions, the king and the
social bandit are usually far apart in politics and in social image,
with only those *Gest* opening moves towards political synthe-
sis. But this situation and the parallel separation of Robin Hood
and King Arthur remains fully true only up to about 1800, after
which an increasing degree of convergence between the two is

seen. During the time of revolutions, political, industrial, literary-romantic, both the outlaw and the king undergo major reworkings, and the effect of this is to make them a good deal more alike in their operations and their significances.

Modernising Robin Hood

Joseph Ritson was not only a profound archival scholar and a serious radical – at once Jacobin, vegetarian and spelling reformer – he also was also in substantial ways responsible for the reconfiguration of Robin Hood in the nineteenth century, and so the present day. His frequently reprinted anthology of 1795 made the ballads very widely known but had a crucial further effect.[14] In his lengthy introduction Ritson provided a full and scholarly compilation of all the known quasi-biographical references and, even though he praised Robin's resistance to tyranny and 'titled ruffians',[15] he also accepted, and asserted, that this active radical outlaw was a lord. Although Ritson did not actually merge the figure of Earl Robin with the energy of the social bandit stories, he juxtaposed them, and succeeding writers were to condense the two discourses of the good outlaw, both yeoman and lord.

This did not happen at once. In *Ivanhoe* Scott deliberately avoided making Robin a displaced lord – that role went to Ivanhoe himself – and the outlaw, here known only as Locksley as if to reduce his impact, is a tough illiterate bandit who fades finally from the text. Scott's conservatism seems to have restrained his fascination with a rough-hewn hero, even more than it did with Rob Roy.[16] John Keats and Leigh Hunt, on the other hand, approved of the liberal, reformist element which they and contemporaries could see in Robin's activities, but in effect they did little more than recirculate and romanticise the yeoman of the ballads Ritson transmitted.[17] The real condensation of the hero's double tradition and the platform for the modern convergence of Robin Hood and King Arthur was Thomas Love Peacock's *Maid Marian* (1822). Very well known through the nineteenth century in its musical comedy form, this retold the lively forest adventures of the yeoman ballads but attributed them to a distinctly aristocratic Robin and Marian. Like Ritson, Peacock was a radical who valued a lord, and his condensation of gentrified status and yeoman vigour is the key to the modern success of the tradition.

Thanks principally to Peacock, a now energetic Lord Robin becomes the default figure of the modern Robin Hood myth. He flourishes in popular novels, in children's television series, in pantomime, in would-be high art like Tennyson's *The Foresters* and the work of the English 'Georgian' poets. There were some dissenters. In 1883 Howard Pyle, a young American illustrator, wrote a Robin Hood text for his splendid illustrations, and he drew on ballads in the yeoman tradition. His Robin may be friendly with the king as in the *Gest*, but he is no lord, and there is no Marian in the stories. This may well demonstrate American republicanism; there were also conscious radical moments from Britain, whether just liberal like the 1912 retelling by the American-born Henry Gilbert, in which Robin is simply a 'freeman' but falls in love with an earl's daughter,[18] or firmly Marxist like Geoffrey Trease's children's historical novel of 1934 where Robin participates as a leader in the Peasants' Revolt.[19] This spirit re-emerged, along with magic and romance, in the 1980s British television series *Robin of Sherwood*, in which Michael Praed played a peasant youth leading localised resistance to the Norman oppressors.[20]

But most accepted Peacock's transmission of an active liberal lord supervising a set of heroic actions and opposing those who themselves oppose true order and hierarchy, all this done in the spirit of romanticism, masculinism and nationalism. This figure of Robin Hood is evidently much closer in both narrative structure and ideological meaning to the long-standing image of King Arthur than was either the medieval tough-guy Robin or the enfeebled Lord Huntingdon temporarily dwelling in the forest. The scale is still different: forest not kingdom, ambushes not wars, natural pleasures not cross-generational magic, and in socio-political terms a bourgeois-friendly minor aristocrat rather than a royal personage. But like the romantic isolate, the Gothic heroine, the professional detective or the emergent scientist, Robin Hood the gentleman outlaw is a central image as urban civil society struggles to displace the weight of the aristocratic past.

It is one of modernity's strongest genres, film, which promulgates and develops most fully the socially enhanced but politically diminished figure of the outlaw. We can guess little about the meanings of the extraordinary number of Robin Hood films – seven – made before 1914,[21] but in the first major version, Robin's role is surprisingly close to royalty. The 1922 United Artists silent, starring Douglas Fairbanks, starts with the drawbridge of a huge castle opening: knights, squires, heralds march out and a major tournament occurs, as in so many Arthurian stories. Robin, Earl of Huntingdon, is the star knight at the tournament, filling the role of Sir Lancelot, and is second-in-command of the royal army as it marches off on crusade. The king is played much like Robin's father, or even older brother: the aura of royalty comes as close to Robin in the film as it did internationally to Fairbanks. Though Robin leaves the crusading army, and is even branded as a coward for that, the end of the film restores him to the position of the king's favourite knight – so making Robin's quest for justice for all an attribute of aristocracy, even royalty, rather than the virtuous vigour of the common yeoman of the past (and indeed also of the relatively recent Howard Pyle).

The film is an American appropriation of past European splendour and a parallel American seizure of moral high ground, and this double move pervades later versions. In the 1938 *Adventures of Robin Hood*, starring Errol Flynn, technical brilliance and vigorous playing by the male leads gave credibility to a contemporary message that combined a New Deal moment (the feast in the forest) with international anti-fascism in making the Normans represent the contemporary Sturmabteilung in Germany,[22] and here too Robin is much like a member of the king's family.[23] In the 1991 *Robin Hood: Prince of Thieves*, family drama lies between Robin and his half-brother, but Marian herself has become heir to the throne, hence the sheriff's desire to marry her – and so, by implication, steal Robin's presumptive royalty.[24] The idea of Robin as monarch was strongly implied in the 1963 film *Siege of the Saxons*, in which King Arthur's daughter Katherine wins the crown through the faithful support of a handsome, leather-clad, bow-bearing outlaw named Robert Marshall, whom she then marries. They have substantial help in the last battle from an outlaw band led by a Little John-like figure and the script seems a consciously coded condensation of the heroic traditions of Robin and Arthur: the outlaw has become a kind of popular king.[25]

Modernising Arthur

If Robin today has become elevated, King Arthur has undergone a range of reductive changes. He became popular rather slowly; the idea that he, like Robin, was a figure of new national and centralised British identity (as Stephanie Barczewski argues in the spirit of Linda Colley[26]) does not stand scrutiny. It was British Celts who first found Arthur of present interest, especially the Welsh and Cornish, with separatist instincts,[27] and Robert Southey's full introduction to the 1817 reprint of Malory did not bear much fruit. Ritson's scholarly *Life of King Arthur*, written just before his death in 1803, was not published until 1825,[28] and Edward Bulwer Lytton's verse epic *King Arthur* only came out in 1848. Tennyson's developing interest was stimulated by Robert Hawker, the Cornish patriot, and when he emerges in the 1849 *Idylls of the King* the nineteenth-century English Arthur is both more centrally active and more human than before. Tennyson consistently adds scenes where Arthur is active and central like one of his medieval knights, notably in 'The Holy Grail' and 'The Last Tournament', and Guinevere finally sees that the king combined elevated status with real manhood: 'Thou art the highest and most human too'.[29]

Arthur's humanity is a crucial formation of the modern period and dominates the tradition through to the present, as it explores and celebrates the king's moral and personal action, nobly resisting evil – and so operating as does Robin Hood. In *A Connecticut Yankee at the Court of King Arthur* (1889) Mark Twain, having started with Arthur representing past European conservatism, realises his personal qualities when he tours deprived and enslaved England. The Yankee concludes he was 'a good deal more than a king – he was a Man'.[30] In the same spirit, the Arthur of T. H. White's *The Once and Future King*, ending like Twain's hero in a despairing confrontation with modern Armageddon, has the position of a moralised individual groping for a system of law and political practice that will strain might into the service of right. The innovative first book, *The Sword in the Stone*, is the work of an idealist teacher outlining a system of humanist and widely ethicised education (where Arthur meets Robin and Marian) that might enable human subjects to order their own world.

What this means in terms of heroic identity and function is that the modern Arthur, from Ritson's biography on through the decreasingly Christianised moralisations, operates as only a broader-scale version of the gentrified and ethicised Robin Hood. Outlaw and king are not only now on the same side, they are effectively avatars of each other. For Twain and White, Arthur stands against corrupt authority, and does not act simply in the name of true hierarchy: he earns his status on moral grounds. The modern Arthur texts, like the more radical Robin Hood stories, are groping for new sources of political and moral order.

That quest can take many forms. In the substantial genre of thoughtful children's fiction, Arthur can represent a morality that finds its vanishing point in the supernatural, whether Christian as with C. S. Lewis or mystical – often partly Celtic – as with

Alan Garner and Susan Cooper. In the historical fictions, from authors such as John Masefield, Henry Treece, Rosemary Sutcliff and Parke Godwin, Arthur tends to represent an idea of moralised enlightenment, reaching back for its validation to Rome and promising to overcome barbarities past and present. In all of these Arthur is a battling, struggling figure, resisting forces that are judged to be evil. His role has become on a grand scale that of one of the knights of the *roi fainéant* and is distinctly similar to the role of the socially and morally elaborated Robin Hood.

Contemporary heroes

In two other modern forms of discourse, feminism and quasi-historicism, Robin and Arthur have received strikingly similar treatment. The modern feminists' Robin, though sometimes a lord (as in Jennifer Roberson's traumatised Crusade veteran) or a capable fighter (as in Theresa Tomlinson's peasant lad[31]), is enfeebled in person and role, though rarely as much as the effete dress designer Robin of Kensington in *Maid Marian and her Merrie Men*, a farce screened by the BBC in 1988 as children's television. Through reducing Robin, these writers' work closely resembles that of feminist Arthurians like Sharon Newman and Marion Zimmer Bradley, where the emphasis on the leading role of the female figure limits the hero not to a mysogynist enemy (presumably because he still bears positive values) but a character of much-reduced significance who participates with the foregrounded woman in promulgating a double-gendered myth in which Marian stands beside Robin or even takes precedence.

A different form of parity between outlaw and king pervades the endeavours of the archivists and historians who dream yet of finding a real Robin Hood – a quest identical to the hunt for the real King Arthur. Both the new British *Dictionary of National Biography* and an unending series of television programmes recycle the same banalities, indicating that the hunger for reified heroic individualisation is only growing, in spite of the absence of any advances in this alleged field of study.

Film has been much more discriminating between the two myths than has fiction. There have been few real successes among Arthur films and no actor has made a name playing Arthur, or even Lancelot. In the period from the end of the Second World War to 1970 nine Robin Hood films were made by large American and British studios and only two on Arthur. Perhaps this is in part the result of American republican – and democratic – attitudes to royalty. But the traditionally dark end of the Arthur story may be a stronger reason. The films usually lack the tragic conclusion, like *Camelot* (1967), or make it Lancelot's opportunity, as in *First Knight* (1995), where (played by Richard Gere) he succeeds Arthur and marries Guinevere. A similarly positive ending is implicit in the 1953 *Knights of the Round Table*, where Lancelot (Robert Taylor) survives, apparently to rule the kingdom in the light of the grail. *Excalibur* (1981) is rare in playing out the tragic end from Tennyson's *Idylls*; perhaps it is no coincidence that the director is British. Strikingly, none of these films names the king in its title. This is very unlike Robin Hood film titles, and presumably is related to the fact that the name Arthur collocates painfully with 'Morte'. Kevin Harty's details show that only four out of eighty-two Arthur films use the hero's name substantively in the title, while thirty-five out of forty-three Robin Hood films do.[32]

The effect of this avoidance of tragedy is to bring the Arthur story closer to the Robin Hood style of heroic comedy. In *First Knight* Richard Gere's Lancelot is a single adventure hero, a rescuer, a warrior and a trickster, in a distinctly Robin Hood-like mould, and Sean Connery, as the dying Arthur, presides over the final marriage just as he did as Richard I in Costner's *Robin Hood: Prince of Thieves*. Such symbolic filmic convergence between the two heroes and their myths, shadowed in *Siege of the Saxons*, moves towards overt condensation in Antoine Fuqua's 2004 film, *King Arthur*. The film can use Arthur's name in its title because it merely starts his career and ends with him being crowned; there is no trace of tragedy, however distant, and Robin Hood features flourish. Guinevere is played in a liberated spirit by Keira Knightley, formerly Robin Hood's daughter in *Princess of Thieves* (2001), and the official poster showed her in Amazon mode, like Ben Jonson's Marian, aiming an arrow at the world. There are other contacts between the two traditions in this film,[33] but when Ray Winstone plays Sir Bors just like his tough cockney Will Scarlet in *Robin of Sherwood*, overlap between the two heroic traditions becomes startling, even ludicrous, condensation.

Arthur and Robin began as apparent opposites, as the king who represents proper authority under strain from various dangerous forces, including internal strains, and the outlaw who represents spirited resistance to improper authority. But a combination of moralist individualism and liberal banality have made the two formerly antithetical heroes of English narrative grow closer. One size seems to fit all in late capitalist consumerism whether it is T-shirts or heroes, a process that seeks to dissolve politics, history and consumer resistance all at the same time. Both the texts and their receptions have become depoliticised – or rather repoliticised – as no more than a passive reception of the politics of the moralised individual, neither king nor outlaw.

Notes

1 See F. J. Child (ed.), *The English and Scottish Popular Ballads*, 5 vols. (1888; New York: Dover, 1965) vol. 2, pp. 415–24.

2 Walter Scott, *Ivanhoe* (1819; London: Penguin, 1986), p. 475. Scott's complex responses to outlawry and authority are discussed by Helen Phillips, 'Scott and the outlaws', in Helen Phillips (ed.), *Bandit Territories: British Outlaws and their Traditions* (Cardiff: University of Wales Press, 2008), pp. 119–42.

3 Christopher Hill, 'Robin Hood' and 'Robin Hood: Possessive individualism and the Norman Yoke' in *Liberty Against the Law* (London: Lane, 1996), pp.71–82, 83–90.

4 See *Robin Hood and His Crew of Souldiers* (London: Davis, 1661); the play is discussed in Stephen Knight, *Robin Hood: A Complete Study of the English Outlaw* (Oxford: Blackwell, 1994), pp. 143–8.

5 For a recent discussion of the meanings of 'yeoman' in the period, see Richard Almond and A. J. Pollard, 'The yeomanry of Robin Hood and social terminology in the fifteenth century', *Past and Present* 170 (2001), 52–77, and ch. 2, 'Yeomanry', of Pollard's book *Imagining Robin Hood* (Routledge: London, 2004), pp. 29–56.

6 See E. J. Hobsbawm, *Bandits*, 2nd edn (London: Penguin, 1985).

7 The two scenes, or perhaps the one play, are reprinted by R. B. Dobson and J. Taylor in *Rymes of Robin Hood: An Introduction to the English Outlaw* (London: Heinemann, 1976), pp. 203–7 and Stephen Knight and Thomas J. Ohlgren, *Robin Hood and Other Outlaw Tales*, 2nd edn (Kalamazoo: Medieval Institute Publications, 2000), pp. 269–80. For a discussion of the relation between the play-games and the ballads, see Knight, *Robin Hood: A Complete Study*, pp. 112–14.

8 For a discussion of Arthur in the saints' lives, see Brynley F. Roberts, '*Culhwch ac Olwen*, the Triads and the saints' lives', in Rachel Bromwich, A. O. H. Jarman and Brynley F. Roberts (eds.), *The Arthur of the Welsh: The Arthurian Legend in Medieval Welsh Literature* (Cardiff: University of Wales Press, 1991), pp. 73–95, see pp. 82–3.

9 See David Wiles, 'Robin Hood as summer lord: I' and 'Robin Hood

as summer lord: II', in *The Early Plays of Robin Hood* (Cambridge: Brewer, 1981), chs 2 and 3, pp. 7–30.

10 Stuart Kane has explored homosociality in 'Robin Hood and Guy of Gisborne' in 'Horse-play: Robin Hood, Guy of Gisborne, and the neg(oti)ation of the bestial', in Thomas Hahn (ed.), *Robin Hood in Popular Culture: Violence, Transgression and Justice* (Cambridge: Brewer, 2000), pp. 101–10 and Thomas Hahn and Stephen Knight explore the topic more widely in '"Exempt me Sire, I am afeard of women": gendering Robin Hood', in Phillips (ed.), *Bandit Territories*, pp. 24–43.

11 Piers Egan, *Robin Hood and Little John, or The Merry Men of Sherwood Forest* (London: Forster and Hextall, 1840).

12 Child (ed.), *The English and Scottish Popular Ballads*, vol. 3, pp. 147–50.

13 Leland describes the poem as 'an old English boke yn Ryme of the Gestes of Guarin, and his Sunnes', see Glyn Burgess (ed. and trans.), *Two Medieval Outlaws* (Cambridge: Brewer, 1997), pp. 127–8.

14 Joseph Ritson (ed.), *Robin Hood, A Collection of all the Ancient Poems, Songs and Ballads Now Extant Relative to the Celebrated English Outlaw (To Which are Prefixed Anecdotes of his Life)*, 2 vols. (London: Egerton and Johnson, 1795).

15 Ritson (ed.), *Robin Hood*, vol. 1, pp. xi–xii.

16 See the discussion in Phillips, 'Scott and the outlaws'.

17 These formations are discussed in some detail in Knight, *Robin Hood: A Complete Study*, pp. 153–78.

18 Henry Gilbert, *Robin Hood and His Merry Men* (Edinburgh: Jack, 1912), p. 15.

19 Geoffrey Trease, *Bows Against the Barons* (London: Lawrence, 1934).

20 Richard Carpenter, creator, *Robin of Sherwood* (Goldcrest Films International, 1984–6).

21 Kevin J. Harty's *The Reel Middle Ages* (Jefferson, NC: McFarland, 1999) identifies seven films on the Robin Hood tradition made before 1914, three British, four American. Although advertising material survives for some, and the 1912 Éclair *Robin Hood* has been restored by MOMA, there is not yet enough information available to analyse the representation of the tradition in this fascinating context – though the increasing riches of film scholarship may well make this possible in the future.

22 Michael Curtiz and William Keighley, dir., *The Aventures of Robin Hood* (Warner Bros., 1938). On the New Deal connection, see Ina Rae Hark, 'The visual politics of *The Adventures of Robin Hood*', *Journal of Popular Fiction* 5 (1976), 3–17.

23 Ernest Callenbach reads the films as realising an Oedipal conflict of son and father in 'Comparative anatomy of folk-myth films: Robin Hood and Antonio das Mortes', *Film Quarterly* 23 (1969–70), 42–7.

24 Kevin Reynolds, dir., *Robin Hood: Prince of Thieves* (Warner Bros., 1991). This theme of royal propinquity recurs in Disney's feebly feminist *Princess of Thieves* (2001) where Robin's daughter loves the imaginary future King Philip, but agrees just to be his mistress. In the Millennium special version of the British television series *Blackadder*, the dubious hero finally ascends to the throne and marries Maid Marian, in the hyper-real, hyper-royal shape of the supermodel Kate Moss.

25 Nathan Juran, dir., *Siege of the Saxons* (Ameran Films, 1963). It is presumably chance that the outlaw's name is very like that of Roger Marshall, who was in trouble in 1498 for organising a Robin Hood riot. The details are described by Dobson and Taylor, *Rymes of Robin Hood*, p. 4; the Marshall tradition was apparently not public in the early 1960s when the film was made.

26 Stephanie Barczewski, *Myth and National Identity in Nineteenth Century Britain: The Myths of King Arthur and Robin Hood* (Oxford: Oxford University Press, 2000).

27 See Rob Gossedge and Stephen Knight, 'The Arthur of the sixteenth to nineteenth centuries', in Elizabeth Archibald and Ad Putter (eds.), *The Cambridge Companion to Arthurian Literature* (Cambridge: Cambridge University Press, 2009), pp. 103–19.

28 *The Byrth, Lyf and Actes of Kyng Arthur. . .* with an intro. by Robert Southey, 2 vols. (London, 1817); Joseph Ritson, *The Life of King Arthur* (London: Payne and Foss, 1825).

29 Tennyson, *Idylls*, 'Guinevere', line 644, *The Poems of Tennyson*, ed C. B. Ricks (London: Longman, 1972), p. 1741.

30 Mark Twain, *The Adventures of a Connecticut Yankee at the Court of King Arthur* (1889; London: Penguin, 1971), p. 326; for the illustration see p. 332.

31 Jennifer Roberson, *Lady of the Forest* (New York: Kensington, 1992); Theresa Tomlinson, *The Forestwife* (London: McRae, 1993).

32 I regard the use of the king's name in the many films of *A Connecticut Yankee at King Arthur's Court* as non-substantive. For details on Arthur see Kevin J. Harty, 'A complete Arthurian filmography and selective bibliography', in Harty (ed.), *King Arthur on Film: New Essays on Arthurian Cinema* (Jefferson, NC: MacFarland, 1999), pp. 233–63, and for Robin Hood see the entries in Harty, *The Reel Middle Ages*.

33 For example, the ambush of a baggage train in a forest (the 1938 Errol Flynn film), a mysterious figure in the forest (*Robin of Sherwood*), tricks with knives and arrows (any Robin Hood film), and the general situation of Arthur as the outlaw-like leader of a small tough band dissatisfied with, and ultimately hostile to, central authority yet heroically determined to bring rescue in the name of international freedom to the poor and oppressed.

2

The Green Knight's balancing act

Gillian Rudd

The Green Knight shares with Gawain the usual title of the famous, anonymous and influential fourteenth-century poem, but it is probably fair to say that he dominates our imaginative reception of it. Without him, the beheading game, the exchange of winnings and the journey through the wilds of the north-west midlands and Wirral would still be a good yarn, but with him, Gawain's challenge rises to a different level.[1] Explicitly and literally green as he is, the Knight also makes the poem an obvious candidate for green reading. Inevitably the Green Knight is read as a representative, if not indeed an embodiment, of the natural world; a point John Anderson made to me while seeing a book through press with his customary mixture of insight, precision, courtesy and continual intellectual engagement.[2] Anderson was not claiming that this was a new or particularly original thought, rather he was gently suggesting that I had overlooked a salient (if not *the* salient) feature of the text when offering what I perhaps presumptuously described as a green reading of the poem. At that point I sidestepped the issue as being too complex and elusive to deal with satisfactorily within a discussion focusing on other elements of the text. Here I want to make a tentative return to it, because for me the Green Knight is both an obvious and an uneasy figure or figuration of nature, whether one capitalises 'nature' or not. This essay will be an exploration of why.

Equilibrium and poise

The image of the great, green knight on an equally large green horse riding into Arthur's hall is a memorable one. After detailing the greenness of horse and rider and the splendour of their garb, the poet finishes the description by focusing on what this knight carries:

> Bot in his on honde he hade a holyn bobbe,
> That is grattest in grene when greves ar bare,
> And an ax in his other, a hoge and unmete,
> A spetos sparthe to expound in spelle, quo-so myght.[3]

This is a display of more than proficient horsemanship, since riding in holding a holly branch in one hand and an axe in the other implies no use of reins, as well as suggesting a highly trained mount and an astute sense of how to make an entrance. The image created is not only faintly surreal, but also begs to be interpreted – and interpret it we do, aided or possibly misguided by the Green Knight's own words. One of the most obvious conclusions to draw is that the knight on his charger, stationary in the king's hall, is a tableau of balance apt for midwinter as one year turns into the next. The holly, with its associations of greenness in winter, signifies renewed life, the natural cycle of the year and also peace, according to the knight's own words: 'Ye may be seker bi this braunch that I bere here / That I passe as in pes, and no plyght seche' (265–6). The axe, on the other hand, may be read as the appropriate tool to cut the holly, thus perhaps suggesting man's use of or rule over natural resources. The knight himself, we are to infer, like all true knights, particularly literary ones, is as much at home in the court with its festivals and rituals and hunting rights as he is on the battlefield.[4] Ostensibly he is choosing at this moment to present his domestic side, his axe as a primarily symbolic woodsman's tool whose blade is noted not just for its size but for the aesthetic qualities of its steel and gold (210–12). But an axe is also a battle weapon, and the momentary focus on the sharpness of this one's blade, 'As wel schapen to schere as scharp rasores' (213), might bring that alternative use to mind, were our attention not so speedily diverted to the shaft with its ornate carvings, decorative lace and tassels (215–20). The warlike aspects of this impressive implement are further suppressed by the knight's rather menacing enumeration of the various military accoutrements he has deliberately left behind:

> For had I founded I fere, in feghtyng wyse
> I have a hauberghe at home and a helme bothe,
> A schelde and a scharp spere, schinande bryght,
> Ande other weppenes to welde, I wene wel, als.

> (267–70)

Armour, shield and spear have been left behind with other weapons, and the conditional mode of this declaration is designed to make us think that *all* other weapons are also 'at home', wherever that may be, increasing the likelihood of our reading the axe as having nothing to do with combat between humans, and everything to do with being a manmade tool contrasted with the naturally growing branch it is designed to hew.[5]

All of this makes it easy to assume that the axe and the branch are not just balanced, but more precisely hold each other in equilibrium,[6] an assumption aided by the image of the knight holding one in each hand and further supported by the description of the knight himself as 'half etayn' (140). 'Half' plays into the idea of two things in equal proportion and encourages the symmetrical image suggested by the knight having branch in one hand, axe in the other. The poet teases us here, invoking the idea of giants only to lay them aside immediately in the next line; while he may think or even wish ('hope') this character is a half giant, he more rationally judges ('mynn') him to be the biggest man ('manne most'). So other elements are introduced and again apparently pitted against each other in equal and opposite modes. Giant is opposed to man, it seems, and the two are united in this figure which, to use the full phrase, is 'half etayn in erde'.

That completing term 'in erde' is the interesting one. While the phrase is being used as an intensifier, it also has literal power here. On the one hand and in the world of the story as a whole, it reminds us that we are on earth, in Arthur's court and so in the real, or at least realistic, mimetic world, not in some magical alternative land, which may be where we find ourselves when Gawain enters Bertilak's castle, Hautdesert. On the other, it offers the notion of a poet who revels in the idea of a half-giant in the real world and rather wishes it could be true, although his more cautious 'but' and 'algate' hint that he knows it cannot. By thus drawing attention to the notion of the giant or half-giant in the actual world, the narrative focuses our imagination on that side of this green figure and encourages us to take as read what the other side of this half creature might be. Just as we automatically assume the holly branch and axe are equal and opposite, so we tend to assume that if this green knight is half giant, the other half must be human. Human is explicit in the 'manne' of line 141 and since no other term is introduced our initial assumption is left unchallenged. Arguably it is not even 'etayn' which intrigues us; rather this is just one extra detail in an already surreal picture of a knight who earns the soubriquet 'green' not just because his garb and shield are green but because his skin and his horse are green too. We are in the realms of romance, where giants and other such creatures require neither explanation nor excuse and their reality or otherwise is neither in dispute nor a matter for speculation. Thus, neither we nor the poem questions the plausibility of the existence of giants, who are as much a part of this natural landscape as the wolves, bears and wildmen who are given a passing reference in line 723 as Gawain travels through the Wirral. So describing the Green Knight as an 'etayn' should create no problems; it is the 'half' that ought to cause concern, as it adds to the ambiguity that began with the phrase 'aghlich mayster' (136) and that continues to resonate throughout the poem.

In his note on these lines, Anderson succinctly comments on the way 'the visitor is between two worlds' and draws attention to the various ways the Green Knight is both beyond and firmly within human social structures. This borderline position is part of the Knight's disconcerting identity, but what is germane for this current discussion is that the use of 'half' reinforces the notion of this green knight being a figure of two equal but opposite elements held together. A tacit assumption of equal halves persists: things come in pairs, are in opposition and are equally balanced. We rarely pause to scrutinise the grounds for this assumption, or to consider that it is not necessarily the case that two different things need be in opposition, nor that balance has to be equilibrium. However, if we return to that arresting initial picture of the Green Knight with his holly branch and axe, it is easy to see where the presumption of static balance comes in. The passage encourages us to envisage an iconic figure whose pose reminds us of symmetrically balanced scales. The imposing knight holds his perfect seat on a horse standing in the middle of Arthur's hall, making both rider and steed the fulcrum for his arms, which hold branch and axe at equal height, as he waits for some kind of response from the awed Camelot. This image is essentially a static one, and invites being read off in a series of binary pairs: human court/magical figure; human civilisation/ natural world; privileged elite/woodsman (as implied by the axe as woodsman's tool); youth/experience; ease and feasting/challenge and adventure; known/unknown. In short Arthur's court stands for all that is secure, homely, familiar and unchanging, while the Green Knight embodies adventure, strangeness, change and the risk inherent in challenge.

However, it is important to remember that right at the centre of Camelot's apparent confident ease and carefully hierarchical seating is Arthur's restlessness, a consequence of his youth, we are told, given that he is 'sumquat childgered' and 'bisied' by his young blood and teeming mind (86–7). It is this inner ferment that instigates the action of the poem and offers a different notion of balance, not that of unmoving equilibrium of scales or of character, but of ceaseless movement, which keeps things in play. This kind of balance prevents any one element achieving lasting dominance because the very process of gaining ascendancy creates a consequence (such as lack of food, over-crowding, or, in the case of the Camelot of this poem, *ennui*) which redresses that success. The scales then tip in favour of another aspect which exploits the weakness opened up by the redressing consequence of the previously dominant element – and the process begins again. This is closer to the kind of balance we associate with ecosystems, a more dynamic and less predictable concept which abhors the stasis associated with perfectly balanced weighing scales. The interdependence that characterises the concept of perpetually moving balance seems to find its emblem in the pentangle, with its five interlocking points and virtues. The poem's description of the pentangle suggests that failure in one virtue results in failure in all, but leaves implicit the equally crucial point that the dominance of one will also upset the balance and result in collapse of the figure as a whole. Although it may be unusual to think of Gawain's failure in terms of excessive adherence to rather than neglect of one or more of the pentangle's principles, it is nevertheless precisely this trap Gawain finds himself in later in the poem, when his wish to keep his word to his host's wife and not reveal the gift of the girdle conflicts directly with his promise to exchange winnings with the host himself. His excess of 'cortaysye' and 'pité', which are explicit elements of the pentangle (653–4), leads to his failure in 'felawschyp' and 'trawthe' towards his host.[7]

Substitution and exchange

On a grander scale, too, the poem reflects this version of balance as something constantly shifting rather than in a state of static equilibrium; that is, balance becomes something to be striven for constantly, rather than a pose that once achieved can be held. This is most evident in the way that the narrative as a whole is full of movement and substitution as both readers and protagonist are forced to reassess and redefine objects, characters and events. Among the most immediately apparent substitutions are Gawain taking Arthur's place as respondent to the Knight's challenge; the shifting of the second half of the exchange of blows from the known of Camelot to the unknown of the Green Chapel; Arthur's court replacing Bertilak's house; the multiple exchanges of kisses and animal carcasses, and the over-arching substitution of the game of the return stroke for the exchange of winnings and of pentangle for girdle. Most of these substitutions appear to work on a simple binary basis, in which one thing is swapped for another, with the added assumption that the booty won by each side in a day will be weighed against that won by the other (but now exchanged for the other's winnings). Balance is thereby invoked in its common role as a method for measuring worth. This process is implied when the exchange of winnings is set up, as the phrase 'quether, leude, so lymp lere other better' (1109) clearly indicates that one will come off worse than the other in this deal. Bertilak explicitly refers to this consequence again at the close of the first day's hunting when he displays the venison to Gawain and demands: '"How payes yow this play? Haf I prys wonnen?"' (1379). Paradoxically, if he has won the prize, he is immediately to lose it, as the deal dictates that he gives the venison up to Gawain, accepting whatever he has won as fair exchange. Implicit, then, in this game of exchange is the expectation that the winnings will not in fact balance each other up at all. Moreover, what you gain, and thus what you have to exchange, is less important than the process of gaining it.

The various elements of the hunt, from the finding of the deer, through the carving up of the beasts which converts deer to venison, the slinging of the carcasses on sticks to carry them home, and the trumpeting that accompanies the journey back to the castle, all feature in the poem and seem as much part of the glory of the win as the fine hoard of venison finally displayed to Gawain in the castle that evening. Meanwhile, and interleaved with this narrative, we have seen the lady of the manor corner Gawain in bed and the flirtation between the two begin. It is inevitable in a narrative poem that narrative should dominate, but in a consideration of movement and balance it is worth noting that while within the deer hunt the power is very much on the side of the hunter and the narrative line moves in one direction with no question over who controls the plot, things are more evenly balanced between Gawain and Bertilak's wife. This first exchange, then, becomes a measuring of a one-way power relation, a descriptive narrative in which the deer are written solely as game with the inevitable outcome of being redefined as venison, against a two-way verbal fencing match in which dialogue is deployed by both parties as they constantly redefine and obscure their positions in the interests of keeping the entertainment going and the power balanced. When Gawain exchanges his kiss for the venison, he refuses to give any details about how or from whom he received the kiss, pointing out that that was not part of the agreement: '"That was not forward," quoth he, "frayst me no more; / For ye haf tan that yow tydes, trawe ye no other ye mowe"' (1395–6). Gawain thus deftly invokes the notion of exact exchange, winning for winning, and in doing so suggests that the value of a narrative that allows for interchange, redefinition and evasion outweighs that of one dealing with fixed definitions, however fast-paced and skilled that narrative may be.

That lesson could be seen to have been learnt when it comes to the second hunt. Here the boar is given some space to make his own point as he gores the men coming after him (1443; 1462). When finally brought to bay, he chooses a place that forces single combat with Bertilak rather than the mass slaughter we saw in the deer drive.[8] This boar has agency; he may be about to lose, and is still at the mercy of a text which defines him as quarry and so dictates the outcome as one in which boar is killed by hunter, but he ensures that an alternative definition of dangerous opponent is also registered within the narrative. The details of his getting the bank at his back and scraping the ground (1571) give this boar identity without anthropomorphising him. Like the deer, he is clearly on the nature side of the nature/human opposition that seems to operate throughout the poem, but his difference from the plural deer indicates that the side of the equation aligned with the holly bush rather than the axe (to continue using that as the defining image of the text) is not made up of just one mode of existence.

Just as this hunting narrative is more complex than that of the deer drive in terms of the points of view permitted, so it is more nuanced in the human/nature relationship it inscribes. The boar is set against a background of rocks, river and gully, natural environments that help him and hinder his foes, but he bites and breaks the backs of the hunting dogs just as he gores the huntsmen who follow him. Some of the oppositions that seemed so secure in that image of holly branch versus axe begin to collapse or at least to be blurred. Where can we draw the line between animal and human here? The dogs are clearly within the human world, being deployed and trained as hunting dogs, but their skill, as with the deer hunt, is their innate, species-related skill of tracking and hunting in packs. Human and dogs on one side, then, as part of a human, civilised framework perhaps, and boars and deer on the other, wild, side?[9] Yet the deer are evidently husbanded, if not exactly farmed, whereas the boar seems to denote a wilder, less governable realm of nature, one that is capable of making unwelcome incursions into the human, literally so in the cases of those gashed by tusks. Those tusks and the boar's strength and anger create a formidable opponent for Bertilak, once again allowing the idea of binary opposition to dominate, inviting us to read the valued side of the binary as the human side, whose worth is proved by his ability to encounter and defeat ferocious nature. So it transpires that after the rush and scramble of the chase, which suggests a less than static state of relations, the final showdown between lord and boar reasserts the framework of one-to-one exact pairing. At the moment when Bertilak enters the gully we are surely to think of the scales as being evenly weighted, man and beast equally matched, the outcome hanging in the balance. This is to be a test of courage and skill between two equally formidable contestants. Yet although this is the conceit upon which the narrative rests, and which it has gone to some lengths to create, it in not in fact the truth of the matter. The boar is in a human story, its role is to be a worthy adversary, yes, but one that must be overcome: he is there to provide excitement, colour, proof of Bertilak's hunting prowess and the assurance that humans win over animals. Exhilarating as the episode is, we are on familiar ground and never doubt the eventual outcome.

A similar process can be seen in the description of the final hunt, which seeks to further refine the divisions within the animal world, while yet resting assured that the human/animal opposition is the one that counts. Despite being defined as 'foule fox felle' (1944) when dead, and thus denied the aesthetic qualities accorded to deer and boar in different ways, the fox is actually given more individuality than the other two hunted species. Reference to him as 'Reynard' (1728; 1898; 1916) links him to the tradition of the tales of Reynard the fox, bringing him into the human world of narrative in a more fully constructed way than that offered the nameless boar. Moreover, although there is no ceremonious carving up of the carcass and no transition from beast to meat to record, there is a loud celebration of the death which is 'raysed for Renaude saule' (1916) and that mention of a soul, however ironic, serves to bring this fox further into a human view of the world than the careful pitting of worthy rivals that ends the boar hunt. Thus another variation of the human/animal binary relation is offered: the fox is not valued as food, adversary or fur, but he is better material for a story. His cunning is legendary, he epitomises the intellectual qualities of wit and guile, not just physical strength and stamina and as such he is closer to the human world than either deer or boar. The use of his stock name invokes his status as one of the most frequently anthropomorphised animals, while the hunting context reminds us of the observed fox behaviour that lies at the root of the anthropomorphic Reynard. The quickness of the fox in both senses of the word serves to point the contrast between him and the other animals. The deer are fleet of foot but timid, running scared; the boar is brave and has wit enough to seek out a place which allows him to guard his back; but neither they, nor indeed the hunting hounds, are credited with the forethought that epitomises the fox. So the final effect of these three hunts is to assert that while a range of animals and relations to them is available, from domesticated dog or horse to various kinds of wild beast, and while it may be possible to envisage a narrative in which the animal takes some active part, nevertheless, each one of those relations ensures that operating human narrative remains intact and dominant at the end of the encounter with the animal. We are encouraged to recalibrate the way we balance the human/animal divide, but not to discard that binary opposition altogether. Or at least not in this section of the poem.

More to the point, this whole process of rebalancing the human/ animal opposition relies upon a notion of exchange that implies entities that can be weighed against each other, that is, that are capable of being brought within the same value system. The non-animal natural world is utterly excluded from this process, overwritten by narratives that focus on the animal/human relation- ships. Significantly, this is most apparent in the last hunt. Whereas the passages that open the other two hunts have moved quickly to the action itself, this last, of the fox, begins with a few lines describing just what the morning was like:

> Ferly fayre was the folde, for the forst clenged;
> In rede rudede upon rak rises the sunne,
> And ful clere castes the cloedes of the welkin.

(1695–7)

Here we encounter what is excluded from a reading of the human/ nature binary which casts human and animal on opposite sides; we see the world occluded by that binary, of vegetation, water and rock, the world of landscape. This description, lovely as it is, is designed to ensure that the non-animal world is securely kept in the position of backdrop to the real drama about to unfold. There is no question of allowing the frost-covered ground the same kind of

access to signification permitted to the animals who are hunted or
who hunt across it. This kind of response to the non-animal world
is indicative of our customary way of reading not only this poem,
but also our relations to the world. Animals can both prove and
trouble our sense of what it means to be human, as Erica Fudge and
others have demonstrated,[10] but we rarely venture into the arena
where there is no division between human and vegetative nature.
This is remarkable in a text which has as its central figure a green
man.

Gome versus green

Of course the green man we have here is not strictly speaking the
Green Man of folklore, despite John Speirs's rather sweeping
assertion that the Green Knight 'can be no other than a recru-
descence in poetry of the Green Man'.[11] Inevitably his arrival in
midwinter, his holly branch, huge stature and above all his colour
suggest an affinity with the Green Man, but, crucially, he lacks the
defining feature, that of being made up of vegetation. His beard
is a beard, not a bush, his face may be green in colour, but it is
made up of skin, not leaves, and there is nothing bark-like about
his clothing. Like the animals of the hunt, this figure is fully part
of the human world, specifically of the knightly one, as his spurs
suggest. In short, he is a figure who has been pulled fully into
human narrative, leaving his vegetative associations as mere hints.

In being presented with a figure who is similar to, but explicitly
not the Green Man, we are forced to ask what exactly he is – the
very question that preoccupies the assembled lords and ladies at
Arthur's court. These unnamed nobles are willing to entertain
any possibility, including the utterly unknown and unfamiliar.
It is they who suggest that the green figure may be supernatural
'fantoum and fayryye' (240), but significantly neither Arthur,
Gawain, nor the narrating voice will have any truck with such an
idea. The court's view is subtly undermined as the narrative com-
pletes the line – 'the folk there hit demed' – which tacitly suggests
that the judgement of these good folk is flawed. The narrative itself
has asserted that its disconcerting antagonist is a 'mon' some one
hundred lines earlier at line 141, and Arthur and Gawain persist-
ently use terms such as 'wyye', 'gome' or 'knyght' when addressing
the green figure. The choice of terminology may well have something to do with politeness, given that Arthur and Gawain talk
to the green knight while the courtiers just talk about him, but it

is worth noting that despite the narrative's insistence on the pre-dominantly human identity of this green figure, the sense of him as otherworldly persists, not least in lines 239–41, which briefly throw into doubt the idea of what it means to be human at all.

An effect is produced through the alliteration on 'f' which begins, scarcely noticeably, in line 239 in the phrase 'fele sellyes'. The attention is all on the marvels ('sellyes') at this point, with 'fele' merely indicating that as they have been so many, the court is used to unusual things, if not indeed a touch blasé about them. Yet they have never encountered anything quite like this, we are told, and it is for this very reason ('forthi') that they deem this figure both 'fantoum and fayryye': doubly strange, doubly other. The 'f's are now piling up and spill over into the next line, where a clue as to what makes this particular marvel quite so remark-able is provided in the word 'freke'. This word is here applied to the people of the court and must bear its primary meaning of 'warrior' or 'lord'. But the word was first used in the poem of the Green Knight, at 149, where it specifically points up the contrast between this figure's bearing ('He ferde as freke were fade') and his colouring ('And overall enker-grene'). Here is the nub of the issue: unlike the familiar Green Man made up of vegetation, the figure who confronts Arthur's court is to all intents and purposes a man, despite his size and allowing for the overriding weirdness of his actually being green. The result is that at the very point of debat-ing this person's strangeness, the otherness that allows them to speculate that he is of fairy origin, the court is brought up against the fact of a kinship of appearance and identity. They, like him, are 'frekes', a word which, as the *Middle English Dictionary* attests, was already carrying connotations of strangeness, particularly strange-ness associated with great size. It is possible that underlying this medieval term for 'warrior' or 'lord' we begin to hear our present-day 'freak' – immediately quashed, but disconcertingly present.[12] For if something that big and green can be some kind of human, what does that mean for the self-identity of Arthur's knights – and indeed of us all?[13]

Here we encounter what Simon Hailwood has described as the necessary otherness of nature. We need to maintain nature as other, precisely because it is an other familiar to us in its very otherness – the one thing that we know we are not, are incapable of dealing with or interacting with, and which thus ensures our own identity as defined and defining selves.[14] Such otherness is not that of a simple binary opposition through which the desirability of one side is assured by the undesirability of the other; rather this is an otherness which ensures that nature remains outside our moral framework, thus ensuring that what lies within that framework does partake of our moral universe, or at least one we can strive to comprehend. Moreover, as necessary and familiar other, nature provides the bedrock for all other comparisons, for concepts of identity and for definitions of what is real. Unlike Kristeva's abject, this other is not taboo, or beyond taboo (for such places are the consequences of an operating moral framework), but is simply outside the system altogether, and as such, verifies the existence of that system. It is necessary, and familiar, but above all it does not identify itself. As such, nature lacks the kind of awareness that we associate with agency and self-realisation, or a sense of self and self-determination, and in lacking those qualities it assures our place as self-determining beings.[15]

For the philosophers, such debates are conducted in terms of abstract concepts of self-realisation, but for readers of *Sir Gawain and the Green Knight* there is the pleasing fact that the Green Knight literally refuses to identify himself. He proclaims his purpose, draws attention to his equipment (including, as mentioned previously, the equipment he has left behind), insults Camelot and lays down the rules of his game; he even demands to know his opponent's name before engaging with him (379–80). But when Gawain points out that he does not know where the Green Knight lives, nor to which court he belongs, nor his name (399–400), any of which would make finding him a year hence a good deal easier, his remarks are brushed aside with the assurance that all will be revealed once he has delivered the blow. In the event, however, Gawain learns his opponent's name only after he has withstood the return blow in the green chapel at the end of the poem, and even then it is debatable how far the Green Knight is in fact Bertilak.[16] When one is transformed by Morgan le Fay into a huge green half-giant, is one, strictly speaking, the same person? Such a question risks taking us into the territory of caterpillars and butterflies, but at the very least such evasion on the Green Knight's part ensures that his identity remains a point of debate, and that in itself lends weight to the idea that he is the ultimate other. This then results in a figure of nature being itself unnatural, but while such a conclusion would fit with the concept of nature as a necessary but familiar other, it is a conclusion that the narrative of the poem or Gawain, its protagonist, goes to some lengths to deny.

As already mentioned, the poem's narrative asserts the human qualities of its central green figure from the start: 'gome' and 'hathel' indicate that this is a man, even if the biggest in the world, and the description of the head being cut off emphasises that this creature is made of flesh and blood. Arthur and Gawain also define this figure as human, Arthur initially in neutral terms, using the simple 'wyye' to greet him (252) and only later moving on to the more elevated 'knight' (276) and 'hathel' (323). Gawain likewise insists on terms that keep his opponent securely in the realms of the human. Given Hailwood's argument that nature lies outside the human moral framework, Gawain's insistence may be seen as canny self-preservation. If he is to have any hope of survival it must rest on fulfilling the terms of the agreement, but such terms will mean nothing to something which is not part of the system in which such laws operate. Thus Gawain's use of 'knight' at line 400, as he asks point blank for some clue to this green figure's identity, may be more than an insistence on courtly etiquette: he is reminding this stranger of his knightly appearance and requiring him to live up to it. It is as knight to knight that Gawain engages with him, not as human to nature. When we see Gawain on his travels later in the poem it becomes clear that 'human' here is a wide term, admitting anything that can itself be brought within the human sphere of understanding. Thus wolves, wildmen, dragons, wild animals and, surely most significant of all, 'etaynes' (723) are numbered among the many adversaries he meets while crossing the Wirral in his search for the Green Chapel. As is often pointed out, none of these causes him half as much pain as the elements: nature itself is a more wearing opponent than any foe, however terrible, that can be dealt with as a single, defined, entity. It is perhaps in recognition of this that Gawain insists on the knightly identity of the Green Man, and it seems that this 'half etayn' accepts the definition as he leaves with the words 'the knight of the grene chapel men knowen me mony' (454). This assertion that many men know him as a knight (an assertion given the lie in the poem's second fitt), coupled with that barely remarked shift of defining green from knight to chapel, serves to place this evasive person within the familiar category of knight known by his attributes and customary abode. He becomes the kind of knight we expect knights errant to encounter, such as, for example, the several different-coloured knights battled by the hero of Malory's 'Tale of Sir Gareth'. Just as the knight deftly deflects his soubriquet, we are reminded of his otherworldliness: not only is he riding out with his head literally held in his hands, but 'to quat kyth he becomen knew non there' (460). He defies definition here, just as he is to do at end of the poem, where again 'the knight in the enker grene / [buskez] whiderwarde-so-ever he wolde' (2477–8).

It is also worth noting that as he departs, the knight leaves behind his axe, now Gawain's by right. In doing so he abandons the potential equal balancing of the properties of the natural and the cultivated world suggested by the pairing of axe and holly branch, and indeed the holly simply slips from sight – we do not know if it is left in Camelot or carried out by the departing knight. This sleight of hand on the part of narrative or knight enacts the process by which the non-animal natural world is quietly relegated to the realm of the unspoken and unnoticed. Without our realising it, our attention has been fully shifted from the idea of a figure representing nature as elements, vegetation and landscape (the Green Man in effect) to one representing a more humanlike non-human realm. Although the tussle over definition is never again as marked, the sway of terms of reference persists within the poem, hinging on the Green Knight's identity and bringing us back to the question of how we read or react to a being who is 'half etayn'. As mentioned above, the assumption is surely that the other half is human, with its tacit definition of 'etayn' as non-human, but it seems that the poem's narrative cannot rest with that assumption. There is a constant struggle between an urge to make the Green Knight a being from another world, straightforwardly supernatural and so somehow more comprehensible, and the assertion that he is in fact part of the world we know but rarely look at. This struggle acknowledges that there is an affinity between giants and humans, as between all animals and humans, which places us all on the axe side of the opening image, as it were, counterbalanced by all that is nature but not animal. Once this is acknowledged, it opens up the possibility that there is a far less humanlike non-human realm, which we might like to identify as simply 'the natural world' without scrutinising what that is or where the boundary between one and the other can be drawn. This then introduces a new element of choice, to recognise and battle with the element which is not human, but is nevertheless humanlike, or to engage with the completely non-human other. No wonder Gawain is so insistent in his choice of terms.

Gawain's definition is borne out by the plot of the poem which reveals the Green Knight to be Bertilak, who laughingly asserts his human position as husband of the younger lady and host to and possible pawn of Morgan le Fay. Although this revelation admits magic and the operation of the supernatural in that sense, it also presumes that Bertilak's court and Arthur's operate in the same plane. Morgan is Gawain's aunt, a relation Bertilak foregrounds as he invites Gawain to return to Hautdesert and there see out the rest of the jollifications. Gawain's outburst and refusal are likewise based on human/human relations, as women are blamed for all men's ills and he curses his own flaw of character, which led him to accept the girdle. Significantly, Bertilak forgives Gawain his flaw explicitly because it is so human – the desire to save one's life. But of course this is also a basic instinct of any living creature, as the details of the hunts have shown. The courage of the stag and the boar and the cunning of the fox have been admired but also expected. The skill of the hunt lies in taking on animals as worthy adversaries; hence the importance of Bertilak's braving of the surging water to tackle the boar at bay on his own. All these details, then – Gawain's insistence on using human terms of reference for his unknown opponent, the equation of the two courts and the acknowledgment of some common ground between human and animal intrinsic to the relation between hunter and hunted – serve to focus attention on a dualism between human and human-like. Even the explicitly supernatural is allowed space in this view because it mimics the human. The knight of the opening section may be 'overal enker grene' but he is a knight; Hautdesert may have a name that suggests an allegorical meaning, and may materialise literally as an answer to a prayer, complete with pinnacles whose resemblance to paper cutouts hints at the generally unreal nature of the place, but it is nevertheless a court run on human lines obeying human structures, codes and feasts; Morgan le Fay may be a witch who transforms Bertilak into a green knight to frighten Guinevere, but she is also Arthur's half sister and herself human. Within the narrative, then, protagonist and minor characters alike work within a human vision which reiterates the inclination to operate in binary terms, creating balancing pairs at every turn.

Yet this is not what that opening image offers. That Green Knight with his holly branch and axe invokes the non-animal natural world, that of vegetation and, we later discover, rocks, as it transpires that the green chapel is not a man-made building but a natural rock formation, possibly created by the stream which runs by it: 'nobot an olde cave, / or a creviss of an olde cragge' (2182–3). Even Gawain is at last forced to notice his environment, for it is only then that he finds he has reached the Green Chapel. He finally admits that the chapel need not be an artefact, or at least not one consciously made by any human or animal agency. It is unclear if it is only the narrative which voices the dismissive 'nobut' or whether the term reflects Gawain's own denigration of a natural phenomenon which takes the place of the chapel that he sought. His reaction to the place, once recognised, reveals his deep-seated anxiety in the face of the presumed inanimate natural world. This place suggests a danger far exceeding that he was expecting or prepared to meet and in response he seeks to make it knowable by invoking religious terms of reference. As a devil's cave it can only be evil and in such a place, godless though it be, his best hope is the combination of faith and valour that has served him so well thus far. It would be far more disconcerting to recognise this place as simply and only the world in which we live but which owes us nothing. This is the world denoted by that holly branch, which has disappeared from view since the middle of the first fitt, but which has been acting upon the poem and us all along.

Regarded in this light, Gawain's fear in these last few stanzas could be rooted in a far deeper sense of crisis than simply anxiety for his reputation and self-image as a worthy knight of Arthur's court. It could be that the merest suggestion that the non-animal world is capable of agency strikes at the very root of what it means to be human. It will not be the Knight he thus encounters, however green, but Greenness itself, anthropomorphised nature now equipped with identity and agency bestowed by his own act of recognition when he admits that this rocky space, carved out by the natural forces of water, is indeed the Green Chapel. It is no coincidence that this fear is increased by the *sound* that suddenly accosts him. This 'breme noyse' (2200) bounces off the cliff edges as if it can break the rocks by force of sound alone. Literally caught between a rock and a hard place, Gawain and the narrative take refuge once again in defining the unknown, making it into something fearful but comprehensible. Thus the sound is quickly transformed from rock-splitting noise into a rock of a different kind, a grindstone that sharpens a scythe, and then, in order to accommodate the water as well as the rock that makes up this place, the noise is further defined and refined to become the sound of water in a mill, still powerful but now comprehensible and appropriate to the notion of the power of streams to alter landscape. Over the course of four lines the powerful, uncontrolled natural force (uncontrolled, that is, by humans) has been normalised and brought into a human sphere of reference. Gawain is now able to speak, to articulate a reaction befitting a knight and a Christian:

'"Let God worche! . . . Drede dos me no lote"' (2208, 2211). 'Lote' as sound or echo may indeed not make him fear now, but that is at least in part because he has brought that 'breme noyse' within the realms of recognisable sound, to the extent of using a word, 'lote', which can also mean 'speech'. It is the Green Knight's words, his term 'grene chapel', which is now no longer a source of fear, once it has been recognised and subsequently defined in terms that Gawain can countenance.

It is only now that Gawain can summon his opponent, significantly using the term 'wyye' (2215), and only now that the Green Knight, eventually, appears. This time there is no ambiguity about the axe he bears; it is a Danish battle-axe, honed to perfection and in no way intended for use on trees. The horse, too, is absent as the Green Knight explicitly walks towards Gawain, 'fayre on his fote he foundes on the erthe' (2229). It seems that Gawain's definition of the mysterious green figure has triumphed. In the stanzas that follow the word 'gome' is used repeatedly (2239, 2259, 2270) as if to emphasise that this is indeed a man, or as near as makes no difference, and it is with this that Gawain deals, all hints of vegetable and mineral natural world expunged.

This then, is the figure of nature the poem offers in the Green Knight – a large, laughing man on a green horse, who gleefully incites someone to cut off his head so that he can demonstrate his ability to go on without it. A power of natural cycles, perhaps, but crucially also one that the poem finally allies not with the many versions of the non-human natural world Gawain actually encounters, from icicles to wild beasts, but with a safer and deliberately included, humanised nature of hunting and hunted, seductive women and laughing men. The narrative thus allows us to forget the non-human half of the initial Green Knight and indeed recasts this being who is 'overal enker grene' as the laughing host, Bertilak, transformed by the comprehensible magic of Morgan le Fay. The sense of necessary but disconcerting swaying balancing act is replaced by one of balance and rest, but for greens this must be an uneasy rest because it allows us to retreat once more from facing the fact that the world is bigger than we know and moves on with us, but without caring much for us.

Crisis without resolution

In the afterword to *Language and imagination in the* Gawain-*poems* John Anderson takes issues with Muscatine's statement that the *Gawain*-poet's art is a defence against crisis, suggesting instead that of the three poets discussed by Muscatine (Langland, Chaucer and the *Gawain*-poet) 'it is Chaucer who is the least committed and most well defended'.[17] This seems right to me; the intricacy and complexity and above all the sense of urgency found in both Langland and the *Gawain*-poet betray a kind of engagement not found in Chaucer's variety and polish. As I hope this discussion has shown, in *Gawain and the Green Knight* we can now find a further level of crisis, one which in the poet's own day would hardly have been articulated in the ways it can be today and which I have presented, with some hesitation, here. Though in very different terms, and with a different focus, the reading I have here presented of *Sir Gawain and the Green Knight* concurs with Anderson's conclusion that the poem presents us with alternative ways of seeing things, ourselves, belief systems and value systems included, all of which relate directly to our sense of our place in the world. The poet presents those alternatives and sees them clearly, even with a desire that one of them might work, yet still, to use Anderson's words again, 'their major doctrines run counter to people's deepest instincts' (239). What this poem presents, then, is recognition of a deep-seated and enduring sense of crisis which is sometimes buried, sometimes at the surface of our sense of self. Perhaps such crisis is necessary in order for us to feel we have an individual identity, much as it is the series of challenges and crises created by the Green Knight that allows Gawain access to his sense of self, as distinct from being one amongst many at Arthur's court. If so, and if my reading is tenable, then our sense of the human rests on an unwillingness to admit identity to those elements in the world which are most foreign, while also most familiar. In short it is not the 'etayn' or 'alvish' side of the Green Knight that disconcerts, but the other, muted and obfuscated side which is finally to be found in the landscape itself. Thus the balance in the poem represented by the Green Knight is not one of two pans of a scales brought to careful equilibrium, but a shifting, swaying balancing act in which one term then the other may dominate for a while before being subsumed by another. This swaying image partakes of Anderson's sense of crisis; it is a crisis without resolution, whose hope, if hope there is, relies on constant movement and lack of secure definition. There is indeed, as Anderson noted, sadness here, a failure of great ideals and an inevitability of imperfection. The best one can hope is that such imperfection resists stasis and allows the balance to keep swaying.

Notes

1 For example, the episode in *Bricriu's Feast* which James Winny thoughtfully provides as an appendix to his edition and translation of *Sir Gawain and the Green Knight* (Peterborough, Ont.: Broadview, 1992) features an ugly churl, Dubthach Dóeltenga, who arrives carrying a tree trunk and an axe and proceeds to issue the beheading challenge, but this 'churl' is finally identified as Cú Rui, come to establish Cú Chulaind's status, and so is thoroughly explained and demystified in a way the Green Knight never is. Moreover, Dubthach Dóeltenga is not green. For those who wish to draw further comparisons, much material may be found in Elizabeth Brewer's *Sir Gawain and the Green Knight: Sources and Analogues*, 2nd edn (Cambridge and Rochester, NY: Brewer, 1992).

2 The book in question is Gillian Rudd, *Greenery: Ecocritical Readings of Late Medieval English Literature* (Manchester: Manchester University Press, 2007). I never clarified with John Anderson if he meant that the Green Knight represented material nature or our human perception and creation of nature, or both.

3 *Sir Gawain and the Green Knight* in J. J. Anderson (ed.), *Sir Gawain and the Green Knight, Pearl, Cleanness, Patience,* (London: Dent, 1996), lines 206–9. All references will be to this edition.

4 Much work has been done on the privileges noblemen enjoyed under forest law, by which land was husbanded with hunting in mind, so it is not impossible to see even a woodsman's axe as a sign of ownership, since trees and shrubs would be cut with the interests of game and hunting prevailing over any other considerations. Distinctions were, however, drawn between domesticated animals and wild ones when it came to who had the right to hunt them. For details and different overviews dealing specifically with *Sir Gawain and the Green Knight* see Anne Rooney, *Hunting in Middle English Literature* (Cambridge: D. S. Brewer, 1993), pp. 194–200 and William Perry Marvin, *Hunting Law and Ritual in Medieval English Literature* (Cambridge: D. S. Brewer, 2006), pp.130–57.

5 This is a definition we should bear in mind when it comes to considering the second axe of the poem, the one wielded at the green chapel.

6 See Joel Kaye, 'The (re)balance of nature, ca 1250–1350', in Barbara Hanawalt and Lisa Kiser (eds.), *Engaging with Nature: Essays on the Natural World in Medieval and Early Modern Europe* (Notre Dame, IN: University of Indiana Press, 2008), pp. 85–113, for an informative and detailed discussion of the changes in the medieval understanding of the terms 'balance' and 'equilibrium' which happily complies with the reading I offer here.

7 The inclination to see things in terms of Gawain's failure is aided and abetted by Gawain's own self-accusation and Bertilak's focus on the failure in the exchange of winnings.

8 Rooney suggests that the deer drive displays the skill of the beaters rather than hunters, and that the encounter with the boar owes more to romance and heroic associations than good hunting practice; see *Hunting in Middle English Literature*, pp. 166–8, 174.

9 My reading here departs from Joyce Salisbury's argument that hunting relies on maintaining a clear division between human and animal worlds as set out in *The Beast Within: Animals in the Middle Ages* (London and New York: Routledge, 1994), pp. 167–78.

10 See Erica Fudge, *Perceiving Animals* (Basingstoke: Macmillan, 2000) and Erica Fudge, Gilbert Ruth and Susan Wiseman (eds.), *At the Borders of the Human* (Basingstoke: Macmillan, 1999) as well as Hanawalt and Kiser (eds.), *Engaging with Nature*, and Susan Crane, 'For the birds', *Studies in the Age of Chaucer* 29 (2007), 21–41.

11 John Speirs, *Medieval English Poetry* (London: Faber and Faber, 1957), p. 219. Piotr Sadowski offers a useful summary of the Green Knight's greenness and responses to it in *The Knight on his Quest: Symbolic Patterns of Transition in 'Sir Gawain and the Green Knight'* (Newark and London: Associated University Presses, 1996), pp. 78–108 and I offer some comments on the figure in *Greenery*, pp. 110–14. Kathleen Basford's book *The Green Man* (Cambridge: D. S. Brewer, 1978, repr. 1996) remains the fullest and most fascinating general study of this intriguing figure.

12 *MED* freke n. (c). The association suggested in the *MED* and used here implies a lengthening of the short vowel of the OE 'freca' to give the Modern English 'freak', thus allowing an association of 'freke/ freak' with weirdness or monstrosity earlier than currently admitted by the *OED*, which prefers to regard 'freke' and 'freak' as distinct words. However, it is surely possible to detect in Montgomerie's 'fy on that freik that can not love' (*Commend of love*, 39, 1605, cited under *OED* 'freke') the same implications of being against nature that form an integral part of the *OED*'s definition of 'freak'. This offers a continuity of association and meaning between 'freke' and 'freak', *pace* the *OED*'s listing of them as discrete words, and allows for the etymology offered by *MED* for 'freke' to be extended to ME 'freak' also.

13 Arthur's court never quite relinquishes its desire to label the Green Knight as some kind of supernatural being; when they bid farewell to Gawain, the courtiers again refer to the Knight's fairy quality in the term 'alvisch mon' (681).

14 See Simon Hailwood, 'The value of nature's otherness', *Environmental Values* 9 (2000), 353–72.

15 Val Plumwood discusses the consequences of thus denying agency to nature in *Environmental Culture: The Ecological Crisis of Reason* (London and New York: Routledge, 2002), see esp. pp. 48–50; 214–17.

16 This belated revelation of the Green Knight's name perhaps prompts a re-reading of line 406. Should 'quen I the tape have' be seen as slightly ambiguous, allowing the meaning 'when I have tapped you' rather than only 'when I have received your blow' as glossed by Anderson?

17 J. J. Anderson, *Language and imagination in the* Gawain-*poems* (Manchester: Manchester University Press, 2005), p. 238.

3

Recasting the role? Brutus in Laȝamon's *Brut*

Carole Weinberg

It is accepted without dispute that Laȝamon's *Brut,* a poetic history of the earliest kings of Britain, is faithful to the content of the *Roman de Brut*, a French verse chronicle by the Jerseyman Wace, completed in 1155 and itself based on Geoffrey of Monmouth's *Historia Regum Britanniae.* As has been pointed out by Françoise Le Saux, 'the faithfulness to the general layout and contents of Wace's *Roman de Brut* is acknowledged by all critics'.[1] But Laȝamon's poem, at 16,095 lines, is more than twice as long as the French version, and although it was thought at one time that Laȝamon's source was possibly an expanded text of Wace, it is now accepted as more likely, given the growing evidence of his conscious artistry, that Laȝamon felt free to embellish Wace. The great difference is not in the matter but in the manner of narration. From the outset Laȝamon sets his own stamp on the narrative, expanding or condensing episodes or adapting them through his own creative imagination. The detailed study of even a single episode of the *Brut* reveals this literary process at work. A brief analysis of the founding of Britain by Brutus will serve to illustrate how Laȝamon's reshaping of Wace serves his own creative purpose.

Unlike Wace, whose introduction to the *Roman de Brut* simply and briefly states that he will truthfully tell the story of the kings who once ruled England as he, 'Master Wace', has translated it, Laȝamon appends a proem of thirty-five lines, written possibly after the body of the poem, which deals with, in turn, his identity, his subject matter, his sources, his method of composition, and the aim and purpose of his work.[2] He introduces himself as 'a priest in the land who was called Laȝamon' and the Christian dimension within which the poem operates is marked already in the proem by Laȝamon's description of the first inhabitants of the island. It came into his mind that he should relate:

> wat heo ihoten weoren   and wonene heo comen
> þa Englene londe   ærest ahten
> æfter þan flode   þe from Drihtene com,
> þe al her aquelde   quic þat he funde,
> buten Noe and Sem,   Iaphet and Cham,
> and heore four wiues   þe mid heom weren on archen.

(8–13)

[what they were called and whence they came who first possessed the land of England after the flood sent by God, which destroyed all living creatures here on earth, save Noah and Shem, Japhet and Ham, and their four wives who were with them in the ark.]

As the periods from the creation to the flood and the flood to Abraham counted as two of the seven ages into which biblical history was divisible, references to the flood were widespread in medieval literature; history for medieval annalists and historians was a continuum, going back ultimately to the Creation. Given Laȝamon's profession, it is not surprising that his view of the past is influenced by his background and outlook as a priest, though one needs also to acknowledge another Laȝamon, one who, while in proper Christian fashion acknowledging Julius Caesar's inevitable damnation as a pagan, is regretful that such a man, the wisest on earth in his time, 'should ever go to hell' (3601). While he is ever mindful of the moral failings of individual rulers, larger political concerns often override personal shortcomings in Laȝamon's vision of history.[3] But at the same time Laȝamon's background as a cleric clearly influences the approach he takes to the story of the past he is telling.[4]

Laȝamon, following Wace, opens his history with the escape of Aeneas from the destruction of Troy, and his taking refuge in Italy, where he marries the daughter of the Italian king and inherits the kingdom. His great-grandson is Brutus, born out of wedlock, but whose future fame is prophesied before his birth. At the age of fifteen he kills his father by accident, is expelled from Italy and, finding refuge in Greece, encounters fellow descendants of Trojan exiles held captive there. We are told in Wace that he quickly gains a reputation 'for daring, bravery, wisdom and generosity' (161–4). Laȝamon is more specific and harks back to qualities in Old Engish heroic literature by noting that within a short time Brutus was beloved by all the people and gained great respect 'for cniht he was swiþe god, / . . . / he was mete-custi, / þat is monscipe steor' [because he was a very good warrior; he was generous in the giving of gifts which is the basis of esteem] (176–7).

But at the same time as using the Old English heroic vocabulary to cast Brutus in heroic mould, Laȝamon also calls upon biblical imagery in his phrasing of the plea of the Trojan slaves to Brutus to be their liberator and leader:

> Heo seiden him mid rede   and mid stilliche runen,
> ȝif he were swa þriste,   and he hit don durste,
> þat he heom wolde leaden   out of þane leoden,
> out of þeowdome   freo þat heo weoren,
> heo hine wolden maken duc   and deme ofer his folke.
>
> (180–4)

[They spoke to him prudently and in confidence, saying that if he were bold enough and if he dared do it, dared to lead them out of that land, out of slavery so that they might be free, they would make him ruler and judge over his people.]

There are clear linguistic echoes here of the biblical Moses, who led the Israelites out of slavery in Egypt, but Laȝamon also invokes the biblical narrative of Joshua, who was chosen to lead his people into the land of Canaan.

When Brutus calls upon Diana, queen of all the forests on earth, for guidance in finding a land to dwell in, she delivers a prophecy of a land to which he will lead his fellow exiles. Wace states succinctly that Brutus 'begged the goddess to teach him by a reply, or show him by a sign, where he could find a good and peaceful land to dwell in' (662–6). Laȝamon, as he so often does, reshapes reported into direct speech, so that we have Brutus speaking directly to Diana:

> Leafdi Diana, leoue Diana,   heȝe Diana, help me to neode;
> wise me and wite me   þurh þine wihtful craft
> whuder ich mæi liðan   and ledan mine leoden
> to ane wnsume londe   þer ich mihte wunien.
>
> (602–4)

[Lady Diana, beloved Diana, great Diana, help me in my need; through your wise arts guard me and guide me where I am to journey and to lead my people to a pleasant land where I might dwell.]

Brutus then makes what amounts to the pagan equivalent of a covenant with the deity, vowing to erect a temple to Diana and to honour her with worship 'ȝif ich þat lond mai biȝeten / and mi folc hit þurhgengen' [if I can conquer the land and my followers overrun it] (605). In both Wace and Laȝamon Diana appears to Brutus in a dream, and tells him of a homeland in the west beyond

France, a new Troy, where the noble descendants of Brutus shall rule, esteemed throughout the world. That Laȝamon wished to stress the concept of Britain as a place predestined to prosperity under Brutus's rule is signalled by his adding to Diana's promise of a home for the exiled Trojans such phrases as 'þaron þu scalt wrþan sæl' [you shall prosper there] (619), and 'þu beo hæl and isund' [you shall be secure and prosperous] (628). The description of this land, called Albion, is more detailed and rhapsodic in Laȝamon with its depiction as a land of plenty, with fowl and fish, wood and water, and fine beasts (618–22). It anticipates details of the island's rich resources given later in both texts (Wace, 1209–18; Laȝamon, 1002–9) at the point when, the island having been colonised by the Trojan exiles and cleansed of the giants who formerly inhabited it, Brutus founds New Troy, later to be called London.

In Geoffrey of Monmouth's *Historia*, Wace's source, it is when Brutus first arrives on the island that a description of it is given:

> At this time the island of Britain was called Albion. It was uninhabited except for a few giants. It was, however, most attractive, because of the delightful situation of its various regions, its forests and the great number of its rivers, which teemed with fish; and it filled Brutus and his comrades with a great desire to live there.[5]

Geoffrey is here consciously tapping into the biblical narrative concerning Canaan, a land said by the spies sent by Moses to be flowing with milk and honey, but occupied by giants, while Brutus's colonising of Albion and his clearing away of the island's giants replays the biblical encounter of Joshua with the giants of Canaan.[6]

Whether Laȝamon had direct access to Geoffrey's *Historia* is still a matter of debate, but it is clear that, unlike Wace, who plays down the biblical echoes, Laȝamon expands and amplifies them. When the exiled Trojan slaves entreat Brutus to be their leader and liberator (180–4 above), it is only Laȝamon who has them plead that Brutus should lead them from slavery 'out of þane leoden' [out of that land]; in both Geoffrey and Wace the slaves simply wish to be delivered by Brutus from their captivity (*History*, p. 56; Wace, 167–70). Again, when Brutus asks Diana where he can find a peaceful land in which to dwell, Laȝamon rephrases the incident to reinforce the image of Brutus as a leader bringing his people out of slavery (Wace, 662–6; Laȝamon, 602–4 above).

On their journey towards the island of Albion, Brutus and his people pass Poitou and put in to land at the estuary of the Loire. The ruler of Poitou prepares for war, but, as Wace states, 'Brutus discovered this through his spies' (843). In Laȝamon (745–56), Brutus, guided by wisdom, sends spies to the court of the king; the spies report back to Brutus, 'heora læuarda' [their lord], giving him the fearful news that the king is threatening to kill everyone: 'nulleð heo leaue nenne of ous aliue' [they will leave none of us alive] (756). Once again Laȝamon expands upon Wace's brief statement to reinforce the image of Brutus as a wise leader to whom his people turn for deliverance in time of trouble.

The giants encountered by Brutus on the island of Albion are described as *gigantes* in the *Historia*; in Geoffrey's sparse prose style the most overtly negative reference is the statement that 'among the others there was a particularly repulsive one, called Gogmagog who was twelve feet tall'.[7] Wace's word for the giants is *gaianz*, and he comments on the strength and power of Gogmagog, their leader (1063–70). In contrast, after identifying the giants on their first appearance as *eotendes*, the Old English word for 'giants', Laȝamon also uses the term *feondes* which translates as both 'enemies' and 'fiends'. Laȝamon describes Gogmagog as 'Godes wiðer-saka / —þe Wrse hine luuede' [an enemy of God —the Devil loved him] (906). When Gogmagog is vanquished, 'þe hæȝe scaðe / ferde to helle' [the great miscreant went to hell] (963). But the term *sceaþa* also carried the meaning 'spiritual enemy, fiend, devil' in Old English and is used to describe Satan.[8]

In his description of Gogmagog, Laȝamon is calling on the Old English tradition which associated giants and other monsters with the race of Cain, an adversary of God and the first outcast — a connection made explicit in the Old English poem *Beowulf*, where the monster Grendel is specifically described as a descendant of Cain.[9] The image of Brutus taking possession of the land promised to him after it has been cleansed of the giants is reinforced by Laȝamon's summing-up statement following the death of the giants that 'nu wes al þis lond / iahned a Brutus hond' [this whole land was now delivered into Brutus's hand] (967).

With the coming of Brutus and the defeat of the giants, the island is colonised and cultivated and Brutus, in both Wace and Laȝamon, beholds and reflects upon the beauty and fertility of the land (Wace, 1209–18; Laȝamon, 1002–9). Laȝamon, however, sums up Brutus's contemplation of the island's prosperity with the comment that 'al he iseih on leoden / þat him leof was on heorten' [everything he saw in the land pleased him greatly] (1009), perhaps a subconscious echo of the biblical words at the completion of the world's creation: 'And God saw everything that He had made, and

behold, it was very good' (Genesis I.31). In a manner of speaking, Brutus, likewise, 'creates' Britain; and he makes it his own by
naming the land after himself:

> Þis lond was ihaten Albion   þa Brutus cum heron;
> þa nolde Brutus namare   þat hit swa ihaten weore;
> ah scupte him nome   æfter himseluan.
> He wes ihaten Brutus,   þis lond he clepede Brutaine;
> and þa Troinisce men   þa temden hine to hærre
> æfter Brutone   Brutuns heom cleopede. . .
>
> (975–80)

> [This land was called Albion when Brutus arrived here; Brutus then
> did not wish that it should any longer be called that, but he devised
> a name for it in keeping with his own. He was called Brutus, this
> land he called Britain; and the Trojans who deferred to him as leader
> called themselves Britons after Brutus.]

This sense of Brutus as 'creator' of the land of Britain is reinforced
at the level of language by the use of the verb *scupte*. One of its uses
in Early Middle English is to describe God's act of bringing the
world into existence;[10] Laȝamon himself has his Christian kings
refer to God, 'þe scop þes daȝes lihte' [who created the light of day]
(7423, 9274, 11769, etc.).

The mythical qualities of Brutus are reflected in the later
description of Arthur, the greatest of the British kings. Like
Brutus, Arthur is born out of wedlock, and his future fame is
prophesied before his birth. It is prophesied by Merlin in an extensive passage original with Laȝamon in which Arthur is described
in dramatic imagery as a heroic saviour whose people are to be
spiritually nourished upon his body and blood:

> Longe beoð æuere,   dæd ne bið he næuere;
> þe wile þe þis world stænt,   ilæsten scal is worðmunt;
> and scal inne Rome   walden þa þæines.
> Al him scal abuȝe   þat wuneð inne Bruttene.
> Of him scullen gleomen   godliche singen;
> of his breosten scullen æten   aðele scopes;
> scullen of his blode   beornes beon drunke.
> Of his eȝene scullen fleon   furene gleden;
> ælc finger an his hond   scarp stelene brond.
> Scullen stan walles   biuoren him tofallen;
> beornes scullen rusien,   reosen heore mærken.
> Þus he scal wel longe   liðen ȝeond londen,
> leoden biwinnen   and his laȝen sette.
>
> (9406–18)

[As long as time lasts, he shall never die; while this world lasts, his fame shall endure; and he shall rule the princes in Rome. All who dwell in Britain shall obey him. Of him shall minstrels splendidly sing; of his breast noble bards shall eat; heroes shall be drunk upon his blood. From his eyes shall fly sparks of fire; each finger on his hand shall be a sharp steel blade. Stone walls shall fall down before him; men shall tremble, their banners fall. So for a long, long time he shall go about the world conquering nations and establishing his laws.]

Arthur is portrayed as a legendary hero whose deeds will be meat and drink to the tellers of tales, but there are also echoes here of his role as a leader of his people before whom, as with the biblical Joshua, walls will fall down.

La3amon fashions Arthur as a saviour for his people, reclaiming the land of Britain from the heathen Saxon invaders. He emphasises the sacred bond between God, the land and Arthur in the dying statement of King Uther, relayed by three bishops and seven knights to his son, Arthur, in Brittany. Wace states baldly:

After the death of Uther the king, he was carried to Stonehenge and there buried within, by the side of his brother. The bishops sent word to each other and the barons assembled; they summoned Arthur, Uther's son and crowned him at Silchester. (9005–12)

La3amon, in characteristic fashion, expands upon this brief statement, setting the scene for the legitimate accession of Arthur by describing a great council in London at which it is agreed that the 'bezst alre 3eo3eðe / þa a þissere weorlden-riche / a þan dæ3en weore, / Ærður ihaten / bezst alre cnihten' [the finest young man who was in this mortal world in those days, the best of all warriors, Arthur by name] (9898–900), be sent for to rule them. Arthur's undoubted credentials thus established, the bishops and knights relay to the fifteen-year-old Arthur in direct speech Uther's dying command that Arthur protect Britain 'swa god king sculdne don, / þine feond flæmen / and driuen heom of londen' [as a good king should, put your enemies to flight and drive them from the land] (9917–18). The emissaries convey the sacredness of the task entrusted by father to son in telling Arthur that Uther 'bad þe to fultume / þene milde Godes sune / þat þu mostes wel don, / and þat lond of Godde afon' [prayed to the gracious son of God to help you that you might do well, and receive the land from God] (9919–9920).

Arthur's immediate reaction on receiving the news of his father's death and his succession to the kingdom is one of silence. Behind the silence, however, the turmoil of Arthur's mind is dramatically portrayed by the colour draining from his face at one moment while at the next it is red with suppressed emotion. When Arthur finally speaks, his first and only words, not in Wace, are directed heavenwards: 'Lauerd Crist, Godes sune, / beon us nu a fultume, / þat ich mote on life / Goddes la3en halden' [Lord Christ, son of God, be a help to us now, that I may uphold God's laws throughout my life] (9928–30). As has been noted by Le Saux, 'La3amon consistently adds a reference to God in Arthur's speeches';[11] this reinforces the sense that Arthur acts in accordance with God's will against the heathen Saxon invaders. And just as Arthur's future greatness as a saviour of his people against the invading Saxons is prophesied before his birth by Merlin, so, likewise, is his messianic return promised, though now, surprisingly, as a saviour to the English.[12] Geoffrey has nothing to say about Arthur's return, and Wace, while noting the stories circulating of Arthur's return, hints at personal doubts and cites Merlin as prophesying merely that Arthur's end would remain uncertain (*History*, p. 261; Wace, 13275–90).

Brutus and Arthur are parallel figures, cast in the same heroic and biblical mode. Brutus is entrusted with the sacred task of founding a homeland for the British and imposing good laws upon the people (1040–6), and Arthur, his descendant and the greatest of the British kings, is entrusted with the sacred task of protecting and defending the kingdom while upholding God's law within it. In La3amon's *Brut* both men are accorded a special, mystical status in the roll-call of British rulers, Brutus the legendary founder of the land named after him, and Arthur, the greatest of British rulers and legendary hero whose reign is brought to an untimely end through internal treachery, but who will return again as a saviour to the people in need of him.

That La3amon wished to stress the concept of Brutus as a deliverer of his people and of Britain as a place divinely predestined as a homeland for the Britons seems clear from his narrative stance. Likewise, at the conclusion of the poem we are told by La3amon, following Geoffrey and Wace, that the loss of the British kings' sovereignty over Britain is in accordance with divine will. Pestilence is ravaging Britain and the British king, Cadwalader, takes refuge in Brittany, but when he wishes to return, and prays to God for guidance, an angelic messenger appears to him in a dream and instructs him to go instead to Rome as it is now the English

who shall possess the kingdom and will do so 'ær cume þe time /
þe iqueðen wes while, / þat Merlin þe wite3e / bodede mid worde'
[until the time comes which has been foretold, which Merlin the
seer prophesied] (16020–1). In Geoffrey's *Historia* an angelic voice
informs Cadwalader that 'God did not wish the Britons to rule in
Britain any more until the moment should come which Merlin had
prophesied to Arthur'. Geoffrey goes on, however, to blame the
British for losing sovereignty over the island, claiming that 'the
famine and their own inveterate habit of civil discord had caused
this proud people to degenerate so much that they were no longer
able to keep their foes at bay'.[13] He comments that the Saxons
behaved more wisely, threw off the domination of the Britons and
ruled over the country under Athelstan.[14]

The impression gained from Geoffrey's concluding statement is
of a relationship of cause and effect between the shortcomings of the
Britons and God's wish that they should no longer rule in Britain.
Wace also views the Britons in a negative light, commenting that,
now known as the Welsh and never again powerful enough to rule
over the land, the Britons 'are quite different and have quite degenerated from the nobility, the honour, the customs and the life of their
ancestors' (14852–4). And just as Wace began his narrative with the
brief statement that he would truthfully tell the story of the kings
who once ruled England as he, 'Master Wace', has translated it, so
he ends the *Roman de Brut* on a similarly brief and self-referential
note stating that 'here ends the story of the British and the race of
lords from Brutus's lineage, who ruled England for so long. One
thousand, one hundred and fifty-years after God became man for
our salvation, Master Wace made this narrative' (14859–66).

La3amon mentions the congregating of the Britons in Wales
where they still live, having ceded sovereignty over the land
to English kings, but there is no derogatory reference to them.
Instead, the concluding lines of the *Brut*, original with La3amon,
note that never since that time have British kings ruled over the
land: 'Þa 3et ne com þæs ilke dæi, / beo heonneuorð alse hit mæi;
/ iwurðe þet iwurðe, / iwurðe Godes wille' [Such a day has not yet
come, whatever may come to pass hereafter; come what may, let
God's will be done] (16094–5).

Clearly La3amon's vision of past history encompasses God's
will, and he sees a divine hand in both the settlement of the land
by the British and their later loss of dominion over it. But while he
does not hesitate to comment pejoratively on the moral failings of
individual British rulers, there is no blanket condemnation of the

Britons, and there is no sense that he regards their loss of dominion as a divine punishment.[15] The island is promised to Brutus, but the actions of subsequent rulers, for good or ill, have consequences for the ownership of the land. The overarching design of God's will is played out at the human level by a secular historiography in which, at the personal and political level and over time, differing communities compete for dominion. At its core it is the land itself, given first to Brutus, and surveyed by him with delight, which is a sacred trust, to be governed in accordance with God's laws, whoever has ownership over it, British, English or Norman.[16]

I end with a note which is relevant to one of John Anderson's research interests. *Sir Gawain and the Green Knight* opens with a historical resumé of the founding of Britain by Aeneas's descendant and Arthur's ancestor, 'felix Brutus'. As Malcolm Andrew and R. A. Waldron note in their edition, the term *felix* 'is unique as a praenomen of Brutus . . . though the epithet is associated in Roman tradition with founders of cities, etc., and in the E.M.E. form *sæl*, it is applied to him [uniquely] by the poet Laȝamon in his chronicle-poem *Brut*'. The Gawain poet's source for this detail is unknown, but it is possible that both he and Laȝamon were drawing on a common tradition.[17]

Notes

1　Françoise Le Saux, *Laȝamon's Brut: The Poem and its Sources* (Cambridge: D. S. Brewer, 1989), p.50.

2　All textual references to Wace are from Judith Weiss (ed. and trans.), *Wace's Roman de Brut: A History of the British* (Exeter: University of Exeter Press, 1999); all textual references to Laȝamon are from W. R. J. Barron and S. C. Weinberg (ed. and trans.), *Laȝamon 'Brut' or Hystoria Brutonum* (Harlow: Longman, 1995). For the possible dating of the *Brut*, see intro., p. ix.

3　See Françoise Le Saux, 'Paradigms of evil: Gender and crime in Laȝamon's *Brut*', in Le Saux (ed.), *The Text and Tradition of Layamon's Brut* (Cambridge: D. S. Brewer, 1994), pp.193–206.

4　For a discussion of the respective roles of Laȝamon as priest and historian, see E. G. Stanley, 'Laȝamon: priest and historiographer', in Rosamund Allen, Lucy Perry and Jane Roberts (eds.), *Laȝamon: Contexts, Language and Interpretation* (London: King's College London Centre for Late Antique and Medieval Studies, 2002), pp.3–24.

5　All textual references to Geoffrey of Monmouth, unless otherwise stated, are from *The History of the Kings of Britain*, trans. Lewis Thorpe (London: Penguin Books, 1966).

6 I discuss further the parallel between Geoffrey and the biblical narrative in my 'The giant of Mont-Saint-Michel: an Arthurian villain', in Ricarda Schmidt (ed.), *Heroes and Villains: A Multi-Cultural Perspective: Proceedings of a Symposium in Honour of Professor David Blamires*, special issue of *Bulletin of the John Rylands University Library of Manchester* 84 (2002), 9–24 (13).

7 For *gigantes* see Neil Wright (ed.), *The Historia Regum Britannie of Geoffrey of Monmouth* (Cambridge: D. S. Brewer, 1985), p.14; Thorpe (trans.), *History*, p. 72.

8 See J. Bosworth (ed.) and T. Northcote Toller (enl.), *An Anglo-Saxon Dictionary* (Oxford: Oxford University Press, 1882–1921), s.v. *sceaþa* (1a).

9 See Bruce Mitchell and Fred C. Robinson (eds.), *Beowulf* (Oxford: Blackwell, 1998), lines 1258–67.

10 Hans Kurath et al. (eds.), *Middle English Dictionary* (Ann Arbor: University of Michigan Press, 1954–), s.v. *shapen*, v. (1a).

11 Le Saux, *Laȝamon's Brut: The Poem and its Sources*, p. 159.

12 It has been suggested that in Laȝamon's reference to 'an Arður' who will return to aid the English there is a supportive allusion to Arthur of Brittany (1187–1203), the designated heir of Richard I. See the notes to the edition of the *Brut*, p. 889. In the Otho manuscript, the only other extant manuscript of the poem – though radically altered in language and condensed in content – Arthur will return to aid the *Bruttes*.

13 Thorpe (trans.), *History*, pp. 283, 284.

14 Two manuscripts of the *Historia* have an *explicit* stating that the Welsh, once they had degenerated, never recovered overlordship of the land, but went on quarrelling with the Saxons and between themselves, and were perpetually in a state of conflict. Geoffrey leaves it to other writers to continue the account of the kings in Wales and those in England. See Thorpe (trans.), *History*, p. 284.

15 For the view that the *Brut* provides a providential mode of reading the past, see Daniel Donoghue, 'Laȝamon's ambivalence', *Speculum* 65 (1990), 537–63. This view is challenged by Lesley Johnson, 'Reading the past in Laȝamon's *Brut*', in Le Saux (ed.), *The Text and Tradition*, pp. 141–60.

16 Christopher Cannon makes the claim that 'the real hero of Laȝamon's *Brut* . . . is no particular person or peoples but the island now generally referred to as Britain, a place Laȝamon characteristically refers to as "þis lond"'. See Cannon, *The Grounds of English Literature* (Oxford: Oxford University Press, 2007), p. 50.

17 Malcolm Andrew and Ronald Waldron (eds.), *The Poems of the Pearl Manuscript* (Exeter: University of Exeter Press, 1996), p. 208 and note to that line; see, also, the Barron and Weinberg edition of Laȝamon's *Brut*, pp. 841–2.

4

'Broad spears broke, shields clashed, men fell': how Laȝamon and Tennyson deal with the problem of combat

Rosamund Allen

Taking John Anderson's abiding interest in medieval Arthurian literature back to its earliest English version and forward to one of the later poets in the tradition, I propose to reconsider, and perhaps to reconstitute, the literary reputation of two poets whose work is interlinked across the span of six hundred years. Laȝamon (conventionally called this, though he may may well have called himself 'Lawman')[1] wrote in the early thirteenth century. His *Hystoria Brutonum* or *History of the British* was first published by Sir Frederic Madden in 1847 in a monumental edition which has never yet been superseded.[2] Alfred Lord Tennyson's poems on battle date from his juvenilia to his last years and like the *Brut* are often regarded as barbaric and old-fashioned. We know that Tennyson read Madden's edition of Laȝamon: he gives Laȝamon's spelling of Arthur's mother Ygerne's name and in a note to the closing lines of 'The Passing of Arthur', the finale (but not the last written) of his twelve *Idylls of the King*, Tennyson points to the dying Arthur's promise in Laȝamon's *Brut* to return to his kingdom and dwell joyfully among the Britons.[3]

But most significantly of all, in the 1908 Eversley edition of *Idylls of the King* published by his son Hallam with Tennyson's annotations, Tennyson actually quotes Laȝamon's description of Arthur, citing Madden's edition. This highlights the features of Laȝamon's Arthur which Tennyson must have found inspirational. The lines Tennyson selects are those in which the fairies bestow on Arthur strength to be the best of knights, to be a powerful (Madden says 'rich') king and have a long life. Tennyson concludes his quotation, for which he supplies Madden's translation, with the lines:

> Heo ȝifen him þat kine-bern:
> custen swiðe gode.
> þat he was mete-custi:

of alle quikemonnen.
þis þe alue him ȝef:
And al swa þat child iþæh.[4]

[They gave to him, the child, virtues most good, so that he was [most] generous of all men alive: This the elves gave him, and thus the child thrived.][5]

This does indeed seem to encapsulate Tennyson's ideal king, one who saves and secures his people by his physical prowess on the battlefield. But not for Tennyson is there chivalric merit in the petty games of joust and tournament, where Launcelot excels but admits that Arthur 'nor cares / For triumph in our mimic wars, the jousts' ('Lancelot and Elaine', 311–12), though as he dies we hear how formerly Arthur, 'a star of tournament / Shot thro' the lists at Camelot' ('The Passing of Arthur', 391–2).[6]

Long life was endowed on Alfred Tennyson himself, but not given to *his* Arthur. Tennyson's Arthurian narratives gradually came together over a period of more than fifty years: the 'Lady of Shalott', not part of the *Idylls* sequence, first appeared in 1832 and was revised in 1842; 'Balin and Balan', last completed of the actual *Idylls*, was published in 1885. The twelve *Idylls* begin with 'The Coming of Arthur' and end with 'The Passing of Arthur'; at mid-point the sixth, 'Merlin and Vivien', sets in motion the inexorable decline of the Round Table.[7] Arthur's aim to cleanse the land of 'wolf-like men' fails as Arthur sees his realm 'Reel back into the beast' ('The Last Tournament', 125). As *Idylls* develops, the rot is seen to set in among the oversexed and under-exercised knights as soon as Arthur has dealt with the Saxon threat. But this is not Arthur's fault: he is a totally balanced man, excelling in the virtues Laȝamon had bestowed on his Arthur, and generous not with wealth but with the power to forgive and to be impartial.

Like Laȝamon's Arthur, Tennyson's is a man of action. For Tennyson, the introspective, solitary life of the hermit or the zealot, or indeed the poet, is far inferior to that of the man who both speaks reason *and* acts. But he must act without the 'maddening strife' which killed the 'gallant band' whose remains lie in 'The Vale of Bones' (64, 43) or 'the cry / Of triumph's fierce delight' uttered by the warriors in 'The Old Sword' (5–6).[8] Tennyson's interest in fearless combat is evident as early as these two poems in *Poems by Two Brothers* published in 1827 with his brother Charles.[9] But even in these early works he tends to bypass hand-to-hand combat by dwelling abstractly on zeal for battle and the native land's 'glory' in conquest ('Vale of Bones', 44).[10] A poem contributed to *The Examiner* in 1852 urges, 'Britons, Guard Your Own' against 'the Emperor', and 'The Charge of the Heavy Brigade' was written in 1854. By the time he began compiling *Idylls of the King*, Tennyson somehow had to accommodate a hero renowned for winning battles in a narrative sequence where the savage beast within man, tamed under Arthur's early rule, re-emerges to precipitate the downfall of a society already made vulnerable by moral delinquency. How can a morally perfect leader be simultaneously a hero in bloody battle? The tactics Tennyson employs to draw a distinction between the carnage which the legend proclaims as Arthur's achievement, and the man of peace Tennyson constructs Arthur to be, matches very closely Laȝamon's own resolution of the way a man who values peace can present war.

Laȝamon's own Arthur has other qualities besides generosity and strength. Unlike Tennyson's, he is not perfect, shows an unwillingness at times to listen to advice and evinces a burning imperial ambition which leads him from a reprisal attack on the nuisance king of Ireland and its annexation (11208) to conquering by intimidation other realms from Iceland (11238), Orkney (11246), 'Gutlonde' (11283) and 'Winetland' (perhaps the land of the Wends, 11309) to Norway (11595), Denmark (11642) and France (11996), finally taking on the might of the Roman empire in retaliation for an insult and almost taking Rome (13969). Tennyson's Arthur, almost in defiance of the British Empire whose figurehead was the monarch who supported Tennyson's writing through his 1845 civil list pension,[11] and which coloured the world-view of his time, is centrally based in the British Isles, though absent on missions in the provinces at crucial times such as the arrival of the Holy Grail. The centrality of the court and its factional weaknesses is vital in Tennyson's *Idylls*, which of course takes this slant from Tennyson's main inspiration, Malory's *Le Morte Darthur*.[12]

Both Tennyson and Laȝamon focus on the power of the word in the governance of the realm. For Tennyson keeping one's word, and speaking out when a situation requires it, is the moral concomitant of physical prowess: it is the danger of gossip, exemplified by the poisonous figure of Vivien, which undermines the attempts of the court to follow Arthur's example. When Merlin succumbs, worn out by Viven's insistence, and yields up his secret information to her, the descent into chaos begins. Laȝamon's use of the spoken word is different but equally shows how the great society depends on the interaction, through the spoken word, of all the constituent and supporting members of the realm. The great Arthur is a man of great powers of oratory too. Laȝamon's important addition to his source text, Wace's *Roman de Brut*, is his supplying of intermediary figures, who have both names and voices, such as the messenger who brings news to Arthur of Modred's treachery (14022–30).[13] A person is his or her word, and both Tennyson and Laȝamon, as poets, demonstrate their own artistic powers in revealing character through speech.

Both poets have nevertheless chosen a topic which, however much they emphasise the individual, employs battle, collective enterprise in martial combat, as a means of exploring the way a great leader is identified. It is not possible to take on the story of Arthur without making him fight. But both Tennyson, son of a country parson, and Laȝamon, a parish priest, are themselves men of words rather than action. Both clearly admire physical prowess when it is ethically exercised, as a means of exploring courage and self-denial. Both, however, I would contend, are troubled by the sheer fact of battle where men set out to damage each other in order to prove valour and justice through fight. Both have been accused of relishing bloodshed and violence; both, I would claim, find that its necessity is disturbing, and seek poetic means to evade and erase the actual moments of impact while never flinching from the resulting carnage.

A recent critic of Laȝamon remarks that he is 'aggressive, violent, heroic, ceremonial' compared to Wace, whom the same critic finds 'calm, practical, rational, with an eye for the realities of war and strategy'.[14] On this reading Laȝamon's Arthur is a 'portrait of extravagant heroism and kingliness' and in contrast to Wace's well-articulated account of the Saxon wars, Laȝamon's 'graphic, violent, often inessential detail', shows 'the love of violence characteristic of those who have occupations that keep them well away from any actual fighting'.[15] But is this really the case? Does Laȝamon really offer pell mell battle in 'scenes of individual combat and melee punctuated with vows of vengeance, boastings, denunciation, execration, scorn and triumph'?[16] And how does Tennyson, another whose occupation 'kept him well away from any actual fighting', actually deal with warfare? Tennyson was accused of being a 'warmonger', a charge he refuted in 1855. 'Considerable resentment was felt at his martial enthusiasm', which he in fact moderated after Sir William Howard Russell's letter to *The Times* after the Battle of the Alma revealed the suffering of the troops.[17] Tennyson thought, however, that his 'war poetry', which figures even among his juvenilia, was 'very important'. When asked by Thomas Edison and Charles Steytler to make phonograph recordings of his poetry, he chose poems like the famous 'Charge of the Light Brigade' and 'Charge of the Heavy Brigade', perhaps because, using the indifferent recording equipment of the time, the sonorous effects of battle would be more audible.[18] Critics of Tennyson today are unmoved by his war poetry; experience of total war has changed our attitudes to fighting, if not to the courage which we admire in those called on to perform what they consider their 'duty', even when they know their superiors have 'bungled'.

Both Tennyson and La3amon do indeed exert their full rhetorical and metrical powers when describing battle:

> Flash'd all their sabres bare
> Flash'd as they turned in air
> Sabring the gunners there,
> Charging an army while
> All the world wonder'd . . .
> Cossack and Russian
> Reel'd from the sabre-stroke
> Shatter'd and sunder'd.[19]

This lyric mode hardly seems to match the causeless slaughter of nearly six hundred men using swords against cannon because of a failure of command. It has almost reduced the fighting to a kind of ghoulish dance. And yet, we might well level the same accusation against Wace, the 'calm, practical and rational':

> Dunc veïssiez vassals combatre,
> Les uns les altres entr'abatre;
> Cez assaillir e cels defendre,
> Granz cops receivre e granz cops rendre,
> Les uns les altres enverser
> E sur les mors lef vifs passer;
> Escuz percier, hanstes cruissir,
> Naffrez chaeir, chaeiz murir.

> [Then you could see warriors fighting, one assaulting the other, these attacking, those defending, receiving and giving great blows, one felling the other, the living trampling the dead. Shields were pierced, lances shattered; the wounded fell, the fallen died.][20]

Slaughter enlivened by deathless rhetoric? Here is how La3amon renders the same fight between Aurelius and Hengest:

þer þa ræ3e men   to-gæderen heom ræsden.
helmes gunnen gullen   cnihtes þer feollen.
stel eode wið þan ban   balu þer wes riue.
urnen inne strete   stremes of blode.
fa3eden þa feldes   & þat gras falewede.[21]

[There the stern men rushed straight together:
Helmets were resounding, knights were falling,
Steel struck against bone, destruction was rife,
Down the roads went gushing rivulets of blood;
The fields were faded coloured and the grass fallow coloured.][22]

There is a difference here which is readily noticeable. Like Tennyson, who describes the flash of light as sabres are twirled aloft, but does not describe individuals pigsticking each other, leaving that to the objectified 'sabre thrust', so too La3amon sweeps into the initial rush and then deflects the human agency in the fighting into the impact of steel upon helmet and bone. Men fall shattered (Tennyson), blood has poured from them (La3amon), but it is the 'urbane' Wace who shows us man attacking man: 'one assaulting the other, these attacking, those defending, receiving and giving great blows, one felling the other, the living trampling the dead'.

The combat Wace presents is much more akin to the way Horn and Havelok fight, where the action is fully personalised:

He yede up to borde
With gode swerdes orde.
Fikenhildes crune
Ther he fulde adune;
And al his men a rowe,
Hi dude adun throwe.[23]
Havelok lifte up the dore-tree
And at a dint he slow hem three.
Was non of hem that his hernes
Ne lay ther-ute again the sternes.[24]

In *The Battle of Maldon* the panoramic technique which Wace also deploys pans in to close-ups of individuals in combat:

Bogan wæron bysige,   bord ord onfeng.
Biter wæs se beaduræs;   beornas feollon
on gehwæðere hand,   hyssas lagon.
. . .
Gegremod wearð se guðrinc: he mid gare stang
wlancne wicing   þe him þa wunde forgeaf.

[Bows were busy, the shield received the spear point; bitter was the battle rush, men fell on either side, young men lay (dead). The Warrior (Beorhtnoð) was enraged: with his spear he pierced the proud viking who had given him the wound.][25]

This is the classical technique for describing battle (as shown here in translations Tennyson might have known):

Fierce Turnus first to nearer distance drew,
And pois'd his pointed spear, before he threw:
Then, as the winged weapon whizz'd along,
'See now,' said he, 'whose arm is better strung.'
The spear kept on the fatal course, unstay'd
By plates of ir'n, which o'er the shield were laid:
Thro' folded brass and tough bull hides it pass'd,
His corslet pierc'd, and reach'd his heart at last.
In vain the youth tugs at the broken wood;
The soul comes issuing with the vital blood:
He falls; his arms upon his body sound;
And with his bloody teeth he bites the ground.[26]

As he spoke he hurled his spear and hit one of those who were in the front rank, the comrade of Aeneas, Deicoön son of Pergasus, whom the Trojans held in no less honour than the sons of Priam, for he was ever quick to place himself among the foremost. The spear of King Agamemnon struck his shield and went right through it, for the shield stayed it not. It drove through his belt into the lower part of his belly, and his armour rang rattling round him as he fell heavily to the ground.[27]

J. Timothy Lovelace shows that Tennyson's early training and consequent immersion in the literature of the heroic age mean that his war poems reflect the imagery of the *Iliad* and *Aeneid*, reinventing for his own age the heroic ethos of ancient texts, particularly where he treats martial subjects. However, while noting that Tennyson's 'Virgilian' war poetry reflects his belief that poets should rouse the spirit of combat, real or figurative, but actually focuses on decay, of weapons as of kingdoms, Lovelace does not address Tennyson's handling of the logistics of combat.[28] Similarly, Jeffrey E. Jackson challenges William Thackeray's allusion to the 'clear clanging of King Arthur's sword' in *Idylls* by noting that for 'many readers and critics . . . Tennyson's Arthurian work appears to be lacking anything like the spirit of red-blooded, boys'-book swordplay that Thackeray suggests' and they are 'left instead with a clearer image of swords breaking throughout *Idylls*'.[29]

If it be objected that Tennyson and Laʒamon had never fought and for that reason avoid direct description of combat, the same lack of experience does not impede classical poets who, as we have seen, know or can imagine the procedures of wounding another human being to the death. The poets of the First World War were both poets and fighters – and were unpopular until the 1940s for bitterly decrying the 'glory' of conquest. I once heard a Second World War combatant observe that fighting in tanks and with long-range missiles does not call forth the courage and dismay of killing someone while looking in their face. Wilfred Owen, writer and fighter, who imagines the words of another poet among the enemy whom he has killed, articulates as Tennyson could not the anguish it entails:

> 'I am the enemy you killed, my friend.
> I knew you in this dark: for so you frowned
> Yesterday through me as you jabbed and killed.
> I parried; but my hands were loath and cold.
> Let us sleep now . . .'[30]

The difference between classical, Old English, Old French, Middle English and early twentieth-century poets' accounts of battle and those of Laʒamon and Tennyson seems to be that Laʒamon and Tennyson only rarely focus on individual combat; they present only the panoramic view and the aftermath. And yet Tennyson had been taught Greek by his father in the Somersby vicarage, could read Homer even before he went to prep school at the age of eight, and was influenced by Virgil and Homer all through his poetic career; interestingly, he also translated *The Battle of Brunanburh* (1876).[31] Laʒamon also knew epic: according to Elizabeth Salter it is highly probable that he took the technique of long-tailed similes in the Arthurian section of *The Brut* from late twelfth-century Latin neo-epics.[32]

And yet both Laʒamon and Tennyson deflect our gaze from human violence, except where the opponent is an outright villain, a heathen Saxon or a Saracen. Laʒamon does in fact present some individuals actually striking an enemy: we see Aldolf kill Hengest with a direct blow to the head, Arthur striking the giant of Mont St Michel (13004), having declined to attack him from behind while he was sleeping, presumably because that would have been unchivalrous (12993), and the brave son of Rumareth of Winetlond, grabbing the carving knives and beheading the man who starts the fight at Arthur's Yule Feast, and killing his brother and five more (11380–4). But most of these individuals are attacking alien insurgents, the disruptive 'other'. Laȝamon seems to fight shy of presenting knights in equal combat, even where Christian forces are fighting pagans. What we see and hear is the gleam of weapon, the crash of sword, the clash of spear on shield – and the after-effects of battle: the trampled and blood-stained grass, the torrents of blood. Laȝamon the priest may not himself have fought (though many priests, besides the Templars, did fight in the Middle Ages, as *The Song of Roland* suggests),[33] but a priest's services would be required after battle to hear the confessions of the dying and to administer to them viaticum and extreme unction. The din of armed men battling hand-to-hand must have been audible miles away, and King John's England was far from peaceful.[34]

Tennyson too is aware of the cacophony of battle, and interestingly he too deploys the same distancing technique of separating the weapon from the man who wields it, endowing the weapon with all the force of human motive:

> And friend slew friend not knowing whom he slew . . .
> And ever and anon with host to host
> Shocks, and the splintering spear, the hard mail hewn,
> Shield-breakings, and the clash of brands, the crash
> Of battle-axes on shatter'd helms, and shrieks . . .
>> ('The Passing of Arthur', 100–10)

Laȝamon's own version of the last battle between Arthur and Modred could almost have served as a model:

> luken sweord longe.   leiden o þe helmen;
> fur ut sprengen.   speren brastlien
> sceldes gonnen scanen;   scaftes to breken . . .
> mon i þan fihte non þer ne mihte;   ikenne nenne kempe.
>> (*Brut*, 14246–51)

> [Drew their long swords, laid into helmets:
> Sparks started out, spears were clattering,
> Shields were shattering, shafts were splintering . . .
> No one in that battle could recognise any warrior.]
>> (p. 364)

Both poets characterise the end of a great society in unbearable pain, and point up the way extreme bloodshed enforces anonymity by depersonalising the event as each becomes unrecognisably covered in gore and the weapons take over. Tennyson's last battle is fought in such a thick mist that opponents are invisible to each other 'and friend slew friend not knowing whom he slew'; again the spears splinter and the swords clash apparently without human control.[35] This is the point: these combatants were fellow knights, they shared an ideal, which was chivalry. Tennyson, born in a rectory and attempting to support his deeply dysfunctional parental family and then his own children by his poetry, was 'a poet haunted by the uneasy feeling that it was the soldier who epitomised action, duty, manliness and courage'.[36] So scoffs Christopher Ricks, himself too young (at six) to have served in the Second World War, whose national service in Egypt was self-confessedly spent guarding rotting potatoes, and who became Professor of Poetry at Oxford.[37] Both Tennyson and Laȝamon seem to have been aware – if uneasily, as Ricks claims – that fortitude *in extremis* is not only the mark of the hero but also the foundation of the uneasy social order he inhabits. Both poets lived in a time of political upheaval: 1848 was known as 'the year of Revolutions' throughout Europe; the years from 1208 to 1213 saw England under interdict from the pope, while in 1216 the French dauphin and his forces invaded the south of England and besieged Dover castle. Both poets must have been keenly aware that the ideals of chivalry and courage were being undermined, in the thirteenth century by the increasing use of mercenaries, and in the early nineteenth century by the steady erosion of patriarchy as female power increased. Both clung to their ideals of the loyalty and honour of the brave warrior: 'Honor the Light Brigade / Noble 600!' (54–5). Male strength guarantees a succession of following generations. Yet Tennyson's Arthur laments before his final battle as his kingdom 'reels back into the beast', '[I] have but stricken with the sword in vain' ('Passing of Arthur', 26, 23).

Some scholars acknowledge that Laȝamon's message is the importance of a strong ruler: 'his strength is proved by his ability to maintain peace and ensure that his officers and knights follow his command. If we detect violence, its purpose is the preservation of order'.[38] Whereas Wace *adds* battle formations to those that Geoffrey of Monmouth enjoys describing in the *Historia Regum Britanniae*, Laȝamon excludes detail; through his 'lack of interest in technical aspects of warfare' he compresses battle scenes and tones down slaughter, as Françoise le Saux confirms, reducing fighting to ritualised formulae.[39]

We can contrast both Laȝamon and Tennyson's versions of Arthur's last battle with Henry of Huntingdon's description of King Stephen at the Battle of Lincoln:

> The mighty king was standing, his enemies trembling at the incomparable ferocity of the blows **he** struck. When the earl of Chester saw this, he envied the king's glory, and rushed at **him** with the whole weight of his knights. At which the king's lightning strength (*uis fulminea*) showed itself, as, wielding **his** great battle-axe, **he** slew some and scattered others . . . Eventually the royal battle-axe **was** shattered by incessant blows. **He** drew out his sword, worthy of a king, and performed wonders with **his** right hand, until **his** sword too, **was** shattered.[40]

Henry of Huntingdon's 'mighty king' has to demonstrate his strength; he is the immediate instigator of the blows inflicted by his weapons, which in the process he destroys, and Henry seems to have no qualms about using violence against his own subjects in civil warfare. But Tennyson's Arthur observes morosely, 'The king who fights his people fights himself' ('The Passing of Arthur', 72).

Tennyson and Laȝamon clearly did find the notion of Christians killing each other disturbing. Gareth is told that Arthur is 'mightiest on the battle-field' but (the corrupt) Lancelot is 'first in Tournament' ('Gareth and Lynette', 485–6). In the early days of Arthur's vision in *Idylls of the King*, Geraint and Gareth, both innocent and young, do actually wield weapons: 'Prince Geraint / Drave the long spear a cubit thro' his breast' ('Geraint and Enid', 463–5; he beheads Earl Doorm, 727–8). Arthur 'lightly' proves his strength in friendly fight against the young challengers Balin and Balan: 'And Arthur lightly smote the brethren down / And lightly so return'd, and no man knew' ('Balin and Balan', 39–40). Equally harmlessly, Gareth conquers the three knights of morning, noon and sunset without killing them, despite hewing great pieces of armour off the third, and reveals the fourth, the ghastly Knight of Night and Death, to be a mere 'blooming boy' in disguise. *Life* prevails. Even when the enemies are clearly renegade, heretic or pagan and full hands-on fighting occurs, the weapons still often take charge:

> Aim'd at the helm, his lance err'd; but Geraint's
> A little in the late encounter strain'd,
> Struck thro' the bulky bandit's corselet home,
> And then brake short, and down his enemy roll'd,
> And there lay still.
>
> ('Geraint and Enid', 157–61)

The one exception in Laȝamon's *Brut* where Arthur actively fights a fellow human (albeit a hated Roman) is Arthur's fight with Frollo with spear and sword, in which Arthur reciprocates his own head wound by splitting open Frollo's skull with Caliburn. Immediately afterwards he demands homage from the Parisians and declares peace, more imperiously than Wace's Arthur: his victory has secured another colonial conquest. In Laȝamon's version, even Modred is not killed by Arthur himself. Unable to evade the magnificent final revenge Arthur wreaks on Mordred in his main source, Malory's *Le Morte Darthur*, Tennyson does allow Arthur this final thrust: 'the King / Made at the man: then Modred smote his liege / Hard on that / helm . . . while Arthur at one blow, / Striking the last stroke with Excalibur, / Slew him' ('The Passing of Arthur', 164–9).

In the Roman War against an alien power, Laȝamon's Arthur's forces engage the pagan enemy actively, but again there is no panning in to individual combat. Once they have been released by men ('heo lette(n)': 'they sent'), the weapons take over:

> To-somne heo heolden   swulc heouene wolde uallen.
> ærst heo lette fleon to   feond-liche swiðe.
> flan al swa þicke   swa þe snau adun ualleð.
> stanes heo letten seoððen   sturnliche winden.
> heoððen speren chrakeden   sceldes brastleden.
> helmes to-helden   heȝe men uellen.
> burnen to-breken   blod ut ȝeoten.
> ueldes falewe wurðen   feollen here-mærken.

(13703–10)

[Together they charged as if the sky would crash down:
First **they sent** flying over, tremendously fast,
Arrows as thick as the snow falling down;
Then **they sent** stone balls crashing their way savagely;
After that spears were cracking, and shields were splitting,
Helmets were caving in, and great men falling;
Coats of mail were shattering, blood gushing out;
The fields were discoloured; their standards tottered.]

(p. 350)

Tennyson's Arthur does indeed battle, until the last, against the heathen Saxons, but this is conducted off stage. Mechanical, ritualised, objective combat is epitomised in Tennyson's opening idyll, 'The Coming of Arthur', one of only four passages where we actually hear of but do not see Arthur as war leader: the song for Arthur's wedding has as variable refrain 'Fall/Clang battleaxe, and flash brand: Let the King reign' (481–501).[41] Arthur's twelve great legendary battles are summarised in two bare lines: '(Arthur) Fought, and in twelve great battles overcame / The heathen hordes, and made a realm and reign'd' (517–18). But by 'The Last

Tournament', the ante-penultimate idyll, combat according to the rule of arms has ceased. Arthur defeats a drunken knight who simply overbalances while trying to hit him and falls off his horse, where his face is trampled out by Arthur's followers, dehumanised as 'a hundred spears' (419), who proceed to slaughter drunken men and women amid 'woman-yells', and then set fire to the place (457–77). Chivalry has disappeared, leaving mere weapons; battlefield and the homestead it should protect coalesce; the 'knights' commit murder on the helpless. Simultaneously the renowned fighter Tristram wins that last tournament with all the rules broken and without striking a blow as his opponents recede to the boundaries in fear ('Last Tournament', 185, 190).

These deflections of human aggression on to the weapons that men wield, with the ultimate erasure of humanity itself, could of course be coincidental solutions by La3amon and Tennyson. It happens that both reduce red battle fury by distancing martial impact, deflecting fighting on to the weapons which make the destructive contact, especially where whole armies of human creatures are being demolished. It is not impossible that Tennyson learned some of this technique from La3amon. It may be argued that both are bellicose poets seeking vicarious excitement amid the thrills of battle but inhibited, by personal physical weakness (Tennyson was famously myopic) or priestly calling, from martial action themselves. But I see this dualistic presentation of man as courage, and weapon as aggression, as a resolution of the problem of demonstrating human bravery in a context of violent action. The animated weapons represent the universal human instinct for destruction but discreetly detached from the nobler aspirations of honour, courage and concern to protect the weak. Tennyson could well have learned from La3amon. Independently or not, both poets have devised an effective solution to the paradox of a ruling martial elite dedicated to removing injustice by exacting harsh reprisal. The reputations of Tennyson's 'blameless king' and La3amon's once noble ('æthele') British race and their English inheritors are preserved by the mysterious operation of weaponry. In my view neither poet deserves the reputation of violent warmonger.

Notes

1 See John Frankis, 'La3amon or the Lawman? A question of names, a poet and an unacknowledged legislator', *Leeds Studies in English* 34 (2003), 109–32.

2 Frederic Madden (ed.), *Laȝamon's Brut, or Chronicle of Britain: A Poetical Semi-Saxon Paraphrase of The Brut of Wace*, 3 vols. (London: Society of Antiquaries, 1847).

3 'I perish by this people which I made, – / Tho' Merlin sware that I should come again'. 'The Passing of Arthur', lines 190–1, in J. M. Gray (ed.), *Alfred Lord Tennyson: Idylls of the King* (Harmondsworth: Penguin Books, 1983), p. 293; unless otherwise noted, quotations from *Idylls of the King* are from this edition. Laȝamon, obscurely perhaps, speaks of Arthur dwelling among 'the English': Merlin prophesied 'þat an Arður sculde ȝete cum Anglen to fulste' [that an Arthur would still come to aid the English] (line 14297) even though it is the Britons ('Bruttes') who still look for Arthur's return (14292).

4 Madden (ed.), *Laȝamon's Brut*, vol. 2, p. 384, line 21 – p. 385, line 3 (Caligula text cited, throughout).

5 Madden (ed.), *Laȝamon's Brut*, vol. 2, p. 384.

6 These lines are present in 'Morte d'Arthur' (lines 223–4), the earlier version of 'The Passing of Arthur', and may represent an earlier characterisation of Arthur than the one Tennyson presents in *Idylls*. 'Morte d'Arthur' was written in 1833, revised in 1835 and published in 1842, while 'The Passing' was not published until 1870.

7 The twelve *Idylls* in their final order (not that of their composition, which took place over the course of forty-three years) are: 'The Coming of Arthur', 'Gareth and Lynette', 'The Marriage of Geraint', 'Geraint and Enid', 'Balin and Balan', 'Merlin and Vivien', 'Lancelot and Elaine', 'The Holy Grail', 'Pelleas and Ettare', 'The Last Tournament', 'Guinevere', 'The Passing of Arthur'. 'The Passing' is a revised version of 'The Epic: Morte d'Arthur' published in 1842; the sequence began in 1859 with 'Enid', 'Vivien', 'Elaine' and 'Guinevere', 'the true and the false', the first later divided and 'Guinevere' enlarged, thus placing 'Merlin and Vivien' at the centre. On the composition of *Idylls* see Kathleen Tillotson, 'Tennyson's serial poem', in Geoffrey and Kathleen Tillotson (eds.), *Mid-Victorian Studies* (London: Athlone, 1965), pp. 80–109.

8 Christopher Ricks (ed.), *The Poems of Tennyson*, 3 vols. (Harlow: Longman, 1987), vol. 1, pp. 108–111.

9 Ricks (ed.), *Poems*, vol. 1, pp. 109–11.

10 Already in 'The Old Sword' (1827), probably by Alfred rather than Charles Tennyson (Ricks (ed.), *Poems*, vol. 1, pp. 105–6), written two decades before Frederic Madden's edition of *Laȝamon's Brut*, Tennyson addresses the weapon metonymically as an index of human bellicosity, partially eliding the human agent in synecdoche: 'what arm hath wielded / Thy richly gleaming brand . . . whose fingers clasped thee?' (17–18, 25), though obliquely referring to the warrior owner in the pronouns 'who/se' and 'his ire'.

11 In Victoria's reign money was still paid out of the sovereign's civil list
    for people in need who, as in Tennyson's case, had given service to
    literature. Tennyson was not expected to be able to make a living from
    poetry at that stage, and received £200 per annum.

12 Tennyson owned Malory's *Morte Darthur* in Wilks's 1816 three-
    volume reprint of Stansby's 1634 edition, which, according to
    Tillotson, is 'inscribed A. Tennyson in Hallam Tennyson's hand',
    though Hallam claims that his father used the 1816 Walker and
    Edwards' two-volume reprint of Stansby. Tillotson suggests that
    'perhaps he possessed one in boyhood and the other in the 1830s'.
    Tillotson, 'Serial poem', p. 84. Southey's edition 'in two handsome
    volumes' appeared in 1817 ('Serial poem', p. 83). The Globe edition of
    Caxton, expurgated and modernised, was published in 1868, by which
    time Arthurian material was very familiar to the public, largely thanks
    to Tennyson.

13 The 'messenger theme' is discussed by Françoise le Saux, *La3amon's
    Brut: The Poem and its Sources* (Woodbridge: D. S. Brewer, 1989), pp.
    47–56.

14 Derek Pearsall, *Arthurian Romance: A Short Introduction* (Malden,
    MA, Oxford and Melbourne: Blackwell, 2003), pp. 16, 17.

15 Pearsall, *Arthurian Romance*, p. 17.

16 Pearsall, *Arthurian Romance*, p. 17.

17 Philip Henderson, *Tennyson: Poet and Prophet* (London: Routledge
    and Kegan Paul, 1978), p. 112.

18 This recording can be heard on: www.bbc.co.uk/arts/poetry/outloud/
    tennyson.shtml.

19 'Charge of the Light Brigade', lines 27–36 in Ricks (ed.), *Poems*, vol. 2,
    p. 510.

20 Judith Weiss (ed. and trans.), *Wace's Roman de Brut: A History of
    the British* (Exeter: University of Exeter Press, 1999), p. 195, lines
    7753–60.

21 G. L. Brook and R. F. Leslie (eds.), *La3amon: Brut*, 2 vols. EETS
    o.s. 250, 277 (London: Oxford University Press for The Early English
    Text Society, 1963, 1978), vol. 2, lines 8187–91. All subsequent quota-
    tions from *The Brut* are taken from this edition.

22 This and subsequent translations from *The Brut* are taken, with
    minor revisions, from Rosamund Allen (ed., trans. and intro.),
    Lawman:'Brut' (London: J. M. Dent and Sons, 1992).

23 *King Horn*, ed. Ronald B. Herzman, Graham Drake and Eve Salisbury
    (Kalamazoo, MI: Medieval Institute Publications, 1999), lines 1496–
    1502.

24 G. V. Smithers (ed.), *Havelok* (Oxford: Clarendon, 1987), lines 1806–
    9.

25 D. G. Scragg (ed.), *The Battle of Maldon* (Manchester: Manchester
    University Press, 1981), lines 110–12, 138–9; my translation.

26 Virgil, *Aeneid*, Bk X, 671–82, in John Dryden (trans.), *The Aeneid of Virgil*, ed. Robert Fitzgerald (New York: Macmillan, 1964), p. 324.

27 Samuel Butler, *The Iliad of Homer Rendered into English Prose* (London: Jonathan Cape; New York: E. P. Dutton and Co., 1825), Book V, lines 533–40, p. 80.

28 J. Timothy Lovelace, *The Artistry and Tradition of Tennyson's Battle Poetry* (New York and London: Routledge, 2003): 'While the glories of battle often appear on the perimeters of Tennyson's pictures, his center of focus is usually rusting swords, vales of bones, or failing kingdoms . . . His belief in poets as the trumpets which sing to battle, even figurative battle, is uncongenial to the modern disdain of Victorian uplift' (p. 165).

29 Jeffrey E. Jackson, 'The once and future sword: Excalibur and the poetics of imperial heroism in *Idylls of the King*', *Victorian Poetry* 46 (2008), 207–29 (207–8). Jackson terms the sword 'synecdoche for violence, its abandonment cognate with Tennyson's oft-discussed "fear of an innate male capacity for irrational violence"' (209), commenting that 'Arthur's noble disdain for violence is couched explicitly as a rejection of the sword' (211); Excalibur must therefore be thrown away. Tennyson does not, as has been suggested, deploy allegory and metonym, but instead, metaphor, so associating the sword with selfish materialism; therefore Bedivere casts Excalibur away as 'a rejection of a profane, unstable materiality'. Jackson's article was published as my paper was nearing completion.

30 Wilfrid Owen, 'Strange Meeting', *The Collected Poems of Wilfred Owen*, ed. and intro. C. Day Lewis (London: Chatto & Windus, 1963), p. 35, lines 39–43. 'At the beginning of the Second World War [Edmund Blunden] declared, "I still regard murder as murder no matter how boldly hidden up in steel helmets and rolls of honour."'; Paul Fussell, *The Sunday Times*, 2 December 1990. 'If we go back we will be weary, broken, burnt out, rootless, and without hope. We will not be able to find our way any more'; Erich Maria Remarque, *All Quiet on the Western Front* (1928/9, as *Im Westen nichts Neues*), written from the German experience, and read to my knowledge by an English survivor of the war. Both cited in www.warpoetry.co.uk/end_of_First_World_War_90th_anniversary.html, ed. David Roberts (November 2008).

31 Tennyson published in *Ballads and Other Poems* (1880) his translation of 'The Battle of Brunanburh' (from the *Anglo-Saxon Chronicle*, year 937). Tennyson's interest was probably sparked by his son Hallam's 1876 translation of the poem. Michael P. Kuczynski identifies Tennyson's interest in the 'complexities of the heroic character' in the poem ('Translation and adaptation in Tennyson's "Battle of Brunanburh"', *Philological Quarterly* 86 (2007)), while Christopher Ricks notes his focus on the horrors of battle (*Tennyson* (London: Macmillan, 1972), p. 292).

32 Elizabeth Salter, *English and International: Studies in the Literature, Art and Patronage of Medieval England*, ed. Derek Pearsall and Nicolette Zeeman (Cambridge: Cambridge University Press, 1988), pp. 63–6. Commenting on the frequent observation that Laȝamon's battle (and seafaring) scenes are less technical than Wace's, Salter also notes that the 'battle-episodes are far less carefully composed than the most famous examples from Old English poetry' (p. 50).

33 See laisse CLXV, 2222–32 where the archbishop takes Oliphant but, weak with wounds, cannot help Roland and dies. F. Whitehead (ed.), *La Chanson de Roland* (1942; Oxford: Basil Blackwell, 1980); D. D. R. Owen, trans., *The Song of Roland* (London: Unwin Books, 1972).

34 On the political involvement of England with Europe at the time, see Alan Harding, *England in the Thirteenth Century* (Cambridge: Cambridge University Press, 1993), esp. pp. 264–71. King John was/ is suspected of killing his nephew, Arthur of Brittany, who had a stronger claim to the throne; he had lost his mother's French holdings through quarrelling with the Lusignan family, and lost Normandy in 1204; he extracted the wealth of the bishopric of Winchester during a vacancy and his quarrel with the pope over the appointment to the archbishopric of Canterbury led to the interdict on England from 1208 to 1213; in 1211 there was an uprising of the Welsh; even before becoming king he had antagonised the Irish; his intemperate lust was notorious; he set exorbitant taxes, and enacted hugely royal lordship rights on the barons, his quarrel with whom culminated in Magna Carta in 1215, and when he died suddenly in 1216 there was civil war and an invasion by the French.

35 Andrew Lynch, in comparing Tennyson and Malory, also comments on the 'ambivalence about Arthurian military violence' in *Idylls of the King*: 'The early victories . . . are nobly vague in representation . . . and emblematic; enemy armies are conquered by . . . weapons, which strike ritually and half spontaneously, without inculpating those who use them'. Lynch argues that 'Tennyson only becomes more explicit about the unpleasant material features of fighting where he doubts its moral and religious basis' and concludes that the poet 'offers a strikingly divided vision of Arthurian war, one whose religion and morality well suit his partisan, imperialist project, but which cannot entirely sustain its self-confidence' ('"Thou woll never have done": Ideology, context and excess in Malory's war', in D. Thomas Hanks Jr. and Jessica G. Brogdon (eds.), *The Social and Literary Contexts of Malory's Morte Darthur*, Arthurian Studies 42 (Woodbridge, Suffolk: Boydell and Brewer, 2000), pp. 24–41 (24–5)). See also Andrew Lynch, 'Archaism, nostalgia and Tennysonian war in *The Lord of the Rings*', in Jane Chance and Alfred Siewers (eds.), *Tolkien's Modern Middle Ages*, 2nd edn (New York: Palgrave Macmillan, 2009), pp. 77–92; '[Tennyson] definitely wanted something else out of Arthur than military prowess,

but couldn't divorce military prowess from the idea of superior right'
(private communication). My thanks to Professor Lynch for this information.

36 Christopher Ricks, *Tennyson* (London and New York: Macmillan,
1972), p. 53.

37 Ricks, in his account of his two years' national service in Egypt as
a 2nd Lieutenant in the Green Howards before going to university,
recalls that 'the army was a bit of a nightmare. I didn't see any of Egypt
because I was behind wire guarding rotting potatoes with killer dogs.
And I loathed the anti-Arab prejudices of many in the army although
the only Arab I actually saw was a man who electrocuted himself and
was killed while doing the ironing'. Ricks became Professor of Poetry
at Oxford in 2004: www.guardian.co.uk/books/2005/jan/29/poetry.
oxforduniversity.

38 Lesley Johnson identifies the 'moralising purpose' of warmaking,
which, in contrast to Wace's *Roman de Brut*, 'is not automatically a
glorious activity' but 'is set against the values of a Christian chivalric
society'; 'wars may be fought on "just" grounds, but there is a linger-
ing recognition in the *Brut* of the cost (and sin) involved in undertak-
ing them' (Lesley Anne Johnson, 'Commemorating the past: a critical
study of the shaping of British and Arthurian history in Geoffrey
of Monmouth's *Historia Regum Britannie*, Wace's *Roman de Brut*,
Laȝamon's *Brut* and the alliterative *Morte Arthure*'; unpub. PhD
thesis, King's College, London University, 1990, pp. 291, 301; I am
grateful to Janet Cowen for drawing my attention to these passages).
David Johnson notes that Arthur's reprisals against those who begin
the fight in the hall 'underpin Arthur's authority and determination to
maintain order'. David Johnson and Elaine Treharne (eds.), *Readings
in Medieval Texts: Interpreting Old and Middle English Literature*
(Oxford: Oxford University Press, 2005), p. 222.

39 Le Saux, cited in Johnson and Treharne (eds.), *Readings in Medieval
Texts*, p. 219; see also Françoise le Saux, *Laȝamon's 'Brut': The Poem
and its Sources* (Cambridge: D. S. Brewer, 1989), pp. 33–42.

40 Diana Greenway (ed. and trans.), *Henry, Archdeacon of Huntingdon:
Historia Anglorum (The History of the English People)* (Oxford:
Clarendon Press, 1996), p. 739. Words in bold indicate the personal-
ised action of the combat.

41 The other passages are: 'Gareth and Lynette', 220–1; 'The Holy
Grail', 311–12, 539; 'The Last Tournament', 92. These were all
composed in the space of four years: 'Holy Grail' was written in
1868 and published in 1869, Tennyson worked on 'Gareth' and 'Last
Tournament' in 1869–72 and published both in 1872, revised the following year (Tillotson, 'Serial poem', 102). Together with the addition of the song 'Blow trumpet' in 'The Coming', the 1873 additions
develop Arthur as an 'off-scene' warrior. Arthur tackles the resurgence

of heathendom in 'The Last Tournament' (122–5, 419–85) and does not deign to strike the drunken rebel Red Knight (457–67), but the total collapse of chivalry is revealed in a horrifying display of butchery: Arthur's knights ride their horses over the fallen Red Knight's face, and then 'sword' both men and women till 'all the pavement stream'd with massacre' (469–76).

5

'For ho is quene of cortaysye': the assumption of the Virgin in *Pearl* and the *Festial*

Susan Powell

Although not conventionally religious, John Anderson was a spiritual man. As such he wrote with sensitivity and generosity about the religious poems of the *Pearl*-poet, as he has come to be known. Indeed, the change of emphasis from *Gawain* to *Pearl* was marked in the placing of *Pearl* first in John's 1976 edition (with Arthur Cawley) of the four poems.[1] In this edition John prepared the texts of *Cleanness* and *Patience* to complement Cawley's texts of *Gawain* and *Pearl*. By the time of the second edition (1996), all four poems were re-edited by John, as Arthur Cawley (who died in 1993) had wished.[2] 2005 saw the publication of John's explication of the four poems: the title, *Language and imagination in the* Gawain-*poems*, expresses not only the strengths of the poet but those of the author.[3]

This chapter will focus on relationships, but not those human networks which John found most stimulating and most intriguing and which led him to write (as the first sentence in a mere two pages allotted him for the poem): '*Pearl* is one of the world's great poems on the theme of human pain and Christian hope'.[4] Indeed, my approach might well not be particularly attractive to John, who made it clear in his introduction to *Language and Imagination* that, while he was prepared, of course, to 'take account of relevant literary and intellectual contexts', his was 'not one of the studies which take a theological approach to them, or any other extra-textual approach'. On the other hand, I hope that I may demonstrate sufficient attention to the text of *Pearl* for John to have agreed that I too see meaning 'as primarily constructed by patterns of words rather than by ideas and scripts which lie beyond the texts'.[5]

The relationships I will deal with in this chapter are those between the Pearl-maiden and Jesus Christ, between the Pearl-maiden and the Virgin Mary, and between Christ and the Virgin Mary,[6] not the relationship between the Pearl-maiden and the Dreamer which is more usually prioritised. I will consider the marriage of the Maiden to the Lamb and suggest connections with the enclosed world of female religious which may (for reasons which I will not hypothesise) have had some relevance to the *Pearl*-poet. From this I will suggest similarities between the Maiden and the Virgin, both essentially and in their relationship to the Lamb/Son. His relationship with them will lead into a brief discussion of a short lyric in one of two assumption sermons in a contemporaneous and extremely popular sermon collection, John Mirk's *Festial*. The chapter will end with an appendix which provides a critical edition of both this lyric and another in the second assumption sermon.

The marriage of the Maiden to the Lamb is crucial to her perception of herself and to the Dreamer's perception of her. The Dreamer can only be given this vital clue after he has submitted to the obedience ('mekenesse', 406) which is essential to a kingdom where the King is figured as a Lamb:

> 'My Lorde ne loves not for to chyde,
> For meke arn alle that wondes hym nere . . .
> My Lorde the Lamb loves ay such chere,
> That is the grounde of alle my blysse'.

> (403–8)

The fact of the peculiar (but not unique) relationship between Maiden and Lamb is not only a direct answer to the Dreamer's question 'What lyf ye lede erly and late' (392), but also crucial to the poem as a whole. At lines 413–16, and again at 757–60, it is laid out in its strange bareness:

> 'Bot my Lorde the Lombe, thurgh hys godhede,
> He toke myself to hys maryage,
> Corounde me quene in blysse to brede
> In lenghe of dayes that ever schal wage . . .'

> (413–16)

> 'My makeles Lambe that al may bete',
> Quoth scho, 'my dere destyne,
> Me ches to hys make, althagh unmete
> Sumtyme semed that assemblé . . .'

> (757–60)

After the first statement, the dialogue focuses on the status afforded the Maiden ('corounde me quene'); after the second, it focuses on the singular choice of the Maiden as bride ('me ches to hys make, althagh unmete'). In each case, the Dreamer initiates the dialogue, in which he plays the role of the unenlightened Boethius (as it were) and the Maiden that of Lady Philosophy:

> 'Blysful', quoth I, 'may thys be trwe?
> Dyspleses not if I speke errour.
> Art thou the quene of hevenes blwe,
> That al thys worlde schal do honour?'
>
> (421–4)

> 'Why, maskelles bryd, that bryght con flambe,
> That reiates has so ryche and ryf,
> Quat kyn thyng may be that Lambe
> That the wolde wedde unto hys vyf?'
>
> (769–72)

In each case, the ensuing explication focuses on the courtly democracy of heaven, where each member is a queen but the Virgin is acknowledged as *prima inter pares*. I will have more to say about the gynocentricity of the New Jerusalem later, but first it will be useful to put the Lamb into context.

The identification of the Lamb with Christ is particularly marked in the Book of Revelation, on which the Maiden's ensuing description of the New Jerusalem (973–1152) depends. The 'Lamb that was slain' (*agnus qui occisus est*, Apoc. 5:12) harks back to the sacrificial lamb of the Old Testament (as in Exodus 12:5 or Leviticus 23:12) but in the Book of Revelation it is no more than an allusion, a synonym for the Lord of the New Jerusalem (Apoc. 6:1, 7:17, 17:14, 21:22, 23) whose cohort consists of 144,000 virgins:

> 'And lo a lamb stood upon mount Sion, and with him an hundred forty-four thousand, having his name, and the name of his Father, written on their foreheads . . . These are they who were not defiled with women: for they are virgins. These follow the Lamb whithersoever he goeth.'[7]

The Pearl-maiden, on the other hand, explicates the reference fully and scholastically: firstly it was the prophet Isaiah who called Christ Lamb in reference to His slaughter at the hands of the Jews (797–816, cf. Isaiah 53:7); secondly it was John the Baptist who called Him Lamb when He came to him for baptism (817–28, cf. John 1:29, 36); thirdly it was John the Evangelist in the Book of Revelation (829–40). And the 144,00 who attend him are 'the Lambes vyves' (785). In Revelation the virgins are notably male ('who were not defiled with women'); they serve as a cohort or bodyguard to the Lord. In *Pearl* they are notably female ('the

Lambes vyves'); the analogy might better (but frivolously) be with a harem and an Eastern potentate.

Although frivolous, the analogy may seem not entirely unfounded. The scriptural emphasis on virginity (while implicit, of course, in the death of the Pearl-maiden before the age of two (line 483)) is obscured (and problematised) in *Pearl* by the courtly imagery of love applied to the Lamb, in particular the use of *lemman*, a word with sometimes a salacious nuance: 'I am holy hysse', the Maiden asserts (418), and He is 'my Lombe, my Lorde, my dere juelle, / My joy, my blys, my lemman fre' (795–6).[8] However, there is an entire lack of force and passion in what might in other contexts be passionate and forceful. This is a Lamb, not a 'noble wohere' who sends presents ahead and then comes to prove his worthiness 'þurh cnihtschipe' and 'dude him i turneiment & hefde for his leoues luue his scheld i feht as kene cniht on euche half iþurlet'.[9]

The analogy with the description of Christ as lover-knight in *Ancrene Wisse* is suitable for my purpose, not just because it offers an example of a more forceful lover than the Lamb, but also because *Ancrene Wisse* was written for an enclosed female audience. While not wishing to argue that this was the audience of the *Pearl*-poet, there are some interesting analogies between the Maiden's marriage to the Lamb (in a poem where no male presence intrudes except for the emasculated Christ) and the dedication to Christ of a young, chaste female through the ceremony of consecration by which a postulant enters a nunnery. The *Pearl*-poet may have had in mind in his characterisation of the Maiden not just the Book of Revelation but the profession of a nun. The 144,000 may perhaps be seen as all those virgins whose marriage is not to earthly men but to Christ Himself.[10]

The image of Christ as bridegroom is persistent in Christian, particularly Pauline, culture, where Christ's spouse is the church, for example, the church at Corinth (2 Corinthians 11:2) and the church at Ephesus (Ephesians 5:23–4). When John the Baptist refers to Christ as the *sponsus* or bridegroom (John 3:29), or Christ refers to Himself as such (Matthew 9:15), even the *Glossa Ordinaria*, the standard commentary on scripture, was silent about who the *sponsa* (bride) might be. However, the use of the term in the Book of Revelation was interpreted unequivocally. When John the Evangelist (as it was thought then) wrote that 'the marriage of the Lamb is come, and his wife has prepared herself' (Apoc. 19:7), or 'I John saw the holy city, the new Jerusalem, coming down out of heaven from God, prepared as a bride adorned for her husband' (Apoc. 21:2),[11] the *Glossa* interpretation was unequivocal: 'Just as the bridegroom sends ahead gifts to the bride before he leads her forth (*sc.* in marriage), so Christ sends in advance faith and virtues and good works to the Church before he takes her up in glory.'[12]

From patristic times, however, the term *sponsa Christi*, bride of Christ, had a secondary referent and was used as a synonym for the woman dedicated to a life of virginity in the service of Christ. The vocation of the nun is conventionally traced to St Scholastica (*c.*480–*c.*547 AD). Broadly speaking, just as her brother, St Benedict, founded the monastic order, so Scholastica founded the female equivalent. However, a ceremony for the consecration of a virgin to Christ existed already in the second half of the fourth century, when Pope Liberius consecrated Marcellina, sister of St Ambrose. At the end of that century a letter of Pope Siricius to an unnamed virgin specifies that the ceremony should be one of *velatio*, putting on a veil such as a married woman would wear.[13] Most relevant for the later Middle Ages is the late-thirteenth-century pontifical of William Durandus, which contains details of the ceremony 'De benedictione et consecratione virginum'. In this consecration ceremony, performed in similar versions throughout western Europe, the bishop explicitly takes the part of the spouse, Christ, blessing and asperging the postulants' new garments, principally the mantle, wimple and veil, and offering them the crown and the wedding ring. In a version of this ceremony as it was performed over two centuries later at the Benedictine convent of St Mary, Winchester, the garments exclude the crown, and it is the ring which is most prominent, placed on the postulant's wedding finger by the bishop, who announces: 'Receive the ring of faith, the token of the Holy Spirit, so that you may be called and may be the bride of God, and may offer it before the Lamb, your spouse Christ Jesus, in the day of the heavenly marriage, if you serve Him faithfully'.[14]

Moreover, in a contemporary note of such a ceremony, the analogy between the postulant nun and the 144,000 virgins of Revelation is absolutely explicit in the bishop's address to the nun:

> 'We invoke you, Lord . . . over these your servants who have vowed to serve you with pure mind and clean heart and body: that you may deign to associate them with those 144,000 who remained virgins and did not join themselves to women, in whose mouth was found no sorrow, and thus may you make these your servants remain immaculate to the end.'[15]

Also dating from a century after *Pearl*, an extant consecration sermon will serve to demonstrate clearly this mystic marriage.[16] 'Desponsacio Virginis Christo', or 'Spousage of a Virgyn to Christ' (fol. A1r), is the title of the sermon delivered to a convent in the Ely diocese by John Alcock, bishop of Ely 1486–1500, which was printed by Wynkyn de Worde *c*.1497.[17] It begins by the calling of the banns:

> I aske the banes betwix the hyghe and moost myghty prynce kyng of all kynges sone of almyghty god and the virgyne Mary in human- yte, Cryste Ihesu of Nazareth of the one partye. And A. B. of the thother partye / that yf ony man or woman can shewe ony lawfull Inpedyment other by ony precontracte made or corrupcyon of body or soule of the sayd A. B. that she ought not to be maryed this daye vnto the sayd myghty prynce Ihesu that they wolde accordyinge vnto the lawe shewe it. (fol. A2r)

The sermon begins as a marriage ceremony, a 'noble spowsage' between 'so grete a prynce & almyghty' and 'a wretche his creature & of a poore lynage'. This is a marriage which exalts not only the nun but all her kin and confirms them 'of cosynage by affynyte to the fader of heuen / our lady all the angels with all the hole Genelogy of Cryste' (fol. A2v). The properties of the new bride must be love ('charyte') and chastity ('virgynyte'); she must be a guardian (*custos*) of the signs of her profession, the veil and mantle, the ring ('in token of maryage'), and (for the ceremony itself) a taper, which represents Christ Himself. She must show obedience to her superiors, remove her thoughts from the world and remain enclosed within the walls of her convent. In doing so, she must learn to experience Christ by meditation on his life at the altars of her own church: 'Soo it is your dewte to seke Cryste Ihesu to whom ye shalbe wedded nother at Nazareth Bedleem nor Iherusalem / but ye shall fynde hym here within your owne chirche the same god and man Cryste Ihesu' (fol. B2r).[18]

The analogies between the nun and the Pearl-maiden are suffi- cient to arouse interest, at least. Both are the brides of Christ; both of low birth, married to one of high birth (the Maiden is 'unmete' (759) and has acquired more of aristocratic status than could any worldly lady (578–9)); both are characterised by love and chastity; both endorse obedience to their superiors ('Maysterful mod and hyghe pryde . . . arn heterly hated here' (401–2)); the Maiden is literally dead to the world, the postulant nun is warned by Alcock: 'though your body be here in this worlde corporally your mynde & your soule to be with Cryste Jhesu' (fol. A6v).

For the postulant nun in the late Middle Ages the ring is the token of her marriage to Christ. Her virginity, which is stressed in the ceremony, is marked by her white garments, such as the Pearl-maiden wears: 'Al blysnande whyt was hir beau biys' (197; cf. lines 1102).[19] However, a different item of her dress, the crown mentioned in Durandus, may serve as a link to the next consideration in this paper: the relationship of the Pearl-maiden to the Virgin Mary. The poet emphasises the crown worn by the Maiden: it is high and made of pearls (205–8); she doffs it when she first catches sight of the Dreamer (237) but replaces it as she rebukes him for his impetuous outburst (255).[20] It is a crown which has been placed on her head by the Lamb Himself (415, 480, 767). To the Dreamer the crown signifies royalty: 'What more worschyp moght he fonge / Then corounde be kyng be cortaysé?' (1479–80) and he protests against the lavish generosity of a God who could exalt a two-year-old to such status: 'That cortaysé is to fre of dede' (481). God might have made her countess, damsel, lady: 'Bot a quene! – hit is to dere a date' (492).

The parable of the labourers in the vineyard which follows develops what is a central feature of the kingdom of heaven (already introduced at 445–68), its democracy: '"Of more and lasse in Godes ryche", / That gentyl sayde, "lys no joparde"' (601–2). Thus, when the Dreamer sees the full cohort of 144,000 virgins, they all wear crowns (1101), as the Maiden had earlier implied (451).[21] However, the Dreamer's mistake (like all his mistakes) is natural for one earth-bound: according to the church the crowned queen of heaven can only be Mary:

> 'We leven on Marye that grace of grewe,
> That ber a barne of vyrgyn flour;
> The croune fro hyr quo moght remwe
> Bot ho hir passed in sum favour?'

> (425–8)

The coronation of the Virgin was a familiar motif of medieval Mariolatry. After the death of the Virgin ('dormition', as used in the Eastern church, expresses rather more clearly the peculiar nature of this death, which involved no decay of the body), the Virgin was taken up into heaven by her Son: 'And Criste sette hyre þer be hym in hys trone and crowned hur quene of heven and emperas of helle and lady of alle þe worlde, and hath ioy passyng alle other seyntus' (London, British Library, MS Cotton Claudius A. II., f. 99v).[22] And, of course, the Maiden does not deny Mary's supremacy: she kneels at her name (as one would kneel at the name of Jesus), turns her face upwards, praises Mary as 'makeles' or matchless (435) and affirms her pre-eminent role:

> 'That emperise al hevens has,
> And urthe and helle in her bayly;
> Of erytage yet non wyl ho chace,
> For ho is quen of cortaysye.'

(441–4)

In the Book of Revelation, there is no specific reference to the Virgin Mary, although she was traditionally identified with the 'woman clothed with the sun, and the moon under her feet, and on her head a crown of twelve stars' (Apoc. 12:1).[23] In *Pearl*, however, the crown is not specific to the Virgin but an adjunct of all the virgins. As such, one might want to suggest an analogy with the crown which formed part of Durandus' consecration ceremony and to suggest that the poet is linking (how deliberately I would not say) his image of the Pearl-maiden as nun and his image of heaven as a royal court.[24] (The essence of the court, as the poet makes clear, is not that it is 'to fre', as the Dreamer has suggested at line 481, but that it extends liberality, generosity, *fraunchise*, all these courtly characteristics, beyond human comprehension.)

The prose quotation above which describes the coronation of the Virgin is taken from an 'assumption of the Virgin' sermon in John Mirk's *Festial*, contemporaneous with *Pearl* and written not far from the *Pearl*-poet's own part of England.[25] It may be relevant to my argument that Marian feasts (the conception, purification, annunciation, assumption and nativity of the Virgin) were often the occasion for consecration ceremonies in medieval nunneries. Linked themes may therefore be expected.[26]

The *Festial* includes two assumption sermons (for the feast celebrated on 15 August), one which describes the death of the Virgin surrounded by the apostles, her assumption and coronation, and then discusses the necessity of her body remaining uncorrupt, and another which allegorises the gospel text of the day (Luke 10:38–42) and applies to the Virgin characteristics of both female protagonists, Martha and Mary, symbols respectively of the active and contemplative lives.[27] Two lyrics from these sermons (the only lyrics in the *Festial*, apart from some rhyming tags) are offered as an appendix to this chapter. One of them will form the conclusion to it.

The Pearl-maiden describes her crowning thus:

'When I wente fro yor world wete,
He calde me to hys bonerté:
"Cum hyder to me, my lemman swete,
For mote ne spot is non in the."
He gef me myght and als bewté;
In hys blod he wesch my wede on dese,
And coronde clene in vergynté,
And pyght me in perles maskelles.'

(761–8)

The death of the Pearl-maiden is thus followed by her assumption into heaven and coronation, a startling analogy with that of the Virgin herself. Just as the body of St Thomas of Canterbury was not washed before burial because it had been washed in the blood of his martyrdom,[28] so the Maiden escaped purgatory and secured heaven through being washed in the blood of the sacrificed Lamb: 'In hys blod he wesch my wede'. In such circumstances, the fact that she did not know the basic tenets of the church (so important to the world-focused Dreamer (484–5)) is trivial. Indeed, in raising her to heaven, Christ barely differentiated between the words He used to the *Pearl*-maiden ('Cum hyder to me, my lemman swete')[29] and those that, according to Mirk, He used to His mother:

'Com, my swete. Cum, my floure.
Com, my coluer. Com, my boure.
Com, my modur, now wyth me,
For quene of heven make I þe.'

And in the *Festial* (as not in *Pearl*), Mary responds to her Son:

'My dere Sone and my loue,
I come wyth þe to þi boure [aboue].
Where þou arte, latte me be,
For alle my loue is leyde on þe.'[30]

The source of Christ's address to His mother is the Song of Songs, where the bridegroom addresses the bride: 'Arise, my love . . . and come', 'Come, my beloved', 'Come from Libanus, my spouse, come from Libanus, come, thou shalt be crowned'.[31] A patchwork of such passages from the fourth to the seventh chapters of the Song of Songs forms the reading at mass on the feast of the assumption.[32] But similar material is also used in the mass celebrated for the birth of a virgin martyr, including an invocation of the type offered by Christ to His mother: 'Veni, electa mea, et ponam te in thronum meum quia concupiuit rex speciem tuam'.[33]

What I believe the *Pearl*-poet is doing in his depiction of the Pearl-maiden is according her (and all those who died as virgins) the role in heaven accorded by Christ to His mother in the traditional teaching of the medieval church. I do not think this treatment is parallelled elsewhere in literary texts. I would suggest that the *Pearl*-poet has meditated on the postulant nun in her role as bride of Christ, on the Virgin Mary in her bodily assumption into heaven, and on the mass for virgin martyrs, and has fused these thoughts into a consolatory narrative of the death of the two-year-old. His is a narrative rooted in the doctrine and liturgy of the church and in the Bible (albeit the volatile Book of Revelation), but it transcends (and subverts) even those powerful media in its daring creativity of 'language and imagination', those crucial features of the poet which John Anderson identified in the title of his last work.[34]

Notes

1 A. C. Cawley and J. J. Anderson (eds.), *Pearl, Cleanness, Patience, Sir Gawain and the Green Knight* (London, Melbourne, Toronto: Dent, New York: Dutton, 1976).

2 J. J. Anderson (ed.), *Sir Gawain and the Green Knight, Pearl, Cleanness, Patience* (London: Dent; Vermont: Tuttle, 1996). References to *Pearl* throughout, by line number parenthetically in the text, are from this edition.

3 J. J. Anderson, *Language and imagination in the* Gawain-*poems* (Manchester: Manchester University Press, 2005). In all three works so far cited, despite differences in the titles, *Pearl* is treated first.

4 Anderson (ed.), *Sir Gawain and the Green Knight*, pp. ix–x.

5 Anderson, *Language and imagination*, p. 10.

6 For useful, popular introductions to some of the topics in this paper, see Marina Warner, *Alone of All her Sex* (London: Picador, 1985), pp. 67–78 (virgins), 81–102 (the assumption), 103–117 (the queen of heaven), 121–33 (the Song of Songs).

7 (Apoc. 14:1, 4). 'Et ecce Agnus stabat supra montem Sion, et cum eo centum quadraginta quatuor millia, habentes nomen ejus, et nomen Patris ejus scriptum in frontibus suis . . . Hi sunt qui cum mulieribus non sunt coinquinati: virgines enim sunt. Hi sequuntur Agnum quocumque ierit.' All scriptural quotations are from the Vulgate Bible and the Douay-Rheims translation. The text is the epistle reading for Holy Innocents' Day: for the Pearl-maiden as Innocent, see Ian Bishop, *Pearl in its Setting: A Critical Study of the Structure and Meaning of the Middle English Poem* (Oxford: Blackwell, 1968), pp. 104–12.

8 *Lemman* ('lover') occurs at lines 763, 796, 805, 829. It is part of the courtly vocabulary used inappropriately (or ironically) by Nicholas to Alison in Chaucer's 'Miller's Tale', *Canterbury Tales* I.3277–81.

9   Geoffrey Shepherd (ed.), *Ancrene Wisse* (London: Nelson, 1959), p. 22, lines 6–10. The punctuation is my own.

10 As an adjunct to the following discussion, see Nicholas Watson, 'The *Gawain*-Poet as a vernacular theologian', in Derek Brewer and Jonathan Gibson (eds.), *A Companion to the Gawain-Poet* (Cambridge: Brewer, 1997), pp. 293–313 (esp. pp. 300–5).

11 'Venerunt nuptiae Agni, et uxor ejus praeparavit se', 'Et ego Joannes vidi sanctam civitatem Jerusalem novam descendentem de caelo a Deo, paratam sicut sponsam ornatam viro suo'.

12 'Sicut sponsus praemittit munera sponsae antequam eam ducat, sic Christus Ecclesiae fidem et virtutes et bona opera antequam eam suscipiat in gloria'. This translation of the gloss to Apoc. 21:2 is my own.

13 These and the following details are dependent on A. Nocent, 'The consecration of virgins', in A. G. Martimort (ed.), *The Sacraments*, vol. 3 of *The Church at Prayer* (Collegeville, MN: Liturgical Press, 1988), pp. 209–20.

14 'Accipe annulum fidei, signaculum Spiritus Sancti, ut sponsa Dei voceris et sis, atque illum praeferas ante agnum, sponsum tuum Christum Jesum, in die coelestium nuptiarum, si ei fideliter servieris'. William Maskell, 'The order of consecration of nuns', *Monumenta Ritualia Ecclesiae Anglicanae*, 2nd edn, 3 vols. (Oxford: Clarendon, 1882), vol. 3, pp. 331–59 (p. 347). The 'order' is taken from Cambridge University Library MS Mm.3.13, given to the nuns of St Mary, Winchester by their bishop, Richard Fox, who held the episcopate 1500–28. As such, he was a contemporary of Alcock, bishop of Ely, whose consecration sermon is discussed next.

15 'Te invocamus Domine . . . super has famulas tuas quae tibi voverunt servire pura mente, mundo corde et corpora: ut eas sociare digneris inter illas centum quadraginta quatuor millia quae virgines permanserunt, et se cum mulieribus non coinquinaverunt, in quorum ore dolus inventus non est'. Maskell, *Monumenta Ritualia*, vol. 3, p. 348. Cf. Apoc. 14:4.

16 The term 'mystic marriage' is usually applied to the quasi-marriages (most commonly envisioned in painting) of (in particular) Saints Agnes and Catherine of Siena (and/or Alexandria). Agnes is treated at some length in Alcock's sermon.

17 John Alcock, *Desponsacio Virginis Christo. Spousage of a Virgin to Christ* (Westminster: Wynkyn de Worde, 1497?) *STC* 286. For details of the few extant consecration sermons, see V. M. O'Mara, 'Preaching to nuns in late medieval England', in Carolyn Muessig (ed.), *Medieval Monastic Preaching* (Leiden, Boston, and Köln: Brill, 1998), pp. 93–119 (pp. 100–15).

18 The sermon is discussed more fully in O'Mara, 'Preaching to nuns', pp. 104–7.

19 The postulants at Winchester are described thus: 'every oon of theym clothed all in whyte, and beryng upon hir right arme the habite that

the relygyon and profession requireth, with the veyle, ryng, and scroll of hir profession attached upon the sayd habite, and in hir left hande beryng a taper wythoute lyght'. Maskell, *Monumenta Ritualia*, vol. 3, pp. 334–5. The white garments of the Pearl-maiden are traditional for heavenly creatures (cf. Matt. 28:3, Apoc. 3:4, 4:4). In the Middle Ages, white was unusual, and the adoption of white clothes by Margery Kempe aroused a variety of (hostile) responses, cf. Sanford Brown Meech, *The Book of Margery Kempe*, EETS o.s. 212 (Oxford: Oxford University Press, 1940 for 1939), p. 84, lines 25–8, p. 116, lines 11–35, p. 124, lines 13–17 (the archbishop of York here understood it to indicate virginity). See Mary C. Erler, 'Margery Kempe's white clothes', *Medium Aevum* 62 (1993), 78–84.

20 For the courtesy of this gesture (swiftly withdrawn), compare the casting of their crowns before the Lamb by the twenty-four ancients (Apoc. 4:10).

21 In the Book of Revelation, only the twenty-four ancients and the locusts wear crowns, and these of gold, not of pearl (Apoc. 4:4, 9:6).

22 Cf. (from a different manuscript) Theodor Erbe, *Mirk's Festial: A Collection of Homilies by Johannes Mirkus (John Mirk)*, Part I, EETS e.s. 96 (London: Kegan Paul, Trench, Trübner, 1905), p. 224, lines 21–4.

23 'Mulier amícta sole, et luna sub pedibus ejus, et in capite ejus corona stellarum duodecim.'

24 For an edition of a nunnery sermon which deals with items of a nun's clothing, see Veronica O'Mara, *A Study and Edition of Selected Middle English Sermons*, Leeds Texts and Monographs, n.s. 13 (Leeds: Leeds Studies in English, 1994), pp. 141–221 (esp. pp. 165–70). In England, by the fifteenth century at least, the crown was distinctive of the Swedish order of Bridgettines and not, it seems, of other orders of nuns (O'Mara, *A Study*, pp. 169–70). However, it was necessary in order to secure the veil to the head, and it may be only that the Bridgettine crown is especially distinctive, with its rendering of the five wounds of Christ as circles of red on a white structure. Admittedly, the crown is not mentioned in the garments described in the texts printed by Maskell, *Monumenta Ritualia*, vol. 3.

25 For a brief synopsis of the *Festial*, see Susan Powell, 'Mirk, John (*fl.* *c*.1382–*c*.1414)', in the *Oxford Dictionary of National Biography* (2004), www.oxforddnb.com/view/article/18818, accessed 5 December 2009; for the fullest details, see Susan Powell, *John Mirk's Festial*, 2 vols., EETS o.s. 334–5 (Oxford: Blackwell, 2009, 2010). The *Festial*'s compiler, John Mirk, was an Austin canon at Lilleshall in Shropshire, but the predominant dialect is north-east Staffordshire, as is that of the *Pearl*-poet. See Angus McIntosh, M. L. Samuels and M. Benskin (eds.), *A Linguistic Atlas of Late Mediaeval English*, 4 vols. (Aberdeen: Aberdeen University Press 1986), vol. 1, p. 105, vol. 3, pp. 37–8 (LP

26). For further refinement of each, see H. N. Duggan, 'Meter, stanza, vocabulary, dialect', in Brewer and Gibson (eds.), *A Companion*, pp. 221–42 (pp. 240–2) and Powell, *John Mirk's Festial*, vol. 2, Appendix IV (forthcoming, 2010).

26 Maskell's text specifies Sundays or solemn feasts, of which 'in festis beatae Mariae' might be one occasion ('The Order of consecration of nuns', p. 331). However, the feast of the assumption may have been the preferred feast. Alcock's sermon was delivered on that day as the text, 'Audi, filia, et vide' (Ps. 44:11), makes plain (cf. J. Wickham Legg (ed.), *The Sarum Missal* (Oxford: Clarendon Press, 1916), p. 309, lines 11–12), and, although O'Mara does not consider her 'nunnery sermon for the feast of the Assumption' a consecration sermon, it is possible that it was so used, since it deals, as consecration sermons seem to have dealt, with the items of the nun's clothing (*A Study*, p. 141ff.). Moreover, if not a consecration sermon, it is (oddly) 'the only extant example of a vernacular sermon in manuscript form for an occasion other than profession' (O'Mara, 'Preaching', p. 107).

27 See text and explanatory notes to sermons 53 and 54 in Powell, *John Mirk's Festial*, vol. 2 (forthcoming, 2010). For the text of these sermons from Oxford, Bodleian Library MS Gough Eccl. Top. 4, see Erbe, *Mirk's Festial*, pp. 221–35.

28 James Craigie Robertson (ed.), *Materials for the History of Thomas Becket, Archbishop of Canterbury*, 7 vols. (vol. 7 by J. B. Sheppard), Rolls Series 67 (London: Rolls, 1875–85), vol. 3, p. 148, line 151.

29 This is the song that the Pardoner and Miller (Christ and the Virgin!) sing to each other on the Canterbury pilgrimage ('The General Prologue', *Canterbury Tales* I.669–74).

30 See the appendix.

31 'Surge, propera, amíca mea, columba mea, formosa mea, et veni', 'Surge, amica mea, speciósa mea, et veni'; 'Veni, dilecte mi'; 'Veni de Libano, sponsa mea: veni de Libano, veni, coronaberis' (S. of S. 2:10, 13; 7:11; 4:8). For a discussion, see Rosemary Woolf, *The English Religious Lyric in the Middle Ages* (Oxford: Clarendon Press, 1968), pp. 298–300.

32 Legg, *Sarum Missal*, p. 308, line 23; p. 309, line 7.

33 'Come, my chosen one, and I will place you on my throne because the king has desired your face' (Legg, *Sarum Missal*, p. 380, lines 3–4), based on the Song of Songs and the Book of Wisdom (S. of S. 6:8, Sap. 7:10).

34 Unlike the Dreamer, the poet dares to think beyond the doctrine of the Church. Because of this, I cannot agree with Watson, 'Vernacular theologian', that he belongs 'with the more matter-of-fact religiosity embodied in pastoral works such as those being produced . . .by John Mirk (the influential *Festial* and *Instructions for Parish Priests*)' (p. 296).

Appendix

The lyrics have been edited from London, British Library, MS Cotton Claudius A.II, collated with the fullest extant manuscripts of the *Festial*.[1] Only one partial manuscript includes an assumption sermon, Cambridge University Library Nn.3.10, fol. 73r (sermon 54). Texts of the *Festial* are either of Group A or Group B.[2] Only Group A manuscripts have two assumption sermons (nos 53 and 54). Group B manuscripts have only sermon 54, but they omit the passage with the lyric and so are not relevant to this appendix. Abbreviations have been silently expanded and only substantive variants are normally noted.

Sigla for the sermons which witness the lyrics are as follows:

Base text
α London, British Library, MS Cotton Claudius A.II

Group A
B   London, British Library, MS Harley 2403
C   London, British Library, MS Harley 2417
D   Oxford, Bodleian Library, MS Gough Ecclesiastical Topography 4
G   Oxford, Bodleian Library, MS Hatton 96
H   Cambridge, University Library, MS Dd.10.50
I   Cambridge, Gonville and Caius College, MS 168/89
J   London, Dr Williams's Library, MS Ancient 11 (*olim* London, New College, MS Z.c.19)
K   Southwell Minster Library MS 7

Sermon 53: *De assumpcione beate Marie virginis sermo*
Witnesses: α f. 99v; B f. 144v, C f. 66r, D f. 128v, G f. 140r, H f. 140r, I p. 255, K ff. 124v–5r.

And it was done also ioyfully, for þe þrydde day, as Cryste sayde, he com doun oute of heven wyth grete multitud[e] of angelus, of prophetus and oþer holy men and seyntus wythoute nombur, and Seynt Mychael be/ring oure Lady soule in hys armes bryther þan þe sonne. Þan seyde Cryste to hym, 'Mychael, do my modur soule into þe body aȝeyne'. And whanne he hadde don so, Cryste sayde to hur:

'Com, my swete. Cum, my floure.   1
Com, my coluer. Com, my boure.   2

> Com, my modur, now wyth me,   3
> For quene of heven make I þe.'

Þan þe body satte vp and lokyd to Criste and sayde:

> 'My dere Sone and my loue,   5
> I come wyth þe to þi boure [aboue].   6
> Where þou arte, latte me be,   7
> For alle my loue is leyde on þe.'   8

1 Com(1)] now *add*. K; swete] modur *add*. H.
2 coluer] dowve K; Com my boure] *om*. H; Com(2)] *om*. DG, to K;
my(2)] own *add*. BCDGIK.
3 my modur] *om*. H.
4 For] *om*. GH; quene of heven] heven quene BCDIK; make I] I
make CDGHIK.
5 dere] swete IK, *om*. H; and my] *om*. H; and] all *add*. I.
6 wyth] to K.
6–7 to . . . be] in to thi ioy thow lede me H.
6 to þi boure] as thyne K; to] in to G; þi boure] þyn D; aboue] *om*.
αBCGI.
7 Where] that *add*. G; arte] now *add*. D; latte me be] þou lede me
be G.

Commentary notes
The lyric is not recorded in *NIMEV* (Julia Boffey and A. S.
G. Edwards, *A New Index of Middle English Verse* (London:
British Library, 2005)), but there are similar elements in *NIMEV*
641, 'Come my dere spowse and lady free' (J. Zupitza (ed.),
'Die Gedichte des Franziskaners Jakob Ryman', *Archiv für das
Studium der neueren Sprachen und Litteraturen* 89 (1892), 167–338
(pp. 184–5)). This lyric is also based on the Song of Songs and
is addressed by Christ to His mother. The Virgin is invoked in
the first four stanzas by the imperative 'Come' with the refrain
'Veni: coronaberis' (S. of S. 4:8). Mirk's version was presumably
influenced by his source for the *Festial*, Jacobus de Voragine's
Legenda Aurea, where the assumption sermon includes the phrases
'columba mea, tabernaculum gloriae, vasculum vitae, templum
coeleste' (T. Graesse (ed.), *Jacobi a Voragine Legenda Aurea vulgo
Historia Lombardica Dicta* (Dresden and Leipzig, 1846), p. 509).
Columba relates to 'coluer' (2); in the same line, 'boure' covers the
three nouns *tabernaculum*, *vasculum* and *templum* and refers to the
Virgin's body as a receptacle for the Christ-foetus, whereas in line
6 the word is used neutrally to mean simply 'chamber' or 'room'.

Textual notes
6 *þi boure aboue*: The conjectural emendation is based on the assumption that in α, *þi boure*, and DK's 'þin aboue', reflect respective omissions of one or the other of the two similarly patterned words 'boure' and 'aboue'.

Sermon 54: *Sermo de euangelio in die assumpcionis beate Marie virginis: hoc modo*
Witnesses: a f. 102r–v; B f. 151r, C ff. 70v–71r, D f. 133r–v, G ff. 144v–145r, H f. 145r–v, I pp. 265–6, J p. 282, K ff. 130v–131v.

Þan schul ȝe knowe þat scheo hadde fyve special ioyes of hure Sone here in erthe, þe whyche gladuth hyr myche whan þei ben rehersyd to hure. But now scheo hath vij special [ioyes in heven], þe wyche scheo schewod to Seynt Thomes of Cawnturbyry and badde hym greton hyr wyth hem in þis wyse, behotyng hym for serteyne þat alle þoo þat vche day devowtely greton hure wyth hem he schal sene hure or he dye, and hys soule schal com to blysse. / Þan schal he say þus:

Be gladde and blythe, quene of blysse,   1
For þine ioy passing isse
In heuen, courte and halle.
In þat courte þou hase no pere
Of ioy, of blysse, of gentil chere   5
Saue þe Lorde of alle.

Be gladde and blythe, swete crem,
Bryter þan þe sone-bem
Whan it is moste schene.
Þe chere of þe it is so brythe   10
Þat alle heven it makuth lytȝh
And seyntus alle bedene.

Be gladde, Lady, and so ȝe mowe
To sene alle infere [b]owe
To ȝow þat ben in blysse.   15
Alle ȝow lowton and done honour –
Þus in heven ȝe haue þe floure
Nexte to God i[w]ysse.

Be gladde and blythe, swete thynge,
Þere ȝe ben quene, ȝoure Sone is kynge,   20
Sytting in hys trone.
Whatte-eure it be ȝe preyor fore,
'Modur', he sayth, 'and quene icore,
I graunte wel ȝoure bone.'

Be gladde and blyþe, Lady free,   25
Syttyng be þe Trenite
In blode and flesse ifere.
Ful of ioye and eke grace,
God hath makyd þer ȝoure place,
As to hys modyr dere.   30

Be glade and blythe in alle wyse,
For alle þat done to ȝow seruise
Ful wel is quitte here mede.
Þin Son is gente – non suche may be –
He bydde[th] alle schulde loue þe   35
And he wil beton þere nede.

Be gladde and blyþe, quene of heuen,
For þese ioyes alle seven
Neure schulle ȝe mysse.
Wel is ȝow þat ȝe were bore   40
Þus to ioy for euremore
Wyth [þ]e kyng of blysse.

Now, swete Lady, I ȝow praye,
Helpe vs at oure endyng daye
And schelde vs from þe fende.   45
And graunte vs alle suche a lytht
For vs of ȝow to haue a syght
Er þen we hennys wende.
Amen   49

1–42 Be . . .blysse] *om.* J.
1 Be] *prec. by* Gaude flore virginali. honoreque speciali. tran-
scendens splendiferum; angelorum principatum. et sanctorum
decoratum. dignitate numerum K.
2 For . . .isse] *om.* H.
3–4 courte . . .courte] crowned H.
3 and halle] *om.* G.
4 courte] contray I; þou hase] ȝe haue DI.
5 of(2)] and BDK; of(3)] and BDK.
6 Saue] sone G; Lorde] kyng.
7 Be] *prec. by* Gaude sponsa cara dei. nam ut clara lux diei. solis
datur lumine; sic tu facis orbem vere. tue pacis resplendere. lucis
plenitudine K; blythe] the *add.* G, thow *add.* H; swete] as *add.* D;
crem] beme GH.
8 þan] than *add.* H; sone] sonus I.
9 it] he B, hoe C, scho D, sche GHK; schene] clene H, clere K.
10 þe(2)] you DI; it] *om.* BCDGHK.

12 seyntus alle] all seyntys G; alle bedene] þat byn deere K.

13 Be] *prec. by* Gaude splendens vas virtutum. cuius pendens est ad nutum. tota celi curia; te benignam et felicem. ihesu dignam genitricem. veneratur in gloria K; gladde] my *add.* BCDGHIK; and so] as BCGHK, for I; ȝe mowe] ȝe may now I, þou well myȝt GH; ȝe] wel *add.* C.

14 To . . .bowe] for angelys bow all ryȝt GH; To] for to BCDIK; infere] to ȝow I, *om.* BCDK; bowe] (a *canc.*) bow D, in *add.* and *canc.* H, howe a.

15 ȝow] the GH, they H; þat] thow H; ben] art GH; blysse] to ȝow *add.* I.

16 ȝow] to þe BCK, *om.* G; lowton] bowen B; done] doþe, the *add.* H.

17 ȝe haue] þou haste BCGHK.

18 iwysse] ywis BCDGHIK, in blysse a.

19 Be] *prec. by* Gaude nexu voluntatis. et amplexu caritatis. iuncta sic altissimo; vt ad votum consequaris. quicquid virgo postularis. a ihesu dulcissimo K.

20 ȝe ben] þou art BCGHK; ȝoure] þy BCGK, they H, oure D; is] ab. l. D, þe *add.* I.

22 be] þat *add.* CHIK; ȝe preyon] þou prayest BCGHK.

23 icore] in core BC, ycrowned H.

24 graunte] the *add.* H; wel] wol D, ȝow I; ȝoure] þi BCGHK.

25 Be] *prec. by* Gaude mater miserorum. quia pater seculorum. dabit te colentibus; congruentem hic mercedem. et felicem poli sedem. regnis in celestibus K; and blyþe] *ab. l.* I; blyþe] my *add.* B.

27 blode and flesse] flesche and blode H.

28 ioye] *over erasure* a; eke] ful of BCDGHI, *om.* K.

29 makyd þer] þere made CGH; ȝoure] thy GK, they H, ȝow a I.

31 Be] *prec. by* Gaude virgo mater christi. quia sola (mater christi *add. and canc.*) meruisti. o virgo piissima; (vt ad votum consequetur *add. and canc.*) esse tante dignitatis. quod sis sancte trinitatis. cescione proxima K.

32 to] *om.* DI; ȝow] þe BCGHK.

33 wel] *om.* H; is quitte] quyt ys C, qwyȝt is H, þou quytest GK, ȝe quit I.

34 gente] gentyl CGHK; non . . .be] as þey may se B, as they mown se GH, as þou may se CK, and dose hem se I, and doþe hym gre D.

35 He byddeth] he bydde a, and byddyth H, and byddeþe hem BCDGIK; schulde] *om.* BCDGHIK; loue] well *add.* G;

36 beton] be at D; qwyȝte HK; nede] mede HK.

37 Be] *prec. by* Gaude virgo mater pura. certa manens et secura. quod hec septem gaudia; non cessabunt nec decrescent. sed

durabunt et florescent. per eterna secula K; quene of heuen] *om.* G; of heuen] *om.* H.
38 þese] *om.* C; alle] *om.* H.
39 schulle ʒe] schalt þou BCGHK.
40 ʒow] þe BCGHK; þat] euer *add.* H; ʒe] þou BCHK, *om.* G.
41 ioy] ioyen CK; for] and G, *om.* BH.
42 þe] BCHK, þe heʒe DGI, hye a.
43 ʒow] þe BCGHJ.
46 a] *om.* BCDGHIK; lytht] myʒt BCDGHIJK.
47 For vs] *om.* BCDGHIJK; ʒow] þe CGHJK; to] for to CDI; haue] suche *add.* BK; a] clene *add.* J.
48 Er þen] er B, ʒer K, or GHJ, or þat DI; hennys] heþen D, hyne I; wend] do wend K, wynd GHIJ.
49 Amen] amen *add.* G, *om.* DIK, et cetera J.

Commentary notes
Boffey and Edwards, *NIMEV* 462. Both the prose introduction (adapted) and the lyric occur in London, British Library, MS Harley 210, ff. 86v–88r (*NIMEV* 462), with a text presumably copied into this book of prayers from the *Festial*, cf. 'These vij ioyus folowynge off owrre lady ben the specyal ioyus that scho hath now and euer schal haue whythowten ende in heuen the wheche scho schewed vnto seynt thomas off cawnturbery' (f. 86v). The connection with St Thomas of Canterbury is common: for example, British Library MS Lansdowne 379 introduces a Latin rubric and the hymn 'Gaude flore virginali' (C. Blume and G. M. Dreves [eds.], *Analecta Hymnica Medii Aevi*, 55 vols. (Leipzig: Reisland, 1886–1922)) with the comment: 'Hereafter ben the vij Joyes shewd by oure lady saint Marye to saint Thomas of Caunterbur' (ff. 81v–84r). It is this hymn which K adds to the *Festial* text (see apparatus, lines 1, 7, 13, 19, 25, 31, 37).

The more familiar five joys of Mary are traditionally the annunciation, nativity of Christ, resurrection, ascension and assumption. These seven joys are somewhat obscure: six appear to be contained in the first six stanzas of the lyric (the Virgin has no equal, she lights heaven, she is next in honour to God, Christ grants her every wish, she is still in the flesh, Christ helps all those who honour her), but the seventh stanza suggests that all seven have now been treated. For lyrics dealing with the Virgin and her joys, see Rosemary Woolf, *The English Religious Lyric in the Middle Ages* (Oxford: Clarendon Press, 1968), pp. 114–58, 274–308. For the history of the topic, see A. Wilmart, *Auteurs spirituels et textes dévots du moyen âge latin* (Paris: Bloud et Gay, 1932), pp. 326–36.

The *ordinatio* of this long lyric (aabccb) has been handled differently in the various manuscripts. α uses double columns and brackets the couplets (ac) and the rhyming lines (b) in each stanza; I uses double columns and brackets the couplets; D sets out the couplets as bracketed pairs with the b line to the right. K is the most elaborate of all, preceding each stanza (except the last) by its Latin equivalent set out as prose, indenting the verse stanzas, and bracketing the couplets and b lines. The final stanza is treated as prose. Of the other Group A manuscripts, BCG present the lyric as prose but make rudimentary recognition of the stanzas by marginal numbering, while H does not offer any recognition of the verse (the text is so corrupt that the verse may not have been apparent to the scribe). J develops a short independent elaboration (illustrated with Latin scriptural quotation) of the active and contemplative lives as demonstrated by Martha and Mary. Only the last stanza of the lyric (229–34) is utilised, as a concluding prayer, set out as prose.

Textual notes

18 *iwysse*: Only α erroneously repeats the previous rhyme (15), 'in blysse'.

35 *byddeth*: The 3rd person present singular inflexion is supplied from the other manuscripts.

42 *þe*: A more doubtful emendation. The adjective cannot stand alone, as it does in α, but the introduction of the definite article (DGI) compromises the metre (unless elision is assumed).

Appendix Notes

1 The lyrics are presented in their prose context, but the prose has not been collated with the other manuscripts.
2 For a still valid analysis, see M. F. Wakelin, 'The manuscripts of John Mirk's *Festial*', *Leeds Studies in English*, n.s. 1 (1967), 93–118. For the fullest details, see Powell, *John Mirk's Festial*, vol. 1, §4.

6

Making yourself 'þer present': Nicholas Love and the plays of the passion

Alexandra F. Johnston

Before he begins his vivid and passionate translation of the *Meditationes Vitae Christi*, Nicholas Love famously tells us who his intended audience is. Unlike his supposed predecessor, Love intends to address his treatise not to the learned and the cloistered but 'to symple creatures þe whiche as childryn, hauen nede to be fedde with mylke of lyȝte doctryne & not with the sadde mete of grete clargye & of [hye contemplacion]'. His intention is to provide for material for the 'edifying to hem þat bene [of] symple vndirstondyng'. His life of Christ will concentrate on the story, not the theology of the incarnation. As, he claims, St Bernard himself has said, the 'contemplacion of þe monhede of cryste is more likyng more spedefull & more sykere þan is hyȝe contemplacion of þe godhed ande þerefore to hem is pryncipally to be sette in mynde þe ymage of crystes Incarnacion passion & Resurreccion so that a symple soule þat kan bot þenke bot bodyes or bodily þinges mowe haue somwhat accordynge vnto is affecion where wiþ he maye fede & stire his deuocion'.[1]

Love's immensely popular redaction of the *Meditationes* serves as a late milestone to a longstanding tradition of pseudo-Bonaventuran writings and synthesises the many English versions of late medieval Christian literature focusing on the retelling of the story of the life of Christ, particularly the story of the passion.[2] The tradition deliberately sets out to play on the emotions of the readers to make them experience the humanity and suffering of Christ as a means to stimulate devotion and penance. The literature takes the form of lyrics, long narrative poems such as the *Northern Passion*, tracts that deliberately call on the reader to repent providing probing questions to guide the spiritual exercise and the biblical plays of the late fourteenth and fifteenth centuries. Each literary form has its own conventions but all respond to the urgent immediacy of Love's exhortation to experience the agony of the passion of Christ as he suffered it: 'Take hede now diligently with alle þi herte, alle þo þinges þat be now to come, & make þe þere present in þi mynde, beholdyng alle þat shale be done aʒeynus þi lorde Jesu & þat bene spoken or done of him.' The recounting of the physical details, though based on the Latin original, is nevertheless graphic in its vernacular vividness:

> And so wiþ þe innere eye of þi soule beholde sume settyng and ficching þe crosse fast in to þe erþe. Sume makyng redye þe nailes & þe hameres to dryue hem wiþ. Oþere makyng redy & settyng vp laddres, & ordeinyng oþer instrumentis þat hem þouht nedeful, & oþer faste aboute to spoile him, & drawe of hees cloþes. And so is he now the þridde tyme spoilece & stande nakede in siht of all þat peple & so bene nowe the þridde tyme renvede þe brosours of þe wondes in his scourgyng by the cleuyng of þe cloþes to his flesh.[3]

The vividness of Love's presentation of the physical detail, the stripping away of dried, blood-soaked cloth from the wounds of the scourging, the nakedness, all carry out his announced intention to emphasise the body and bodily things. Simple men and women can come to an understanding of the faith through the contemplation of the suffering body of God.

Most works of literature based on versions of the *Meditationes* are just that – meditations – aids for the *private* devotion of the reader or hearer. But the drama is a public medium; the experience is a corporate one. Yet it is also an immediate one. Rather than having to make themselves 'þer present' in their minds with reflection, the plays force the audience to be part of the passion event. The familiar streets of York, Chester and Coventry *became* Jerusalem. For the time of the performance, the physical quotidian surroundings of the sponsoring cities were transformed. Similarly, in the parishes where many more such plays were performed,[4] playing spaces were fashioned in familiar surroundings to create the physical reality that Love enjoins his readers to imagine with their 'inner eyes'. Plays such as the *N-Town Passion* were performed in what is called a 'place and scaffold' arrangement with stages representing such locations as Pilate's court, Herod's court and Gethsemane, set in a field or a large enclosed space.[5] The audience is in the space between these stages and the movement between the stages takes place through the audience. There is nowhere for the audience to be but among the players; spectators are literally within the action. In the production of the *N-Town Passion* in Toronto in 1981,[6] special provision had to be made after

Christ's 'daughters of Jerusalem' speech for just the action that Love describes in the passage cited above.[7] The crosses had to be carried into the playing area, the hammer, nails and ladder had to be 'set'. On these grounds alone it is possible to argue that the dramatised versions of the familiar meditation narrative fulfil most completely the purpose Love set out to achieve – to bring an appreciation of the suffering of Christ to the unlearned folk through an emphasis on the physical details.

The literature of 'affective piety' had flourished in England for well over a century by the time Love produced his *Mirror of the Blessed Life of Jesus Christ*. The conception of at least one set of surviving plays, those at York, pre-dates the *Mirror* but the text that has come down to us was written down in the 1470s. Almost without exception the dramatic texts survive in fifteenth- and sixteenth-century manuscripts and show the marks of revision. The play texts share many of the characteristics of the meditation texts. In the tradition of the Pseudo-Bonaventuran texts, they retell the story of the incarnation in the vernacular drawing on such material as the writings of Richard Rolle, and such long narrative pieces as the *Gospel of Nicodemus*, *The Stanzaic Life of Christ*, the *Cursor Mundi* and *The Northern Passion*. The two civic so-called cycles, *York* and *Chester*, have Old Testament prologues, drawing, as Pamela King has shown particularly for *York*, on the liturgical calendar for their choice of episodes.[8] Some episodic plays may not have had Old Testament sequences. There is, for example, no evidence for any Old Testament episodes in Coventry indicating that the plays there may have begun, as the meditation texts typically do, with the Christmas story. Some non-cycle plays such as the *N-Town Passion* and perhaps the passion play at New Romney treat only the passion story, as do such meditation texts as the *Meditations on the Supper of our Lord and the Hours of the Passion* once attributed to Robert Manning of Brunne.[9] Others, like the *N-Town Mary Play*, begin (as does the *Meditationes*) with the childhood of the Virgin and the parliament of heaven. The influence of the literature of meditative affective piety is all pervasive in the dramatic texts that have survived.

Denise Baker, in her introduction to her translation of *The Privity of the Passion*, explains that her text, like the *Meditationes*, emphasises the role of the Virgin and the other women in the story, introducing the Virgin specifically on the road to Calvary, expanding her role at the foot of the cross and introducing an episode (brilliantly dramatised in the *N-Town Passion*) where the resurrected Christ appears first to his mother. She writes, 'As witnesses to

Christ's suffering, the two Marys (the Virgin and Mary Magdalen) become surrogates for the meditator as they dramatize the compassion that this devotional practice was designed to induce'.[10] In a slightly different way, in many dramatic texts, the Virgin, the other Marys and Veronica in particular also become surrogates for the audience as they give voice to the emotions of the audience over the spectacle of the torture and death of Christ. In the 'Burial of Christ' from Bodleian E Museo 160 what action there is derives from the laments of the Virgin.[11] Here her mourning (rather than the act of torture and execution) dominates the piece although the body (or image) hanging on the cross remains the focus of meditation. This text is from the early sixteenth century and seems to be one of the few remaining examples of a genre of parish Easter plays that was popular in England just before the break from Rome.[12]

In the more narrative plays such as the *Chester Plays*, the women provide a lamenting counterpoint to the bustle of the crucifixion as the Virgin and the three Marys – Magdalen, Jacobi and Salome – speak sixty-three lines between the fastening of Pilate's sign '*Jesus Nazarenus rex Iudeorum*' to the cross and the exchange between Christ and the thieves.[13] They remain kneeling at the foot of the cross, the physical presence of mourning. In the version in the Towneley manuscript, just over a quarter of the entire play is taken up by a dialogue between the Virgin and St John inserted in the text between the agony of the dropping of the cross into its mortice (a second time) and the words from the cross.[14] This passage takes place at the foot of the cross with Mary lamenting and John explaining to her (and to the audience) the reason for the sacrifice. In a twist on the convention, the first part of the *N-Town Passion* ends with Mary Magdalen running to the Virgin with news of the arrest of Christ. The lament of the Virgin that follows directs the audience to the reason for the suffering. But, characteristic of the *N-Town* Mary, she does not minimise her own desolation. Passion Play 1 ends with these lines:

> Now, dere sone, syn þu hast evyr be so ful of mercy
> > Þat wylt not spare þiself for þe love þu hast to man,
> On all mankend now haue þu pety –
> > And also thynk on þi modyr, þat hevy woman.
>
> (Play 28, 189–92)

In Passion Play 2, after the thieves have been crucified, the stage direction indicates that the dicing for Christ's garments has begun and then continues:

> And in þe menetyme xal oure Lady come with iij Maryes with here
> and Sen Johan with hem, settyng hem down asyde afore þe cros, oure
> Lady swuonyng and mornyng. (Play 32 between lines 92 and 93)

The party of mourners has arrived and, as in *Chester* and *Towneley*, they stay until Christ is dead, serving as a focus of identification for the audience. In two of the eleven plays of the long and gruelling passion sequence in the *York Cycle*, the women serve a similar function. As in the *Meditationes*, they meet Christ on the road to Calvary in Play 34 (the ninth of the sequence) and in the last, Play 36 (the *Mortificacio*), they serve the same purpose at the foot of the cross as they do in the other dramatic versions.

The English plays of the passion, then, share many of the characteristics of the meditation texts and to a greater or lesser degree provide surrogates for the emotional responses of the audience in the women followers of Christ. But in two of the texts – the *N-Town Passion* and the passion sequence in the *York Plays* – other things are happening as the playwrights explore other ways to make the audience feel that they are 'there present' at the death of Jesus.

In the *N-Town Passion* play, the extraordinary naturalism of the characterisation of the mature Virgin fulfils this role. In 1984, when the *Poculi Ludique Societas* of Toronto was asked to take a passion play to an Easter play festival in Rome, we went with a shortened version of the *N-Town Passion*. I played the Virgin in that production and learned this character from the inside. Her characterisation provides the possibility for a close identification between Mary and the mature women, possibly patrons of the play, in the audience. This Mary makes an extraordinary emotional journey; she is no hieratic mourning saint but a woman who moves from self-pitying despair to joyful confidence.

She enters at the mid-point of Passion Play 2, as we have seen, supported by the other three Marys and John to confront Christ as he hangs on the cross. Her first outburst of anger, shock and shame is followed by a descent into self-pity:

> A, my good Lord, my sone so swete!
> What hast þu don? Why hangyst now þus here?
> Is þer non other deth to þe now mete
> But þe most shameful deth among þese thevys fere?
> A, out on my hert – why brest þu nowth?
> And þu art maydyn and modyr and seyst þus þi childe spylle!
> How mayst þu abyde þis sorwe and þis woful owth?
> A, deth, deth! Why wylt þu not me kyll?

(Play 32, 93–100)

And, as the rubric tells us, here she swoons.

To readers who have not been called upon to act this role, and are familiar with the other lamenting Marys in medieval meditation texts and drama, speeches like this one can be passed over as painful but formulaic. However, when you have to examine every word to understand fully what is being said and convey that understanding to an audience, you discover that this is anything but formulaic. The tangle of emotions represented here and the implications of what she is saying for the characterisation of this Mary are quite astonishing. All the complex stages of grief are here: the anger at the loved one who is dying, the sense of outrage that such a thing is happening to the mourner, the conviction that somehow this situation has been created simply to make her suffer. Mixed in, as well, is the sense that by dying between thieves, Christ is bringing shame to his respectable mother.

Christ, seemingly ignoring his mother, forgives the thieves and an outraged Mary snaps at him 'þu hast spoken to alle þo þat ben here / and not o word þu spekyst to me' (Play 32, 136–7). Christ then commits her to John's care but in her violent despair she cries that she will die with him and, as the rubric directs here, 'xal [she] ryse and renne and halse þe crosse'. At this point this Mary is completely given over to hysterical grief and must be cared for by others as John and Mary Magdalen support her in her grief. When Christ dies she moves forward, this time to lament in measured eight-line stanzas before she stoops to kiss the dead feet. When the body has been taken from the cross, Joseph of Arimathea lays the body on Mary's knees and in a living icon of the pietà she prepares the body for burial speaking stark, poignant lines in a conscious recalling of the Mary of the nativity caring for the helpless body of her son. Here this Mary finds again the centre of her being as she accepts Christ's death. She takes leave of Joseph of Arimathea and Nicodemus like a great lady dismissing her servants – regal, gracious and controlled.

The Mary of the *N-Town Passion* moves from self-centred hysteria to outward-looking dignity as she is carried through the stages of mourning. Yet there is still another emotion the actor is called upon to portray. Following the tradition of the *Meditationes*, the resurrected Christ appears first to her. She at first greets him formally but, as they part, her tone moves from ritual to lyric:

Farewel, my sone! Farewel, my childe!
Farewel, my Lorde, my God so mylde!

Myn hert is wele þat fyrst was whylde,
Farewel, myn owyn dere love!

(Play 35, 121–4)

The *N-Town* playwrights captured the complexity of Mary developed over the long years of the meditative tradition. She interacts with her child, her God and her beloved in a complex way. The *N-Town* Mary is both a mourning mother and a bereaved lover. This is a mature woman who has experienced all emotions from ecstasy to despair, a woman set apart by God yet at one with all women as the mother and mourner, caregiver and lover. Gail McMurray Gibson has called her 'God's bride and God's mother'.[15] She is also God's widow. Through this extraordinary characterisation of Mary, the playwrights provided a compellingly real character with whom the audience could identify drawing them to be 'þer present' at the passion through the sheer naturalism of her portrayal.

The situation in the *York Plays*[16] provides another approach to the idea of being 'þer present'. The York passion sequence as it has come down to us in the 'register' was significantly altered between 1415, when the Ordo Paginarum or 'Pageant Order' was first written down in the A/Y Memorandum Book, and the compilation of the register more than fifty years later in the 1470s. The evidence from the guild records is complex but the general consensus is that the plays as we now have them date from the decade between 1422 and 1432, long enough after the date of Love's *Mirror of the Blessed Life of Jesus Christ* for that treatise to have an effect on the reviser. Nine of the eleven plays, from the first play when the high priests plot to rid themselves of Jesus to the *Mortificacio*, are written in long alliterative lines frequently identified as those of the reviser or revisers. Three are not. One is the fragmentary play of the last supper. The other two plays are *The Road to Calvary* and the *Mortificacio*, which, as we have seen, use the conventional device of surrogate mourners. However, in the other eight plays of this sequence, the revisers developed an entirely different approach to affective piety. Here there are no surrogates. In these episodes there is no mediation between the audience and the suffering isolation of Christ. To make these revised plays compelling, their creators 'thought themselves there present' and opened a fifteenth-century world of folly, fear, legalism, sadism and hysteria. Not only is the city of York the city of Jerusalem, the first-century judicial murder takes on the overtones of a contemporary one where the victim is isolated and alone.

The technique they have adopted is clear in the contrast between the crucifixion play (Play 35) and the *Mortificacio* (Play 36). Play 36 has a complete cast of characters – Christ and the thieves on their crosses, Pilate and the high priests, the mourning women with John, the centurion, Longeus, Joseph of Arimathea and Nicodemus. Play 35 has, famously, only five characters – Christ and the soldiers, who nail him to the cross with efficient brutality, raise it and then jeer at him. Play 36 has the surrogate mourners, the comfort of familiar iconography and, at the end, with the praise of Longeus whose sight has been restored by the blood of Christ, a powerful statement of the divine purpose. In Play 35, as in the long series of trials that precede it, Christ stands alone and helpless in the hands of his enemies. There is no one there to help him and each member of the audience must stand impotent and suffer with him.

The *York Plays* are a complex work of art interwoven by many hands over the centuries of their production. Unlike the meditation texts, they have their own interpretation of the Christian story that is overlaid on the biblical narrative. The plot turns on the confrontation between the old and the new law and the revisers of the passion sequence, recognising this, rewrote the trial scenes giving them a distinctly contemporary twist.[17] In these plays it is Annas and Caiphas who spearhead the animosity to Christ. Pilate is a weak and vacillating civil servant, jealous of his own power, and Herod is a buffoon. The key to the animosity of the high priests lies in Caiphas' line in the trial before Annas and Caiphas, 'þis ladde with his leysyngis has oure lawes lorne' (Play 29, 387). The York playwrights chose to make the issue of the law pivotal in their dramatising of this segment of the story. Both Elza Tiner[18] and Pamela King[19] have analysed the trial scenes, explicating their sources in civil and ecclesiastical court proceedings. The revisers of the passion sequence trial scenes, taking their cue from earlier episodes in the cycle such as Christ and the doctors, the transfiguration and the woman taken in adultery, wrote a stinging indictment of the legal world of fifteenth-century England.

In these plays, there is no one with whom the watcher can identify as the Son of God stands, largely silent, as his enemies seek to destroy him by manipulating the law. There are only tiny hints of support for Christ within these plays. For a brief moment in Play 30, the first trial before Pilate, the beadle stands up and testifies to what he has seen at the entry into Jerusalem and bows to Christ. Suddenly the pain is eased; the grinding inevitability of the judicial process is lightened for the watcher. In the second trial before Pilate (Play 33), the banners bow to Christ and the judges rise involuntarily from their seats. For a moment this mute recognition of Christ as king provides relief but the incident only increases the frenzy of Pilate and the high priests to get rid of this man they are now convinced is a 'warlowe' (Play 33, 190). He is beaten, mocked, subjected to every humiliation his enemies can think of and yet he will not acknowledge their right to judge him or entertain them. He turns their arguments against his judges again and again, ultimately enraging them because they know that they are wrong.

His stoicism is the stoicism of God and yet, in the tradition of the *Meditationes*, the playwrights make it very clear that he is a man. The masterful alliteration of the play of the agony in the garden near the beginning of the sequence emphasises that his flesh 'dyderis and dares for doute of my dede' (Play 28, 2). Although he is 'mased' in his 'manhed' (91) he prays for the strength to be obedient to the will of God. What follows is not easy to watch. As the long sequence of verbal and physical abuse continues, the watchers become horrified voyeurs privy to, indeed present at, the torture. Each one witnesses what mankind has done to the Son of God and what the Son of Man accepts willingly to save mankind. The contemporary references create a paradoxical sense of complicity as the watcher is both drawn to identify with these characters (whom he recognises from his everyday world) and, at the same time, to reject them. The revisers planned their unrelenting horror carefully and did not edit out the episode on the road to Calvary. After the claustrophobic atmosphere of the trials, this pageant provides an enormous emotional release when, at last, the solitary watcher can identify with the mourning women and disciples within the play world. But the revisers have one more stark lesson to teach. The sense of Christ's isolation returns in the actual crucifixion, as we have seen, as the watcher is once again a helpless witness to the death of Christ. He or she is 'þer present' when the judicial murder is committed and is unable to stop it. However, the revisers again chose not to alter the *Mortificacio* and the audience is able to join in the final mourning as the nascent Christian community buries the body of the saviour.

The meditation texts of the late Middle Ages share a didactic and pastoral impulse with fifteenth-century biblical drama. The drama, however, is able to use a wider variety of techniques to respond to the exhortation from Nicholas Love to allow the watchers to be 'þer present' in their minds to experience the passion and to repent. The dramatic form of affective piety had a life of its own at every level of late medieval English society with different genres based on different poetic and theatrical principles. Yet, ironically, it seems possible that the similar impulses behind meditation literature and biblical drama have preserved for us, almost by accident, more than half the surviving play texts that would otherwise have been lost. Four major collections of biblical drama have come down to us, once thought to be four 'cycles' of plays. Of these, two – the *York* and *Chester* plays – are what they have always been thought to be: plays performed by the guilds of the two northern cities under the watchful eyes of generations of city councils. However, codicological studies prompted by new editions and the performance of most of the canon over the last few decades have made it clear beyond any shadow of doubt that two of the four major collections of plays – *N-Town* and *Towneley* – are not dramatic units but rather compilations, anthologies of plays with eclectic staging demands gathered together for some other purpose – and that purpose seems to have been to function as meditation texts. In much of the *N-Town* manuscript, conventional speech headings are mixed in with such lines as '*Adam dicit sic:*' or '*Hic ardent decimum Abel, et Caym quo facto dicit:*', as if the scribe anticipated that readers, as much as actors, would use his text. The *Towneley* manuscript is so late and so closely identified with a recusant family that it is unlikely that the text as it has survived was ever used as anything *but* a meditation text. This is not to say that all the plays, long and short, single episode or sequences in all the manuscripts were not played. They were, all over the country.[20] But at least half of the canon has been *preserved* not because the episodes belonged together as plays but because their episodes could be arranged to serve the purpose of meditation texts. Had there not been a strong and continuing demand for individual spiritual exercises using the techniques of meditation laid out by Nicholas Love, the surviving canon of medieval English drama would be reduced to the cycles of York, Chester and a few fragments.

Notes

1 Nicholas Love, *Mirror of the Blessed Life of Jesus Christ: A Full Critical Edition Based on Cambridge University Library Additional MSS 6578 and 6686*, ed. Michael G. Sergeant (Exeter: University of Exeter Press, 2005), Text p. 10.

2 See further the website *Geographies of Orthodoxy: Mapping English Pseudo-Bonaventuran Lives of Christ, 1350–1550*, by John Thompson and Ian Johnson; www.qub.ac.uk./geographies-of-orthodoxy/discuss.

3 Love, *Mirror of the Blessed Life of Jesus Christ*, p. 174.

4 Alexandra F. Johnston, 'An introduction to medieval English theatre' in Richard Beadle and Alan Fletcher (eds.), *The Cambridge Companion to Medieval Theatre*, 2nd edn (Cambridge: Cambridge University Press, 2008), pp. 10–15.

5 The *N-Town Passion Play* is embedded in London, British Library, MS Cotton Vespasian D.VIII. See Stephen Spector (ed.), *The N-Town Play*, 2 vols., EETS s.s. 11 (Oxford: EETS, 1991). See also Peter Meredith (ed.), *The Passion Play from the N-Town Manuscript* (London: Longman, 1990).

6 The production was by the *Poculi Ludique Societas*, the medieval and Renaissance drama group of the University of Toronto. The text was modernised by Stanley J. Kahrl.

7 Spector (ed.), *The N-Town Play*, Play 32, line 21; vol. 1, pp. 314–16. All quotations from *The N-Town Play* are from this edition.

8 Pamela King, *The York Mystery Cycle and the Worship of the City* (Cambridge: D. S. Brewer, 2006).

9 The evidence for the complex passion play in New Romney is found in James Gibson (ed.), *Kent*, Records of Early English Drama (Toronto: University of Toronto Press, 2002) vol. 2, pp. 738, 745–95.

10 'The privity of the passion', trans. Denise N. Baker in Anne Clark Bartlett and Thomas H. Bestul (eds.), *Cultures of Piety* (Ithaca: Cornell University Press, 1999), pp. 85–106 (89).

11 Donald Baker, John L. Murphy and Louis B. Hall, jr. (eds.), *The Late Medieval Religious Plays of Bodleian MSS Digby 133 and E Museo 160*, EETS o.s. 283 (Oxford: Oxford University Press, 1982), pp. 141–68.

12 See Alexandra F. Johnston, 'The emerging pattern of the Easter play in England', *Medieval English Theatre* 20 (1998), 3–23.

13 Robert M. Lumiansky and David Mills (eds.), *The Chester Mystery Cycle*, 2 vols., EETS s.s. 3, 9 (Oxford: Oxford University Press, 1974, 1986), Play XVIa, lines 241–88.

14 Arthur C. Cawley and Martin Stevens (eds.), *The Towneley Plays*, EETS s.s. 13, 14 (Oxford: Oxford University Press, 1994), Play 23, lines 311–502; vol. 1, pp. 296–302.

15 Gail McMurray Gibson, *The Theater of Devotion* (Chicago: University of Chicago Press, 1989), p. 137.

16 Richard Beadle (ed.), *The York Plays* (London: Arnold, 1982). For a discussion of the revisions see also Richard Beadle, 'The York cycle' in Beadle and Fletcher (eds.), *The Cambridge Companion to Medieval English Theatre*, pp. 104–22.

17 See Alexandra F. Johnston, '"His langage is lorne": The silent centre of the *York Cycle*', *Early Theatre* 3 (2000), pp.185–95.

18 Elza Tiner, 'English law in the York trial plays' in Clifford Davidson (ed.), *The Dramatic Tradition of the Middle Ages* (New York: AMS Press, 2005), pp. 140–9.
19 Pamela King, 'Contemporary cultural models for the trial plays in the York Cycle', in Alan Hindley (ed.), *Medieval Texts and Cultures of Northern Europe* (Turnhout Brepols, 1999), pp. 200–16.
20 Johnston, 'An introduction' pp. 7–15.

7
Reading a procession: Bishop Blase at Bradford

Peter Meredith

John Anderson and I first met in Adelaide, South Australia, in the early 1960s. Neither of us at the time had anything to do with cities and their entertainments. My interests lay in the texts and performance of medieval drama and John's in the *Gawain*-poet. But time changes all things. Medieval drama inevitably led me to an interest in the places where it was performed, and so to civic government and city structures, and most recently to my own locality of Leeds and Bradford, while John's physical path long ago led him back to England and Arthur Cawley, and so to the Records of Early English Drama project and the civic entertainments of Newcastle-upon-Tyne. John branched out widely and successfully in many directions. I have stayed with the drama, so my small homage to John is in the area of study where, for a while, we touched; not, however, medieval drama but a much later civic ceremonial.

The 1825 Bishop Blase celebration in Bradford

St Blase, or, as he is in this later period more frequently called, Bishop Blase, was the patron of the woolcombers, who celebrated his day, 3 February, with a procession and merrymaking. He was believed to have been bishop of Sebaste in Armenia in the fourth century and to have been put to death under the Emperor Licinius, and is usually so described in nineteenth-century newspaper reports. Woolcombing was a specialist part of the process of preparing wool for making worsted cloth, and Bishop Blase was reputed to be the inventor of the wool comb and to have been tortured with it – hence his adoption as the woolcombers' patron.[1]

The development of the Bishop Blase celebrations and their appearance in different parts of the country are described with varying levels of detail by a number of commentators. The fullest account, and one which puts the Bradford event in a national context, is a paper by H. Ling Roth read to the Society of Antiquaries in December 1914.[2] From 1900 onwards, Roth was much involved with the Bankfield Museum in Halifax, as honorary curator and later keeper. He was, therefore, by personal choice a local man. Other less extensive accounts are given by two local Bradford men, James Burnley and John James.[3] The earliest mention of a celebration being held under the auspices of Bishop Blase is given by Burnley (pp. 191–2). It is an account of the wool-combers in London in 1730 celebrating the queen's birthday with a procession and a loyal address. It took place on 3 March, however, not the true February date.

The poet John Dyer presents the Blase celebrations in idealistic terms as regular annual processions and feasts in *The Fleece* (1757):

> Hence the glad cities of the loom his [i.e. Blase's] name
> Honour with yearly festals: through their streets
> The pomp, with tuneful sounds, and order just,
> Denoting labour's happy progress, moves,
> Procession slow and solemn: first the rout;
> Then servient youth, and magisterial eld;
> Each after each, according to his rank,
> His sway, and office in the commonweal;
> And to the board of smiling plenty's stores
> Assemble, where delicious cates and fruits
> Of ev'ry clime are pil'd; and with free hand
> Unsparing, each his appetite regales.
> Toil only tastes the feast, by nerveless ease
> Unrelish'd. Various mirth and song resound;
> And oft they interpose improving talk,
> Divulging each to other knowledge rare,
> Sparks, from experience, that sometimes rise;
> Till night weighs down the sense, or morning's dawn
> Rouses to labor, man to labor born.[4]

Dyer's 'cities of the loom' are deliberately generalised, but as he was living in Leicestershire while writing *The Fleece*, it is possible that his reference is to the midlands, east or west. There are Blase celebrations in various parts of the country, including Loughborough in Leicestershire, during the eighteenth century, but they appear nevertheless to cluster in Yorkshire.[5] Besides Bradford (1769), there are early examples quoted by Roth and James from Leeds (1738), Halifax (1738), Stainland, near Halifax (1757), Masham (by implication, 1794) and Wakefield (by implication, 1794) in the eighteenth century, and Keighley (1812) in the early nineteenth century. The earliest so far noted in this area are the celebrations in Leeds and Halifax in 1738, of which, according to James, an account appeared in the *Leeds Mercury*.[6]

The best recorded of all the Bishop Blase celebrations, however, is that held in Bradford in 1825 – the best recorded and, ironically, the last ever held there.

> Hail to the Day, whose kind auspicious rays
> Deign'd first to smile on famous Bishop Blaize!
> To the great Author of our Combing Trade,
> This day's devoted and due honours paid;
> To him, whose fame through Britain's Isle resounds,
> To him, whose goodness to the poor abounds:
> Long shall his name in British annals shine,
> And grateful ages offer at his shrine . . .

So begins 'The Original and Correct Speech to be spoken at the Grand Septennial Festival at Bradford, on Thursday, February 3rd, 1825', as recorded in one of the handbills that were produced for the occasion.[7] After praising Bishop Blase himself the poem goes on to extol the wool trade, the value of it for rich and poor, and the part that Britain, and Bradford in particular, had played in it. It closes: 'To celebrate our Founder's great renown, / Our Shepherd and our Shepherdess we crown' (lines 29–30).

'Original and Correct' is not just padding. 'Hail to the Day' was the 'official' speech certainly from as early as 1804 (hence 'Original'), and at least one other, 'A New Speech proposed to be spoken at the approaching Festival at Bradford', had been put forward, almost certainly in 1825, as an addition or a substitute (hence the emphasis on 'Correct'). The alternative speech, 'Our rising Commerce now her arms extends', follows much the same lines as 'Hail to the Day', but with further, and perhaps what were felt to be more pertinent, details added. For example, the seven-year gap between celebrations is mentioned, the fears for their trade (as it turned out, unfounded), and the building of 'extended walls', 'charming villas' and 'spacious halls'. 'Hail to the Day' appears not to have been a local production. James says it was written by Thomas Rawnsley, Woolbroker, of Bourne in Lincolnshire,[8] and it may well be significant that in the alternative speech, 'Our rising Commerce', no mention is made of crowning the shepherd and shepherdess, for which there is no certain evidence in Bradford at this date.

Some of the handbills also record the order of the procession and the route to be taken. The report in the *Leeds Mercury* records full details of the procession on that day, together with some historical information on Bishop Blase himself,[9] and there is also a more personal record in the diary of a young local physician, Dr John Simpson.[10] As a result of these combined sources, we know the state of the weather, the route taken, the numbers involved and whether they were on horseback or on foot, the speeches given (and up to a point, where they were spoken and by whom), the costumes of the participants, the refreshment given to them and where they received it, where people watched from and the reactions of at least one member of the audience. The *Leeds Mercury* also includes an account of the dinner which followed on the evening of 3 February in the large room at the courthouse in Bradford 'attended by nearly a hundred gentlemen', and the ball on the following evening. There is no doubt that this 1825 occasion was not only the best recorded in Bradford but one of the best recorded of all the Blase celebrations of the eighteenth and nineteenth centuries. To one coming from the world of medieval and early renaissance provincial civic ceremonial, with its sporadic and haphazard information, this is wealth indeed.

The information begins with the preparations, and the anticipation. John Simpson writes in his diary on 2 February:

Tomorrow is the day on which is celebrated the septennial festival of Bishop Blaise. For the last two months preparations have been making for it by the different individuals connected with the trade of the place. It has been much talked of lately & noticed in the newspapers, so that we may expect a great influx of strangers, indeed great numbers have arrived already.[11]

The *Mercury* also commented on the large numbers coming to Bradford: 'As early as seven o'clock, strangers poured into Bradford from all the surrounding towns and villages, in such numbers as to line the roads in all directions: and almost all the vehicles within twenty miles were in requisition.' At an earlier celebration of Bishop Blase in Bradford (1811), some spectators certainly came from as far away as Bramley (one of the outer townships of Leeds and on the road to Bradford) and beyond. Joseph Rogerson, who owned a mill in Bramley, records in his *Memorandums*:[12] '4 [Feb] There are a very many people going today to Bradford to see the Bishop Blase celebrated: hundreds go by here. I may say thousands. Mill standing [idle], all our men gone to Bradford.' The weather, however, in 1825 looked bad, as Simpson recorded: 'Feb.

1. A handbill for the 1825 Bishop Blase procession, printed by R. Blackburn, Westgate, Bradford.

2nd . . . I hope the day will be favourable, but I very much doubt it as it has been blowing all day a tremendous gale of wind attended with heavy rain . . . Feb. 3rd. The wind has been blowing most tremendously all night attended with snow and rain. I looked out of my window at five o'clock. It was then very cloudy and raining.' Despite his doubts, by eight o'clock he was able to report: 'the morning was beautiful. The wind had ceased, the clouds had dispersed & the sun was shining most beautifully.'[13]

'The different trades began to assemble as early as eight o'clock in the morning', the *Mercury* recorded. The assembly point was the foot of Westgate, near the junction of the three old streets of Bradford – Westgate, Kirkgate and Ivegate – the site of the old market. Bradford in 1825 was still at an early stage in its huge and rapid expansion from a small country town to industrial 'Worstedopolis'. Though there had been some new streets built and considerable infill housing, spatially it was still largely confined within its old limits. At the foot of Ivegate, by Bradford Beck, there were mills but there were also open spaces. The iron foundries to the south were well developed, but they were at some distance. Much of the beck was still open and the townships of Manningham, Little Horton and Bolling were still separated from Bradford by open fields. The route which the procession was to take is described in the handbill which announced the coming celebration (see fig. 1). It differed from previous routes in that it took in the newer Darley Street and Rawson's Place before joining up again with the old route which took it downhill to Church Bridge, up the very steep Church Bank past the parish church to Mr Garnett's Mill, back down to Mr Duffield's, up to another private house, Mannville, and back down near the beck for refreshments at the Holme, an open space at Mr. Fawcett's mill not far from the foot of Ivegate. The procession then went to Little Horton, before returning via Kirkgate and Ivegate to the Sun Inn, at the foot of Ivegate, where it dispersed.[14] Altogether, the processional route was between four and five miles.

The order of the procession is listed in the handbills but the fullest description is given by Simpson:

A Herald came first supported by two constables. Then a band of music. Afterwards the Woolstaplers on horseback riding on fleeces ornamented with sashes. Then the Spinners on horseback, with sashes & slivers of wool, blue coats & white stuff waistcoats: their horses covered with white worsted nets. Next a band of music & the Masters' Sons & Apprentices on horseback most gaily dressed in scarlet stuff coats, white waistcoats, blue pantaloons, blue sashes & most beautiful caps ornamented with ostrich feathers, artificial flowers, gold chains, beads & various other trinkets. Several of these caps cost ten or fifteen pounds and some it was said even thirty. Next came the Merchants on horseback; blue coats, white stuff waistcoats & crimson sashes. Music. King & Queen with Guards on horseback with drawn swords: the horses of their majesties led each by two grooms richly dressed. Then Jason & Medea with Guards likewise on horseback and grooms. Afterwards came Bishop Blaise with Mace-bearer, Chaplain, and Guards as before; the horses of the Bishop & Chaplain led by grooms. Next the Shepherd & Shepherdess, surrounded by a troop of Shepherd Swains, all beautifully dressed in green jackets, white trousers & ornamental caps. The horse of the Shepherdess was led by grooms & she supported a fine lamb on a fleece. The Swains on horseback carrying crooks. Then came the Combmakers on horseback with combs & rams' heads with gilt horns. A band of music & Wool-Sorters on horseback with red & white slivers & ornamental caps. The charcoal-burners on horseback. Afterwards Wool-Combers on foot, ornamented dresses, wool wigs and caps. Another band of music. Master Diers on horseback with sashes & coloured slivers, their horses covered with coloured nets. Diers on foot with coloured sashes, slivers & caps. There were several flags carried in the procession with appropriate devices.[15]

Simpson is the only one to go into such detail in describing the costumes of the participants, but great stress is everywhere laid on the woollen element in costume and decoration as a sign of the beauty and the flexibility in the use of wool – though the effect sometimes sounds comic. It is worth adding to this description the approximate numbers that the *Mercury* estimated were in the procession: '24 woolstaplers, 38 spinners and manufacturers, 6 merchants, 56 apprentices and masters' sons, 160 wool-sorters, 30 comb-makers, 470 wool-combers, and 40 dyers', making a grand total of 824, not counting the woolsorters and charcoal-burners, the bands of music and the named characters and their grooms and guards.

On the route the Bishop Blase poem was declaimed. At the very beginning, Richard Fawcett, mill-owner and one of the organisers, doffed his hat and spoke the speech, 'with great animation' according to the *Mercury*:

The lines were afterwards several times repeated, in the principal streets and roads through which the cavalcade passed, by Mr Lister, Mr John Rand, Jun., and others: among the rest, by the youngest member of the train, a fine boy five years old, the son of Mr

> Thompson, who was mounted on a Shetland pony, and repeated the commencing and concluding lines, with great distinctness and animation opposite the house of Miss Preston in Kirkgate.

This is not quite how 'the fine boy' remembered it some years later, by which time he was an MP for Bradford:

> My father thought it right that I should take part in the procession, and he had me up every morning at breakfast until he had drilled into me a certain number of verses. I was put on top of a door or out of a window at the bottom of Kirkgate, and spouted these verses to an immense number of people, although I dare say nobody heard me three or four yards off. I was then taken on a pony down into the Holme, and spouted the same verses to a number of workmen assembled round a table.[16]

There was also a pause for refreshment at Mr Fawcett's mill on the Holme – the 'workmen assembled round a table', no doubt the one that young Thompson remembered – 'where the men were refreshed with sandwiches and ale, of which they partook freely, some of them too freely' (*Mercury*). John Simpson went to see the refreshments: 'There was beef and ham for them also about a hundred gallons of punch. Some of them got very tipsy' – some difference of opinion about what they ate and drank, but not about the outcome.[17]

John Simpson watched first from the windows of Mr Lister's house in Darley Street (presumably Thomas Lister, a surgeon, who had a house there) and then later from Miss Preston's in Kirkgate – the same house that featured the young Matthew Thompson, though Simpson remembers hearing John Rand deliver the speech there. Simpson was greatly impressed by the show: 'The sight was most beautiful & I had not the least idea that it would be so interesting and imposing.' Not only were the streets crammed with people but the houses along the route too. 'The windows of the houses situated where the procession had to pass were all filled. Our windows were filled.'[18] Inevitably, not everyone's visit was trouble-free. The *Mercury* reported two pockets being picked; though if that was all, it was a remarkably orderly event.

Simpson had been invited to attend the dinner which followed the day's celebrations at the 'Court-house' (presumably the Court of Requests in Darley Street), but, because he had a visitor (from Halifax), he cried off. The occasion is reported at length by the *Leeds Mercury*; not the meal itself but the speeches, the toasts and the entertainment. Speeches were given in praise of Bradford and

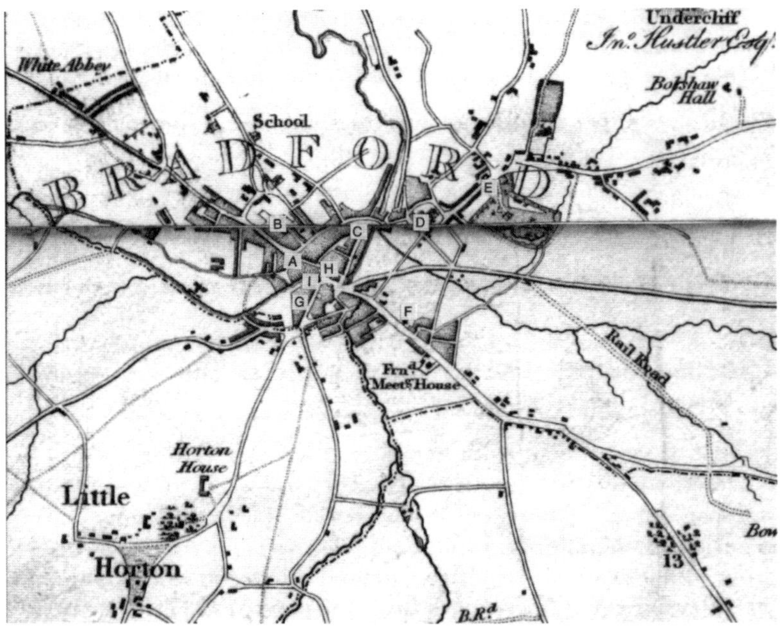

2. The route of the Bishop Blase procession. A. the junction of Westgate (running NW–SE), Ivegate (almost a narrower continuation of Westgate) and Kirkgate (running SW–NE) – gathering place of the procession; B. Darley Street and Rawson's Place – two of the newer elements in the route; C. Church Bridge – one of the crossing places of Bradford Beck; D. Church Bank, the steepest uphill part of the route, and the parish church; E. Garnett's mill in Barker End; F. Mr Duffield's, a large private house on the Wakefield Road; G. Mannville, another private house, the home of Mrs Mann; H. the Holme, the refreshments stop, next to Fawcett's Mill; I. the Sun Inn at the foot of Ivegate – the dispersal point in 1825, after the return from Little Horton. Based on a detail from a map by Joshua Thorp, surveyed 1819–21, and therefore showing the extent of Bradford around the time of the 1825 procession. North is at the top.

its wool trade, management and worker solidarity, and the success of the Blase festivities. Toasts were proposed by, amongst others, Matthew Thompson, the organiser of the celebrations and father of the young orator, and George Thompson Lister, a local surveyor and auctioneer, John Rand Jun., a worsted spinner and manufacturer, and Richard Fawcett, all of whom had been speakers of the Bishop Blase verses. Speeches were followed by toasts, toasts by songs and 'glees'. On the following night there was:

THE STUFF BALL

That the Ladies might partake in the hilarity of this Festival, and that the manufactures of the place might be promoted by it, a splendid Ball was given last night at the Court-House. One hundred and forty tickets were issued, and the whole number was engaged early in the day. At eight o'clock in the evening, the company began to assemble, and before ten the room was crowded. The dresses of the Ladies, though uniform in fabric, assumed all the forms that fashion and taste could impart. The masters' sons appeared in the scarlet stuff coats which they had worn in the procession of Thursday . . . At the conclusion of the banquet [provided at midnight], dancing was resumed and kept up to an early hour in the morning, when the company separated, highly delighted with the entertainment of the evening, and rapturous in their praises of the festival of the Golden Fleece. (*Leeds Mercury*, 5 February 1825)

Not everyone was as delighted with the ball as the newspaper implies. John Simpson wrote: 'Nothing particularly interesting occurred. I only danced one quadrille for there was such a dust arose from the chalked floor that I could not breathe. The company was very mixed, but all went off well. There was such a dust from the chalk that we were all coughing & sneezing during the whole of the evening. I got to bed about 3 in the morning.'[19] The atmosphere seems not to have been so bad that he had to leave early.

George Walker's *Costume of Yorkshire* (1814)

One further, and important, element in the Bishop Blase evidence needs to be mentioned here, because, though it does not depict the events of 1825, it nevertheless gives a clear visual impression of the appearance of one Bishop Blase procession. This is the watercolour by George Walker reproduced in his *Costume of Yorkshire*.[20] The painting was reproduced again by Roth in his paper on 'Bishop Blaise', but because he knew only of a Darlington connection, he entitled it 'Grand Festival of Woolcombers, Comb-makers and Dyers at Darlington on 3rd. Feb., 1825', thus obscuring its Yorkshire provenance and its true date.[21]

In two horizontal panels, the painting shows a Bishop Blase procession lined up across the page from the masters at the front, top left, to the woolcombers at the end, bottom left. In as much as Walker is primarily interested in the dress of the participants, the picture is almost certainly selective rather than comprehensive, giving examples of each of the types (masters, masters' sons, apprentices, etc.) rather than an accurate impression of the whole mass of the procession. Similarly he is not concerned with creating an urban setting; the procession looks rather as though it were crossing open moorland. But in categories, order and appearance of participants, the painting matches in every detail the description given in the *Leeds Mercury* account of the 1811 celebration in Bradford, and in fact Walker's written commentary seems to have been taken word for word from a handbill or the newspaper account of that procession.[22] The masters are described as on horseback each with a white 'sliver'; the masters' sons come next, also on horseback, followed by their 'colours'; then the 'apprentices on horseback in their uniforms'. This first group is linked to, or separated from, the next by 'music', shown by Walker as six members of a military band and two apparently black (but probably blacked-up) performers, one with a drum and the other with a tambourine. Then come the first of the characters: 'the king and queen; the royal family; their guards [a group of eight soldiers with rifles, led by an officer – probably members of the First West York Militia who are pictured elsewhere in Walker's volume] and attendants'. They are followed by the second of the characters, Jason, with the golden fleece held up on a pole behind him, and attendants; the third character, Bishop Blase with his chaplain and their attendants (see fig. 3a); and the fourth and final characters, the shepherd and shepherdess, and their swains and attendants. Then come the rest of the industrial section: 'foremen and wool-sorters on horseback; combers' colours; wool-combers two and two, with ornamented caps, wool wigs, and various coloured slivers' (see fig. 3b; *Costume of Yorkshire*, p. 86). The 'ornamented caps' are combed wool (usually coloured red, white and blue) wound into a conical shape. The 'slivers', worn by the masters, Jason's attendants and the foremen and woolsorters as well as the woolcombers, are long lengths of combed wool, worn as sashes, either a single one diagonally across the chest and tied at the waist, or two crossed over.

The picture, because it is selective, perhaps over-emphasises the extent to which the procession was mounted. Of the sixty-two people shown, twenty-five, or nearly half, are on horseback. This compares with the 284 specifically said to be on horseback out of the total of 824 noted by the *Mercury*; nearer to a third. It is, nevertheless, still a high proportion. The largest body of those on foot in the 1825 procession is that of the woolcombers (470), whereas in the picture there are only four shown. The pictured procession

3a. Jason and the Golden Fleece and his attendants; Bishop Blase and his chaplain.

3b. The woolcombers bringing up the rear of the procession. Their wool hats are striped red (actually pink), white and blue.

is also less colourful than that described in 1825. There are, for example, no scarlet coats, white waistcoats, blue pantaloons and highly decorative caps for the masters' sons and apprentices, and the shepherd swains are not dressed in green jackets, white trousers and ornamental caps.

The picture also seems to show a rather caricatured presentation of the bishop, Falstaff-like in build, with a large nose and red face, and his mitre tilted over his forehead. This contrasts with the extremely thin and Puritan-looking chaplain. Jason, too, is not the heroic figure of Greek myth. He wears a 'classical' helmet and carries a drawn sword, but looks back over his shoulder, apparently nervously, at his rather frozen-looking band of attendants. Is Walker deliberately undermining the occasion, or was this how it appeared? Nowhere in the written record is it suggested that the bishop is a figure of fun, but on the other hand it could be that all the praise lavished on him is tongue-in-cheek. Is it significant that, as far as we know, he was not given a place of honour at the celebration dinner? Roger Young considers Walker, who was the son of a wealthy Leeds industrialist, to be a product of his background, unsympathetic towards the working class. In discussing the Blase procession, Young presents Walker as one unable to appreciate 'the social and cultural significance of such protracted and riotous occasions to local working people', who depicts working people in a less than flattering light.[23] It is true that the upper levels of society in the procession are presented straight, but so are the walking woolcombers and the shepherd group. It seems to be not the working-class figures but the 'theatrical' ones that are given a slightly comic flourish: Bishop Blase, Jason and even the king. Something also worth bearing in mind is that the bishop and the king are performed by seasoned 'specialists'. James, whose *History of Bradford* was published in 1841, and therefore within living memory of the final celebration, records that the king was played by William Clough from Darlington, who had played the part on four previous occasions, and the bishop by John Smith, who also had performed 'on several other commemorations'.[24]

Reading the procession

How should the 1825 procession be read? Is it self-indulgence on the part of the organisers or a response to popular demand? Is it a sop to the workforce, many living in insanitary and over-crowded conditions, or is it a communal effort? Is it a demonstration of worker coercion, or of worker–management solidarity? Is it a calendar custom still in the hands of the people or is it a 'bread-and-circuses' reinvention? As is so often the case, the only voices that are heard are those of the upper ranks of society. In their own words (heard in the speeches at the dinner afterwards) the organisers and their friends and colleagues present the procession as a celebration of the success of Bradford, the wool-manufacturing businesses and the harmonious relationship between workers and masters. It would be easy to present this simply as self-congratulatory, self-deluded wishful-thinking, or even deliberate ignoring of the plight of the workforce, especially in view of the intractable positions taken up in a devastating strike which followed later in the year.[25]

To some extent it would be reasonable to do this. But the dinner is, in its own way (and certainly in the way it is recorded in the pages of the *Mercury*), another set-piece, like the procession: a speech leads up to a toast; a toast leads on to a 'glee' or a song, which in turn gives way to a speech, and then the process is repeated. It is a celebration, not a post mortem. There is no dispute, no upsetting of the ritual pattern. Dr Simpson, unfortunately, did not attend the dinner, otherwise we might have had a less formalised presentation of the events. It could be said that the organisers, representing the masters, are celebrating their own view of an ordered and benevolent society, which in the procession they have imposed upon their workers and upon the town as a whole.[26]

Certainly that seems to be the message of 'Hail to the Day':

> By this our Trade are thousands daily fed,
> By it supplied with means to earn their bread [.]
> In various forms our trade its work imparts,
> In different methods, and by different arts,
> Preserves from starving, indigents distress'd,
> As Combers, Spinners, Weavers, and the rest.

(9–14)

Equally it is the tenor of part of the alternative speech:

> Our rising Commerce now her arms extends,
> The rich she blesses, and the poor befriends!
> Seven prosperous years again have circled round,
> Since last we heard the animating sound
> Of his great name who first found out our trade,
> And for our wealth a sure foundation laid.

(1–6)

This is even more the case in the alternative 1804 speech:

> In various modes our stuffs are made,
> Which greatly doth promote our trade;
> The poor have means to earn their bread,
> Thousands by it are daily fed;
> Pale poverty can find no place,
> A smile there sits on every face.

Our Manufacturers become
Respectable, their friends among;
And many by their diligence,
Possessed are of Opulence;
And all their workmen's glad to see,
Their welfare and prosperity.[27]

On the other hand, the procession represents a real commitment on the part of everyone involved. It would have to have been a communal effort. Matthew Thompson, the main organiser, is clearly committed to the success of the event, but so too, in their different ways, the woolcombers or the apprentices or the masters' sons must have been, by the simple act of taking part and perhaps providing the costumes to play their parts. Altogether around nine hundred people are involved. It is worth observing that the normal position of honour in a procession is the rear; everything leads up to that position. At the rear of Bradford's processions are the workers, most prominently the woolcombers. Not far in front of them are the shepherd and shepherdess, then Bishop Blase and then Jason – so the whole procession, though it turns Dyer's order of 'rout . . . servient youth . . . and magisterial eld' on its head, has what could be seen as an 'order just'. Is Simpson thinking only of the masters when he says, 'For the last two months preparations have been making for it by the different individuals connected with the trade of the place'? People flocked from all around to see the procession because it was a sight worth seeing and a genuinely popular spectacle.

However, there were those who doubted its value. This is indicated in the words of John Rand, Jun., at the dinner, when he says: 'It is not, Sir, as a mere pageant that I regard our septennial procession . . . however others may term it a piece of foolery, or attempt to ridicule its celebration'. The objections levelled against it may well be implied in his later words: 'Amply rewarded have we all been for the expense and labour of this day's proceedings' (*Leeds Mercury*). 'Expense and labour', money and effort, were directed towards the celebration which could have been better expended elsewhere. There was a dispute in Keighley in 1819 over the Blase procession there, when a small group of manufacturers suggested through the *Leeds Mercury* and through handbills that the money put towards the celebration would be better spent on blankets for the poor. Rand may well have been thinking of this, as the Keighley proposers suggested that perhaps the people of Bradford would make a similar stand.[28] These two strands of civic life, celebration and charity, are juxtaposed, probably accidentally but nevertheless tellingly, in the *Leeds Intelligencer*'s report of the 1776 celebrations:

> On Saturday last, being Bishop Blaze Day, a grand procession was made by the Wool-Combers through the streets of this town.
>
> And, we hear from Bradford, that the Wool Combers of that town and neighbourhood, never made so splendid a show, on any former similar occasion.
>
> A collection for the relief of the poor, was last week made in several of the divisions of this town.[29]

Bradford's long-lasting devotion to Bishop Blase may well have had its origins in a popular calendar custom. Its first recorded celebration in 1769 would have taken place at a time when Bradford was a very small country town, where there was no large-scale manufacturing presence. The crowning of the shepherd and shepherdess, which appears in the 'official' speech and may well not represent a local custom as its author was from Lincolnshire, does not appear in the alternative 1825 speech. But it is referred to, with additions, in the alternative 1804 one (both alternative speeches were presumably locally written):

> This Day the Streets we do Parade,
> With Implements each of our Trade;
> Our Shepherd, and our Shepherdess,
> We do them Crown and richly dress.

If this was a locally produced verse it suggests that the crowning of the two characters may have been part of the celebration; perhaps, because of the time of year, a lambing-season custom, as the shepherdess is always said to be carrying a lamb in her lap.[30] The fleece of the sheep was after all the basis of Bradford's trade. That the custom, if it existed, had died out by the 1811 celebration is suggested by the fact that there is no sign of crowns or of rich dressing on either the shepherd or shepherdess in George Walker's picture.

As will have become apparent, it is not a question of reading one procession. The 1825 event is the culmination of a series for which there is plentiful evidence from 1804 onwards, and newspaper references for 1769, 1776, 1783, 1790 and 1797. From the point of view of Bradford, the dates are significant. It is always called the *septennial* celebration, and all the dates fit into the chronological pattern shown in the early nineteenth-century celebrations. Dyer calls the celebrations in his poem annual, and, certainly, it is usual for calendar customs to be so. I have not so far found any comment on why the Bradford event occurred every seven years rather than annually, but it is something which was clearly felt to be important.[31]

The medieval connection

There is no direct connection between the processions and the Middle Ages. However, anyone working in the earlier period will constantly be reminded of it by Bishop Blase. In considering the origins of the York play, I remember worrying about whether it was likely that a Corpus Christi procession would be stopped in order to perform brief theatrical pieces. It seemed to me unlikely. Did the Blase procession of around nine hundred people stop for the brief utterance of a speech? Or did it march inexorably on while the speeches were given to one side? It is certainly true that the debates about the interpretation of the Fouquet miniature representing the martyrdom of St Apollonia, apparently as a stage performance, would be a lot easier to resolve if we had not only the picture but information about the performance pictured.[32] Even more enlightening would be pictures of something like the N-Town plays in performance.[33] The Records of Early English Drama survey of dramatic records in Britain includes lists of food and drink bought for celebratory feasts.[34] For Bradford, we do not know what was eaten, but we do know the content and conduct of the celebratory part of the Blase dinner. How different our understanding of the earlier feasts might be if we knew what was said and how people conducted themselves, as well as what was eaten. And would that we knew as much about the procession of Yule and Yule's wife in York as we do about the Bishop Blase procession in Bradford.[35] But even with Bishop Blase we do not know how people kept warm or whether they processed in any weather. In nineteenth-century Bradford, we have Walker's picture of the Blase procession *and* detailed information about the celebration it records. Because of that many things become clear: who the band were, for example, and how Bishop Blase or the king and queen were presented, and what the 'colours' looked like. But nevertheless the debate about the meaning of the evidence continues; it simply shifts into a different mode.

After 1825

Just as we have the ending of the performances of religious plays in York, so we have the ending of the Bishop Blase celebrations in Bradford. One is stopped, the other stops, but there are odd echoes in the ways those endings are presented by 'authority'. On the one hand it is the authority of church and state, on the other the authority of 'public opinion' mediated through the columns of a newspaper. Dean Hutton writes to the lord mayor and aldermen of York in 1568 about the Creed Play: 'as I finde manie thinges that I muche like because of thantiquitie, so see I manie thinges, that I cannot allowe, because they be Disagreinge with the senceritie of the gospell . . . ffor thoghe it was plausible 40 yeares agoe, & wold now also of the ignorant sort be well liked: yet now in this happie time of the gospell, I knowe the learned will mislike it and how the state will beare with it I knowe not'.[36] The *Leeds Mercury*'s account of the Bradford Blase celebrations states: 'Thus has been sacrificed another old English custom and pageant which cannot but excite a feeling partaking of regret; yet reason commends the sacrifice; the age is growing superior to childish shows, and we hope to degrading dissipation; and intellect and religion are getting the better of sensual indulgences'.[37] Two very different authorities from very different circumstances, but both in their own ways apparently concerned with 'antiquity', both shedding perhaps crocodile tears for the demise of a venerable custom, and both adopting the moral high ground of religion and the values of a new age.

For many years Bishop Blase did not fade away in Bradford. The following two extracts will perhaps give some flavour of his later manifestations:

Bishop Blaize – The commemoration of the septennial festival of Bishop Blaize was not quite neglected in Bradford. Amongst the festivities got up in honour of the 'Great Author of our Combing Trade,' may be mentioned the ball which took place in the evening in the large room of the Exchange Buildings, when about two hundred persons assembled. Horabin's band was in attendance, and the dance was kept up to a late hour in the morning. The stewards were distinguished by a rosette of white yarn. There was also a ball in the large room of the Odd Fellows' Hall, which was numerously attended. Several of the masters gave their men treats, and about 200 children in one of the mills, disappointed in not having a holiday, refused to work after breakfast, and paraded the streets in high glee. As it was St. Monday, a number of workmen not connected with the worsted business made a holiday, in consequence of which the streets were busy during the day with saunterers, and in the evening, a great many drunken people were observed rolling about. On Tuesday, there was a dinner at the Talbot Inn, at which M. Thompson, Esq. presided.[38]

> The Bishop Blaize Anniversary. – The society of Masters and Foremen connected with the wool trade, held their annual meeting, in honour of Bishop Blaize, at the Church Steps Inn, Bradford, on Tuesday last, when about forty of the members sat down to an excellent entertainment. The room was tastefully decorated with flags and banners, and festooned with wool, in all its different stages of manufacture. The usual loyal toasts were given, and heartily responded to. The chairman (for twenty years foreman to W. C. Haigh, Esq.) delivered an address in which he showed the good results that had followed the associating together of the employers and employed, impressed upon the foremen the responsibility which rested with them, and wished them to notice the many breaches of trust that had occurred in the country since last he addressed them, and always to bear in mind the motto 'Honesty is the best policy.' 'The town and trade of Bradford' was given by Mr. J. Smithies, and responded to by Mr. T. Tetley, who delivered the popular 'Blaize speech.' The vice-chairman (Mr. R. Sutcliffe, wool-stapler), in a long address, showed the regular progress of trade, from the first mill being built in the town to the present time. 'The ladies' (proposed by Mr. C. J. Elgey), and many other toasts were given, interspersed with songs, and the company separated after spending a very agreeable evening.[39]

However dubious, and indeed tedious, these occasions and their sentiments may now sound, Bishop Blase remained a popular symbol of the prosperity of Bradford. Despite the mock burial announced in February 1832, there continued to be gatherings of friends to toast his memory or dinners given to the workforce by the firm; until late in the nineteenth century there were letters to the newspapers from strangers to the district enquiring who Bishop Blase was or about some aspect of the celebration, and occasionally, at various functions, talks were given about Bishop Blase and his day[40] – including performances of the official speech with its pious but ultimately unfulfilled assertion:

> Long shall his name in British annals shine,
> And grateful Ages offer at his Shrine.

Who now remembers Bishop Blase?[41]

Notes

1 For a brief account of St Blase, see D. H. Farmer, *The Oxford Dictionary of Saints* (Oxford: Clarendon Press, 1978), p. 44, *s.v.* Blaise.

Leeds newspapers sometimes substitute Diocletian for Licinius as the emperor responsible for Blase's martyrdom. For a description of hand woolcombing as part of woollen manufacture, see James Burnley, *The History of Wool and Woolcombing* (London: Sampson Low, Marston, Searle and Rivington, 1889), pp. 87–90.

2 'Bishop Blaise, saint, martyr and woolcombers' patron', *Proceedings of the Society of Antiquaries of London*, 2nd ser. 27 (1914–15), 6–44. Roth was an anthropologist of some repute in Australia before returning to England and settling in Yorkshire; see *Dictionary of Australian Biography* (Sydney 1949), *s.v.* Roth, Henry Ling.

3 Burnley, *History of Wool and Woolcombing*, pp. 186–210; John James, *The History and Topography of Bradford* (London: Longman, Brown, Green and Longmans, 1841), pp. 163–7 and *Continuations and Additions to a History of Bradford and its Parish* (London: Longmans, Green, Reader, and Dyer, 1866), pp. 94–7.

4 *The Poetical Works of John Dyer L.L.B.* (London, 1765), p. 56, book II, lines 526–59 (quotation 541–59, quoted in part by James, *History and Topography of Bradford*, p. 164).

5 Roth refers to celebrations in Wellington (late eighteenth–mid nineteenth century), Worcester (1781), Saffron Walden (1778), Coggeshall (1778), Colchester (1782), Norwich (1783) and Loughborough (by implication, 1773). Withington refers to the probable appearance of Bishop Blase in a guild merchant procession at Preston, Lancashire, *c.*1762; amongst many other characters in a procession which was part of an operetta entitled *The Lord Mayor's Day* at the Theatre Royal, Covent Garden, in January 1783; and at Coventry in 1826 as the culmination of the Lady Godiva procession; see Robert Withington, *English Pageantry: An Historical Outline*, 2 vols. (Cambridge, MA: Harvard University Press, 1918; repr. New York: Benjamin Blom, 1963), 1:34; 2:99; 2:168. Roth's 1783 Norwich procession is the one attended by Parson Woodforde and described in some detail in his diary (James Woodforde, *The Diary of a Country Parson, 1758–1802*, ed. John Beresford (Oxford: Oxford University Press, World's Classics 1956), pp. 198–200). I am grateful to John Marshall for reminding me to look in Withington, and to Jill Golzen for remembering Parson Woodforde.

6 James, *Continuations and Additions*, p. 94.

7 Lines 1–8. The handbill, reproduced as fig. 1, is also reproduced in *The Journal of Dr. John Simpson, 1825* (Bradford: City of Bradford Metropolitan Council, 1981), p. 8. The alternative 1825 speech is quoted from a handbill printed by W. H. Blackburn, now West Yorkshire Archives Service: Bradford, DB3/15/9d. Roth quotes the opening of the same speech (except 'arm' for 'arms') but printed by a different Bradford printer, G. & E. Nicholson.

8 James, *Continuations and Additions*, p. 96.

9 *Leeds Mercury*, 5 February 1825. There is a later account of the

celebrations, printed in booklet form as *A Full and Particular Account of the Septennial Festival Held in Honour of Bishop Blase which was Celebrated in Bradford on Thursday February 3rd, 1825 Being the Last Public Demonstration of the Kind* (Bradford: Charles Denton, [1862]). '1862' has been added in ink below the title in the York Minster Library copy (Y–BRA/Z 77.31 FUL). This follows the newspaper account closely for the procession, the dinner and the ball, except for putting it into the past tense and adding two speeches at the end of the dinner and further details regarding the decorations at the ball.

10 *Journal of Dr. Simpson*, pp. 6–9.

11 *Journal of Dr. Simpson*, p. 6.

12 Emily Hargrave and W. B. Crump, 'The diary of Joseph Rogerson, scribbling miller, of Bramley, 1808–1814', in *The Leeds Woollen Industry, 1780–1820*, ed. W.B. Crump, Publications of the Thoresby Society 32 (1929), pp. 59–166 (113–14).

13 *Journal of Dr. Simpson*, pp. 6–7.

14 For the early development of Bradford, its industry and class relations, see Theodore Koditschek, *Class Formation and Urban-Industrial Society: Bradford, 1750–1850* (Cambridge: Cambridge University Press, 1990) and Gary Firth, *Bradford and the Industrial Revolution: An Economic History, 1760–1840* (Halifax: Ryburn Publishing, 1990). The procession visits and turns at two important private residences, Town Hill (Mr Duffield's) and Mannville (Mrs Mann's), and two important industrial sites, Garnett's Mill and Fawcett's Mill. Are these simply courtesy calls or the remains of earlier visits for refreshment or reward? The *Intelligencer* report of the 1818 celebration observes that after the Holme 'The assemblage then moved in procession to the Gentlemen's seats in the neighbourhood' (9 February 1818). The combers in the Keighley procession were still, according to the *Mercury*, being 'liberally regaled at the houses of the wool-staplers' (quoted in Roth, 'Bishop Blaise', p. 32). The combers in Leeds in 1769 'collected upwards of 23£ which they divided; and were entertained at night at the joint expence of their masters' (*Leeds Intelligencer*, 7 February 1769). How was the celebration financed? The 1804 hand-bill ends with the announcement that 'The Committee will attend at the Golden Fleece, on Saturday and Tuesday Evening next, the 28th. and 31st. of January, to receive Subscribers names and no longer'. These are presumably subscribers to the costs of the procession. The 1862 pageant in Coventry was supported in this way, see Withington, *English Pageantry*, 2, pp. 170–1.

15 *Journal of Dr. Simpson*, p. 7.

16 Quoted in Burnley, *History of Wool and Woolcombing*, p. 202.

17 *Journal of Dr. Simpson*, p. 7.

18 *Journal of Dr. Simpson*, p. 7.

19 *Journal of Dr. Simpson*, p. 9.

20 George Walker, *The Costume of Yorkshire, illustrated by a series of forty engravings being fac-similes of original drawings* (London: Longman, Hurst, Rees, Orme and Brown, 1814) was reprinted in 1885, with a new introduction containing some biographical information on Walker by Edward Hailstone. The originals of the watercolours are in the library of the Yorkshire Archaeological Society. The beard which the shepherdess appears to have in the engraving is revealed by the water-colour to be just a smudge, but the bishop is unchanged.

21 Roth, 'Bishop Blaise', facing p. 30.

22 Walker, *Costume of Yorkshire*, p. 86.

23 R. Young, 'George Walker's *Costume of Yorkshire* (1814): the representation and negotiation of class difference and social unrest', *Art History* 19.3 (1996), 393–417 (407).

24 James, *History of Bradford*, p. 166.

25 For description and discussion of the strike see Koditschek, *Class Formation*, pp. 471–4, and the works there cited.

26 This is Koditschek's view of the event: 'The graduated social structure of traditional manufacturing was disclosed along the streets for all to see. The organic ideal of mutual interdependence was set forth in a symbolism articulated by the masters and organizers and ratified silently by the mass of the workers who contributed their bodies for the visual effect. Worsted production depended on their labor; in turn it would ceremonially acknowledge their place' (*Class Formation*, p. 470). This almost certainly overstresses the silence and the lack of individuality, and possibly underestimates the positive involvement. Did the woolcombers make their own 'ornamented caps'? It seems likely. Even if not before, after the refreshments, the silent mass must have been a little more self-expressive.

27 Lines 11–22. The 1804 handbill is West Yorkshire Archives Service: Bradford, DB3/16/9a. It contains the official speech alongside the alternative. I am grateful to the staff at Bradford and at Keighley for their ready assistance.

28 The handbills containing the protest and the response to it are in Keighley Local Studies Library, BK321. The newspaper advertisement is in the *Leeds Mercury* for 9 January 1819.

29 *Leeds Intelligencer*, 6 February 1776.

30 Shepherd, shepherdess and lamb appear regularly in the processions of other towns. As Roth observes in relation to the Essex towns, 'the shepherdess with a lamb seems to have been quite as important as the Bishop' ('Bishop Blaise', p. 28). In Coventry in 1824 the lamb was a living one for the first time (Withington, *English Pageantry*, p. 168, n.1). It is not clear what the situation was at Bradford.

31 Evidence for the celebration for the three years between 1776 and 1804 is contained in the *Leeds Intelligencer* for 4 February 1783; 1 and 9 February 1790; and 30 January and 6 February 1797. There was

a celebration in Leeds as well in 1783, but not thereafter. Given its association with prosperity, the seven-year pattern may be related to the lean and fat kine of Pharaoh's dream (Genesis 41); but there are many possibilities. Annual celebration on the scale that was apparently acceptable might well have been beyond the resources of the town. Bradford seems to have been unusual in its regularity. In Yorkshire and elsewhere, the celebration does not appear to have been regularly observed (see, for example, Roth, 'Bishop Blaise': Leeds and Masham, p. 29, Wakefield, p. 33). A procession is sometimes held on a day other than 3 February, or may be said to be 'under the auspices' of Bishop Blase. The 1783 Norwich procession was held on 24 March; in 1788, one was held in Leeds on 3 July, to celebrate the act preventing the export of wool from England, and, in the last week of January 1758, one was held there 'under the Auspices of Bishop Blaize' to celebrate the birthday of the king of Prussia (see Roth, 'Bishop Blaise', pp. 29, 27).

32 See, for example, the debate between Gordon Kipling and the late, and much missed, Graham Runnalls in *Medieval English Theatre* 15 (1997), 26–120.

33 The plentiful staging evidence in the stage directions remains wide open to interpretation. For the evidence only, see *The N-Town Play, Cotton MS Vespasian D. 8*, ed. Stephen Spector, 2 vols, EETS s.s 11 and 12 (Oxford: Oxford University Press, 1991), *The Mary Play from the N.town Manuscript*, ed. Peter Meredith (Exeter: Exeter University Press, 1997) and *The Passion Play from the N.town Manuscript*, ed. Peter Meredith (London: Longman, 1990).

34 See, for example, *Expense in ffesto Corporis christi* at York for 1520, 1521 and 1522, where apart from food and drink, which is plentiful, we know only of the hanging of the chamber, the nails used for it and the odd payment. Alexandra F. Johnston and Margaret Rogerson (eds.), *York*, 2 vols., REED (Toronto: University of Toronto Press, 1979), pp. 221–2, 225–6, 229–30. At least at Chester feasts there were some minstrels (for example, Elizabeth Baldwin, Lawrence M. Clopper and David Mills (eds.), *Cheshire including Chester*, 2 vols., REED (Toronto: University of Toronto Press, 2007), pp.133 (painters, etc.), 177 (smiths, etc.)) even if we don't know what the diners talked about.

35 This was another winter celebration; see *York*, pp. 359–62 and 369.

36 *York*, p. 353.

37 *Leeds Mercury*, 4 February 1832.

38 *Leeds Mercury*, 9 February 1839.

39 *Leeds Mercury*, 7 February 1857.

40 Burnley describes the mock burial (*History of Wool*, pp. 206–7). There are events of one kind and another recorded in the *Leeds Intelligencer* and the *Leeds Mercury* at least until the end of the nineteenth century; see, for example, *Leeds Mercury*, 5 February 1857, 20 February 1873,

19 April 1879, 19 March 1881, 1 January 1887, for recapitulations of the history (sometimes in answer to queries, sometimes in reports of meetings) and frequent reprintings and recitings of the Blase speech. Blase also appeared in the procession celebrating the opening of the Bradford Town Hall in 1871, see *Yorkshire Notes and Queries*, ed. C. F. Forshaw, 4 vols. (Bradford: Henry Casaubon Derwent; London: Elliot Stock, 1905), 1:30. William Hone might have created a more generalised awareness of the Blase celebrations by reprinting the 1825 account from the *Leeds Intelligencer* in the entry for 3 February in his *Every-Day Book or Everlasting Calendar of Popular Amusements*, 2 vols. (London: Hunt and Clarke, 1826), 1, coll. 209–12.

41 A postscript: Ralph Thoresby, visiting Leicester in 1712, wrote in his Diary: 'the feast of St. Blase, a bishop, is celebrated yearly about Candlemas by those who deal in wool, he being said to be the first who invented the combing thereof.' Joseph Hunter (ed.), *The Diary of Ralph Thoresby*, 2 vols. (London: Henry Colburn & Richard Bentley, 1830) vol 2, p. 166. The remark seems to suggest that Thoresby had no previous knowledge of such a celebration in his own locality of Leeds, as he undoubtedly would have done if it had existed. The date and annual celebration link it with Dyer's poem and demonstrate early celebration of the feast in the Leicester area.

8

'Trewe techyng and false heritikys': some 'Lollard' manuscripts of the *Pore Caitif*

Kalpen Trivedi

The interaction between Lollard material and texts of a more orthodox nature in manuscript books has increasingly become the focus of recent scholarship, as in, for instance, Anne Hudson's important pieces, 'Some aspects of Lollard book production' and 'The expurgation of a Lollard sermon-cycle', which explore the scope of such literary activity.[1] As she writes, however, the line between orthodoxy and heterodoxy is not easily defined:

> How often have I read through a set of sermons or a tract and felt, by the itching of my palms, that a Lollard wrote them; yet, trying to isolate anything that could be regarded as decisively Wycliffite, I have had to admit that the text could be just radically ortho-dox. . .[In] the centre was a large grey area where the authors at best did not wish to define their position, and at worst did not understand the issues sufficiently clearly to be able to do so.[2]

Inevitably, these studies on Lollard literary history have concerned themselves with the questions of Bible translation into English and the case for or against evidence indicating early literary activity in English among Wycliffite circles. An early and important contribution to this debate is Michael Wilks's 'Misleading manuscripts', which tackled head-on the problems of dating early translations of the Bible into English, and suggested that such activity might have started earlier than was hitherto accepted.[3] While these studies differ in scope and focus, they almost all make it clear just how convoluted a problem it is to classify rigidly and date much of the minor religious prose of the late fourteenth century, and yet they almost always reinforce a sense of dichotomy between orthodox and heterodox material.

In the passage quoted above, Hudson is referring to 'writing on ecclesiastical issues around 1410–30', yet the confusion may well be seen in an earlier period.[4] Just how easy is it to distinguish clearly between 'trewe techyng' and 'false heritikys' in the case of texts of the late fourteenth century, when the Wycliffite movement was merely nascent? Surely, it can be argued that writers of this period, like their later counterparts, would have felt no obligation to wear any badges, either as marks of persecution or as signs of belonging to the establishment. In past centuries, cataloguers and editors habitually attributed anonymous texts or texts of doubtful origin to either Wyclif or Purvey on the one hand, or to Rolle on the other.[5] While twentieth-century scholarship has spent much effort correcting these spurious authorial ascriptions, it has still managed to preserve this sense of dichotomy between orthodox and heterodox material.

The *Pore Caitif* is a very good case in point, as the narrative surrounding this text has invariably been organised along these two lines. This late fourteenth-century manual of doctrine and devotion, usually comprising fourteen tracts covering the basic spiritual syllabus and encouraging more sophisticated devotion, used to be attributed, on tenuous grounds, to Wyclif. In the light of Sr. M. T. Brady's researches on the text it is now usually thought of as 'an entirely orthodox one', but one which nonetheless shows some sign of Lollard infiltration. To quote from Sr. Brady's article, 'The Lollard sources of the *Pore Caitif*':

> Despite a long history of attribution of The *Pore Caitif* to Wycliffe and/or the Lollards, I believe the text is uncontaminated by heresy. . . . It should be noted, however, that interpolations and omissions that seem to be work of Lollard sympathizers occur in twelve manuscripts of *Pore Caitif*.[6]

This chapter, however, seeks to present quite a radically opposite position, namely, that one must view the genesis of this treatise as being from within the Lollard movement in its incipient stages – for want of a better term, the *proto-Lollard* movement – or as a result of some literary activity concomitant and similar to the gospel translations being undertaken at this time. This view is based on the examination of codicological evidence from surviving manuscripts and has some implications, notably to do with its probable date of composition, and also the understanding of the interaction between so-called heretical and orthodox literature in the fifteenth century, which will also be touched upon briefly in the course of the chapter.

It is commonly acknowledged that the author of the *Pore Caitif* was skilled at weaving together his disparate sources, both orthodox and heterodox, to form a single unified manual of doctrine and instruction. These sources have been examined by Sr. Brady in two articles and it is useful to summarise her investigation of the Lollard sources of the *Pore Caitif*.[7] The treatise borrows quite substantially from a number of works popular in Wycliffite circles. The first and probably the most important Lollard source of the *Pore Caitif* is the *Glossed Gospels*. The *Short Matthew* and *Short Luke* are the basis for several passages in the exposition of the creed and the tract called the 'Counsel of Christ'. The *Short* and the *Long Matthew* are further used in the 'Mirror of Chastity' tract. The second source noted by Brady is the *Early Version* of the Wycliffite Bible. Studying the scriptural quotations found in the 'Mirror' tract, she concludes that they are fairly similar to the *Early Version*, but also notes some differences, which may be attributed to the compiler of the *Pore Caitif* himself. The third source investigated is *De salutaribus documentis*. This treatise, thought to be the work of Paulinus of Aquilaea, was known in the Middle Ages as *Augustinus ad Julianum Comitem*, and the *Pore Caitif* is usually referred to as 'St Austin's book to þe eerl'. Excerpts from this source may be noted in four tracts of the *Pore Caitif* – brief passages may be found in the creed, commandments and 'The Counsel of Christ', while one half of the 'Charter of Heaven' is dependent upon the *De salutaribus documentis*. The fourth and final source noted by Brady is the encyclopaedic *Floretum*. The *Pore Caitif*'s dependence on this reference aid is altogether more problematic to prove than its debt to the other three Lollard works.[8]

Of course, the use of Lollard source material is not in itself proof that the author shared Lollard views or indeed was a part of the movement. However, it is peculiar that in the light of the evidence that Brady has herself gathered, she does not seek to problematise her wholehearted attribution of orthodoxy to the compiler based on his use of sources such as the Fathers, Rolle and Grosseteste. This endorsement of the *Pore Caitif*'s orthodoxy, however, proves even more tricky when one actually examines the manuscript contexts of the texts thought to contain heterodox interpolations or omissions.[9]

Several features revealed by the study of the manuscripts militate against the view that the text of this treatise was adulterated in some manner by adherents or sympathisers of the Lollard movement. The first, and quite remarkable feature is that most of the volumes testifying to this so-called Lollard infiltration tend to be among the earliest copies of the text. I have elsewhere examined some patterns of circulation of the *Pore Caitif* as attested by the earliest codices containing the orthodox version of the treatise and it is worth noting that these copies testify to either the circulation of parts of the *Pore Caitif* separately in anthologies, or in a variant order from the 'definitive' form and number of tracts as established by Sr. Brady.[10] In fact, most of the stand-alone copies of the orthodox *Pore Caitif* with the 'definitive' order of tracts are later than these early Lollard or variant-order manuscripts. The second feature is the extraordinary coherence of these Lollard manuscripts as a group, both textually and in physical features such as the size, the layout and presentation of the text, the use of Latin quotations, and so on.

When one considers these factors together with the nature of the interpolations – a deletion here, a couple of sentences there – the patterns revealed do not bespeak random interpolation. What one observes instead is a highly coherent early group of manuscripts with certain interpolations and omissions that may be *interpreted* as 'Lollard' in sympathy: for instance, the omission of the passage that declares that 'ymagis schulen be as kalenders to lewide folk' or the passage that allows oaths as lawful under certain circumstances, or the interpolation regarding suffering tribulation meekly.[11] Most of these examples of textual anomalies are matters of omission rather than interpolation, and such is their nature that I believe they represent an effort to 'clean up' the *Pore Caitif* once the business of Lollardy had became too distasteful. Moreover, the care exhibited in the presentation of the text in these books – the delineation of Latin and English, the marking off of the 'glose', etc. – have long been considered hallmarks for Lollard book-production. Anne Hudson identifies such features as being typical of Lollard book-production, features which she notes the *Pore Caitif* shares.[12] In my view, then, the uniformity exhibited by this group of manuscripts in codicological and textual matters is indicative of the fact that the *Pore Caitif* had its genesis in Wycliffite circles. The problems arising from such a statement are, of course, a reconsideration of the dating and possible authorship of the text.

I have thus far been using the terms *Lollard* and *Wycliffite* quite indiscriminately, and this is partly the problem I wish to highlight. It is quite difficult to fix any watertight definitions for these terms, and the matter is particularly problematic in the case of a text like the *Pore Caitif*, which, while seemingly orthodox, betrays certain complexities. Earlier in the chapter I used *proto-Lollard* for want of a better term, as *Lollard* is associated as a mark of opprobrium

with the heresy in its extreme form as it flourished at the end of
the fourteenth century and the few decades thereafter, and as was
prosecuted by Archbishop Arundel. I suggest, then, that in the
case of the *Pore Caitif* the so-called Lollard interpolations in these
manuscripts are not, as has been previously thought, the *ad hoc*
work of some Lollard sympathisers. In her discussion of the early
Wycliffite movement, Hudson notes that 'during the period 1381
to 1413 much of the Wycliffite literature, and almost all of the
lengthy writings, were composed and revised'.[13] It is my conten-
tion that the *Pore Caitif* is produced as part of this movement, very
probably within Oxford circles, during the early 1380s or even
before, containing those parts we have come to regard as interpolations, these last being excised at some later stage to produce a
more orthodox text. It is a text, then, that must come early in the
history of the movement, during that period when, as Hudson puts
it, 'people . . . may have encountered Wyclif's ideas before they
were condemned and when the significance of the Blackfriars decision for the church as a whole was not clearly understood', rather
than later (the period after 1401) 'when consciousness of a divide
between two opposing, and incompatible, groups was beginning to
emerge'.[14] Wyclif's own *De mandatis divinis*, for instance, on which
the *Pore Caitif* occasionally draws, is a moderate tract that did not
attract much criticism during his lifetime.

If one looks beyond Hudson's statement, the very idea of
'Lollardy' as a condemned notion before the early 1390s becomes
untenable. The watershed of 1382 (when Henry Crumpe report-
edly called some of his colleagues at Oxford '*Lollardi*'), taken
as a starting point in traditional accounts of Lollard history, is
essentially a date provided by later, orthodox narratives about
the heresy, both ecclesiastical and historical (e.g., the *Fasciculi
Zizaniorum*, Knighton's *Chronicle*), which have been accepted at
face value.[15] Even sensitive and complex recent studies by modern
scholars like Kantik Ghosh, who explores how academic dissent
becomes popular and achieves radical force outside the schools,
and Rita Copeland, who provides a comparative account of two
Lollard writers and their engagement with late-medieval learning,
nonetheless participate in this narrative where Wycliffism transi-
tions seamlessly into Lollardy.[16] Most recently, however, Andrew
Cole provides a compelling new history of the invention of Lollardy
when he re-reads these accounts of the 'lollardization' of the 1380s
in terms of the creation of a heresy by orthodox authorities, first
Courtenay and then Arundel, and concludes that 'we should,

therefore, remove 1382 as a starting point for our critical "lollard" histories', suggesting also that 'as late as 1386 there were no "lollards" in England', and possibly not even until the early 1390s; but there certainly were Wycliffites.[17] I believe that it is these misunderstandings about the nature of early Wycliffite activity that lead scholars to attempt to distinguish between orthodox and 'Lollard' material from this period, a distinction that is, in my opinion, ultimately futile. As the studies of Ghosh, Cole and Fiona Somerset show, Wycliffite ideas and genres become increasingly popular in non-clerical and vernacular circles from the 1380s on, so if the *Pore Caitif* shares in some of these, it should come as no surprise to us.[18] In light of this, I view the early ascriptions of 'Wycliffism' to the *Pore Caitif* as essentially accurate, although there is no suggestion that Wyclif had any part in the text's composition.

As a possible clue to dating the *Pore Caitif*, one can examine the scriptural references in the treatise and attempt to correlate it to the activity surrounding the Wycliffite translation of the Bible. As mentioned earlier, in the *Mirror of Chastity* tract the biblical references are close to the *Early Version* of the Wycliffite Bible.[19] A similar examination of the scriptural quotations from the ten commandments tract paints a slightly different picture. The texts of different commandments are close variously to the *Early Version* and the *Late Version*. There is a parallel version of scriptural translation found in the Wycliffite sermon cycle with which it may be instructive to compare the versions found in the *Pore Caitif*. The complication in this picture is that it is hardly easy to date the work on the Wycliffite Bible with certainty. Dates as early as the 1370s in Oxford have been suggested by S. L. Fristedt and David Fowler; J. Forshall and F. Madden believed the first part (to Baruch 3:20) to have been completed by 1382. But it is difficult to disagree with Hudson, who says that 'the last twenty years of the fourteenth century would seem to be the right period for the operation' and that the *Late Version* was completed 'some time between 1395 and 1397'.[20]

It is also in these last twenty years of the fourteenth century, and possibly at Oxford, that work is being carried out on the *Floretum*, the *Glossed Gospels*, *English Wycliffite Sermon Cycle* and the revision of Rolle's Psalter commentary. Certainly, Hudson prefers a 'centre' for the production and dissemination of early Lollard literature, possibly even at Oxford, which resulted in the publication of the *Floretum* and the *Glossed Gospels*. The *Glossed Gospels*, which Sr. Brady enumerates among the sources of the *Pore Caitif*, is dated by Hudson to between 1390 and 1407, once again at such a centre which offered the resources of a publishing house and a library.[21] However, the nature of the similarity between the *Glossed Gospels* and *Pore Caitif* is far from clear: it is possible for both the *Pore Caitif* and the *Glossed Gospels* to share material if the circumstances of their production were analogous, so that the former may be simultaneous with, or even precede, the latter rather than being indebted to it. The point here, then, is to suggest that the *Pore Caitif* is contemporary with such early group activity, before 'Lollardy moved fairly rapidly away from the original standpoint of its founder in the direction of a more radical, populist, lay-centred church'.[22] The comprehensive nature of a treatise like the *Pore Caitif*, drawing variously from a number of orthodox and heterodox sources, could only have been produced in a location well supplied with books and scholars, and given the astonishing uniformity and cohesion among these heterodox manuscripts, as will be shown below, one may posit its genesis as part of the kind of group activity or centre (not necessarily a scriptorium) mentioned above.

Let us turn first to the question of the dating of these manuscripts. The probable earliest *Pore Caitif*, thought to date from late in the fourteenth century, is a Lollard copy – New York, Public Library, MS 68. This is not exceptional: two other late-fourteenth century copies of the text are found in Hunterian MSS 496 and 520, both of which are miscellanies containing a number of other religious works, both orthodox and heterodox. An approximate dating of the so-called Lollard manuscripts is as follows:

Late fourteenth century	Hunterian MS 496, Hunterian MS 520, NYPL MS 68
Early fifteenth century	MS Bodley 3, MS Add. B.66, Trinity College Cambridge MS B.14.53, CUL MS Ff.vi.55, Lambeth Palace MS 484, MS Harley 2322
Mid fifteenth century	MS Bodley 938, BL MS Add. 30897, MS Lyell 29?

By contrast, the earliest orthodox copies of the *Pore Caitif* (Oxford, Bodleian Library MS Ashmole 1286, and Paris, Bibliothèque Nationale MS Fonds anglais 41) have been dated to after 1400, both miscellanies that, as we have noted, preserve an ordering of tracts different from the 'definitive' order. Stand-alone orthodox copies of the orthodox *Pore Caitif* date from the second quarter of the fifteenth century or later. The brief excerpts and single tracts that are found in very varied manuscripts proliferate, by and large, in the third and fourth quarters of the fifteenth century. Of course, as is generally the case with such late manuscripts, it is very difficult to make any precise affirmations about dating in the absence of extra-palaeographical evidence. This dating of the *Pore Caitif* manuscripts, which I consider to be of conservative estimate, does, however, have some value in that it establishes general trends for the circulation of the treatise. It is clear, then, that the earliest copies of the text testify to the circulation of a heterodox treatise – or at least a seemingly heterodox one. Of course, the survival of the heterodox version in earlier manuscripts does not necessarily mean it was composed first; yet we cannot discount the fact that the early cluster of heterodox copies shows itself to be remarkably coherent in other ways as well.

This group of early Lollard manuscripts displays certain other peculiarities not seen in the 'definitive' orthodox copies of the text. The first of these is the use of Latin in the text. For the purposes of argument these Lollard volumes may be considered in two groups: those that include quotations and citation in Latin, generally from biblical sources, within the text, and those that do not contain such quotations. It is noteworthy that such use of Latin is only observed in some manuscripts of this group rather than the orthodox one. The following Lollard manuscripts contain material in Latin: MS Add. B.66, Trinity College Cambridge MS B.14.53, CUL MS Ff. Vi.55, Hunterian MSS 496 and 520, and Lambeth Palace MS 484. In all of these the method of presentation of the text involves first the copying of the Latin text of the commandment or the article of the creed, followed by a translation of the text in question. A certain uniformity of presentation is to be observed: the Latin text in these manuscripts is frequently copied in red or underlined in red; the translation is generally preceded by the words 'þat is', also usually in red; and finally, the rubric 'þe glose' is interposed between the translation and the exposition of the particular text. Thus, the text of the first commandment is set out as follows in Cambridge, University Library MS Ff.vi.55:

Here bigynneþ þe ten comaundementis of god
Locutus que est dominus cuntos [sic] sermones hos. Ego sum dominus deus tuus qui eduxi te de terra egipti de domo seruitutis.

Non habebis deos alienos coram me. Non facies tibi sculptile neque omnem similitudinem que est in celo desuper et que est in terra derosum nec eorum que sunt in aquis sub terra. Non adorabis ea necque coles. Ego sum dominus deus fortis zelotes visitans iniquitatem patrum in filios vsque in terciam et quartam generacionem erum qui oderunt me, et faciens misercordiam in milia his qui diligunt me et custodiunt precepta mea. **þat is** þe lord spak alle þese wordis: I am þe lord þi god þat ladde þee out of þe lond of egypt out of þe hous of þraldom. Þou schalt not haue alien goddis bifore me. Þou schalt not make to þee agrauen ymage ne ony licknesse þat is in heuene aboue and þat is in erþe byneþe, ne of þo þingis þat ben in watris vndir þe erþe; þou schalt not worschipe hem ne loute hem. I am þi lord god a strong ielous louer, visitynge þe wickidnes of fadris in sones in to þe þridde and þe fourþe generacioun of hem þat hatiden me, [and doinge] mercy in to þoussandis kynredis of hem þat louen me and kepen myn heestis. **þe glose** Alle þese wordis seide oure lord god, and þei ben chargid wiþ more witt þan we kunne telle. (ff. 30v–31v)[23]

Such precision of presentation is also observed in manuscripts of this group which do not contain Latin. So, for instance, the text of the first commandment from London, British Library, MS Harley 2322:

The firste heeste of god is þis: God hym silf spak alle þese wordis. I am þe lord þi god þat ladde þee out of þe lond of egipt and brouhte þee out of þe hous of þraldom. Þou schalt not haue aliene goddis bifore me. Þou schalt not make to þee an ymage grauen wiþ mannes hond, neiþir any lijknesse of þing þat is in heuene aboue ne in erþe byneþe ne of hem þat ben in watris bineþe þe erþe. Þou schalt not worschipe hem ne loute hem as god. I am þe lord þi 'god´ astronge gelous louere visitinge þe wickidnesse of fadris in children into þe þridde and þe fourþe generacioun of hem þat haten me and I do mercy into þousandis of kinredis of hem þat louen me and kepen myn heestis. Þese wordis of godd ben chargid wiþ more wit þan we kunne telle. (ff. 39r–v; the English text underlined in red ink)

This uniformity of presentation is to be remarked not only in the case of the commandments, but also in that of the petitions of the *Pater Noster* and the articles of the creed. Of interest comparable to the uniformity of presentation is the English text of the commandments that is used in these manuscripts. All the manuscripts of this group, whether or not containing Latin, use the same English text of the commandments – a version which is unique to this group. A comparison of the orthodox manuscripts shows that they are equally consistent in their use of a different translation from the Latin. Let us look at the English text of the first commandment from the orthodox version to be found in London, British Library MS Harley 2336:

> The firste comaundement god hotiþ in þese wordis seiynge himsilf: I am þi lord god þat ledde þee out of egipt, out of þe hous of þraldom eþir bondage. Þou schalt not haue straunge goddis bifore me. Þou schalt not make to þee a grauun ymage, neþir ony licnesse which is in heuene aboue and which is in erþe byneþe, neþir of þo þingis þat ben in watris vndir þe erþe. Þou schalt not praie to hem neiþir worschipe in soule. I am þi lord god, a strong gelous louer, visitinge þe wickidnessis of fadris in þe children in to þe þridde and ferþe generacioun of hem þat hatiden me, and doynge merci in to a þousynd of hem þat louen me and kepen my comaundementis. (ff. 17r–v)

It will be at once apparent that the text differs in a number of ways. While the variations are not significant in themselves – they do not substantially change the meaning of the text or offer problematic interpretations – what is significant is the fact that both the orthodox and heterodox manuscripts are constant in their espousal of one particular version. So, for instance, the version in the orthodox manuscripts adds the redundant phrase 'eþir bondage' after 'þraldom'; it replaces the word 'aliene' with 'straunge', and the phrase 'þou schalt not worschipe hem ne loute hem' with 'þou schalt not praie to hem: neiþir worschipe in soule'; and finally, the word 'kynredis' is dropped. Similar examples may be cited from the texts of the other commandments. In the case of the second commandment, the orthodox version adds the otiose phrase 'eþir withouten cause' to the phrase in CUL Ff.vi.55, 'þat takiþ þe name of his lord god idilly', and it replaces the Cambridge manuscript's 'innocent or vnponyschid' with 'withouten gilte'. In the third commandment the heterodox lists 'hondmaiden' among those bound to keep the Sabbath, as it does 'þe see' among the list of God's creations; both are missing in the orthodox version. The significance of these quotations from the commandments is not so much in how they differ but in the fact that they *do* differ, and yet agree consistently within their own groups.

Other instances of consistency in this group may also be mentioned. For instance, with the exception of British Library, MS Add. 30897 and the first hand of MS Lyell 29, all the manuscripts of this group are copied in uniform book hands. Standard blue and red flourished initials are used throughout the texts, and Cambridge, Trinity College MS B.14.53, CUL MS Ff.vi.55 and

MS Harley 2322 make use of very similar pink, blue and gold initials at the beginning of major tracts. While I have not examined MSS Hunterian 496 and 520, the very full descriptions in the catalogue indicate the use of such initials. Conversely, such sumptuousness is not the norm in orthodox manuscripts. Those that use any gold decoration at all – Paris, Bibliothèque Nationale MS Fonds anglais 41, Lambeth Palace MS 541 and London, British Library MS Stowe 38 – employ initials and borders of a very different style. Even in the case of Paris and Lambeth manuscripts, which otherwise betray a close relationship, the decoration and illumination is far from consistent. Further uniformity is also observed in the physical appearance of the manuscripts themselves of this group: invariably, the codices tend to be small enough to be carried in pockets, very probably priests' books. The average dimensions of a typical volume would be in the region of $5\frac{1}{2}' \times 3\frac{3}{4}''$ or 141 mm × 96 mm, with 22–29 lines of writing per side.

From the evidence about the manuscript books discussed so far, it would not be unreasonable to posit that they were produced in similar, possibly controlled circumstances, at about the same time. There are other matters of layout and decoration that may be added to this argument, but not much will be served by overelaboration. By contrast, even the early manuscripts of the orthodox group evince a greater variety of sizes and scripts. What we can conclude, then, is that these early Lollard manuscripts form a group that is codicologically very consistent, in addition to being textually so, and this is borne out by further investigation.[24]

In the discussion of the first commandment, the text of the orthodox group grudgingly allows the use of images, for they are helpful to the unlettered.[25] So, having elaborated the fickleness of the Jews and the 'greete mawmetrie' that is in idols, the author nonetheless states:

> Alle suche symilitudis and ymages schulden ben as kalendris to lewyd folk: þat rihtte as clerkis seen by her bookis what þei schulden do, so lewyd folk whanne hem lackiþ techynge schulden leerne by ymages whom þei schulden worschipe and folewe in lyuynge.[26]

He is however quick to reiterate that 'to do goddis worschipe to ymages; eche man is forfendid'. Most manuscripts of this group omit this passage, and include interpolations against the use of images. A comparison of the texts shows the following groupings: $CC_1G_1G_2LLa$ add a passage on how images are 'grauen hoten and peyntede amys and contrarie to oure feiþe'. G_1G_2 also add a brief passage observing that the uses of images may have good and bad effects, a view resembling that of Wyclif in his *De mandatis divinis*, a similarity which is also noted by Sr. Brady. B_2L_1 further add a sentence on how the worship of images may not avail a man in difficulty.

This last noted similarity is merely one of many shared by these two manuscripts, to whose unique relationship we will presently return. It is interesting to note, however, that the sentiments expressed in this sentence are not unlike a unique interpolation in the lower margin to be found in that anomalous manuscript MS Lyell 29 after the discussion of the sun and moon as false gods in the context of idolatry:

> Alle such ben fals goddis to trist upon þat mown not delyuere hem silf ne her worshipers fro þe veniaunce of almihti god at the dredeful dome as god witnessiþ bi his prophete: Iere. X. (f. 15ᵛ)

That the scribe of this manuscript thought this reading to be significant is evidenced by the fact that it is set out exactly in the manner of other marginalia. In this manuscript, marginalia are used not merely to indicate biblical or patristic references, but also points of interest to the reader or scribe: so, for instance, on this page, we have 'poule glotenye', 'poule leccherie', 'ymages', and 'gregor to serene'.

The *Pore Caitif* is largely silent on the matter of oaths, a subject which is usually a great favourite of the Lollards. It is only in the discussion of the eighth commandment that this matter is raised, and then it is in the form of a grudging acceptance of oaths in a just cause. Such sentiments are also expressed in the discussion of the second commandment, when false-swearing is counted as the taking of God's name in vain, and in the seventh commandment false witness-bearing an infringement of the injunction against manslaughter. Of the manuscripts which omit the acceptance of idols as noted above, CC_1LLa are also consistent in the omission of the allowing of oaths in the discussion of the eighth commandment.

The matter of oaths by creatures is discussed in the second commandment, and swearing by Christ's body is specifically forbidden. Even in this matter MS Lyell 29 is enthusiastic, amplifying the standard injunction not to swear by Christ's body in the following manner:

> but also dismembren him and crucifien hym, in as mych as is in hem, swering bi his herte and bi hise woundis, bi hise sidis, and nailis, and

bodi and soule, feet, ihen, and face, and oþire membris. Suche doen more dispijt to crist þan þe iewis diden þat nailide him to þe cross as seynt austin and gregor seien. (ff. 19v–20r)

In an early article, Sr. Brady has discussed how some manuscripts of the *Pore Caitif* present individual articles of the creed as ascribed to the twelve apostles, whereas others specifically forbid such speculation.[27] While she looks at this matter again in her article on interpolations, the fact that all the manuscripts which omit the references to individual apostles belong to this Lollard group is never brought to attention. With two exceptions, the manuscripts of this group all contain the stern warning against vain speculation. The two exceptions, B_2L_1, omit the ascription to the apostles as well as the warning against speculations. Thus, this pair of manuscripts, which we have already seen as exhibiting certain peculiarities in the case of the commandments, proves to be internally consistent here as well, and the unique nature of their relationship is further discussed in the next section.

In order to understand the close relations between B_2L_1 it is necessary to return to the ten commandments. One of the omissions in the heterodox group of manuscripts not noted by Sr. Brady occurs in the conclusion of the commandments tract in B_2L_1. In most manuscripts, both heterodox and orthodox, the exposition of the commandments is followed by some small tracts, often collectively rubricated as 'The Charge of the Heestis'. The first of these tracts, beginning 'These be þe ten comaundementis of god aftir þe whiche it bihoueþ alle men and women to rule her liif, if þei wolen be saued', goes on to recapitulate the necessity of keeping the commandments and the duty of each man to teach them to his subjects. A tract beginning 'Uppe þat ech man kepiþ þese comaundementis of god yuel eiþir wel' follows, and contains a further recapitulation of the commandments and some remarks on prayer which might link it to the *Pater noster* tract that generally follows. The commandments are rounded up with a third tract that elaborates the relationship of the commandments to love: 'And ech man þat kepiþ þese ten heestis of god, þe whiche ben conteyned in loue to god *and* to þi neihbore.'[28] The twofold division which is the subject of this last tract is to be found at the end of a number of commentaries on the commandments, both heterodox and orthodox. This scheme of tracts, however, is not followed in the B_2L_1 group, which omits the last two tracts, preserving only the first of these three short tracts.

There is, thus, no discussion of love, or any lead into the *Pater noster* tract, but then, in both these manuscripts the latter precedes the commentary on the commandments.

What further compounds the grimness of this ending is the truncated discussion of the tenth commandment and the omissions from the first recapitulative tract. A comparison of the beginning of the two versions will serve to illustrate my point:

> These be þe ten comaundementis of god aftir þe whiche it bihoueþ alle men and wommen to rule her liif, if þei wolen be saued . . . and þerfore god comaundiþ generali to his peple þat ech man telle to his sones how god ledde his peple out of Egypt. And it schal be as a tokene in þin hond as seiþ god and as a þing of mynde bifore þin ihen and the lawe of þe lord euere in þi mouþ. And in anoþir place god seiþ þese wordis whiche I comaunde to þee þis day **schulen be in þin herte and þou schalt telle hem to þi sones and þou schalt þinke on hem sittinge in þin hous and goinge in þe weie and sleepinge and risynge. And þou schalt binde þo as a signe in þin hond, and þo schulen be moued bitwixe þin ihen**, and þou schalt write þo in þe doris and lyntels of þin hous. **Þat is þou schalt rule alle þi þouhtis, wordis and deedis priuy and apeert with inne hous and wiþ oute and in ech place bi þe comaundementis of god**. Kepe þi silf and þi soule bisily, ne forhete þou not þe wordis whiche þin ihen han seen, and falle þei not fro þin ihen in alle þe dayes of þi liif. (Paris, BN MS Fonds anglais 41, ff. 64rv–65r)

> These ben þe ten hestis of god aftir þe whiche eche cristen man and womman owen to reule her lijf if þei wolen be saued . . . And þerfore god comaundide generaly to his puple: be þe lawe of þi lord euere in þi mouþ. And in anoþir place god seiþ þese wordis þat I comaunde to þee to day **schulen be in þin herte, and þou schalt telle hem to þi sones. And þou schalt þenke on hem sittinge in þin hous and goinge in þe weie and 'so´ þou schuldist þenke on goddis word in al þing þat þou doist**. And god seide þou schalt write hem in þe lintels and doris of þin hous. **þat is þou 'schalt´ reule þi þouhtis wordis and deedis and þo þat ben in þin hous boþe priuy and apert aftir þe biddinge of god** and passe not þe word of god out of þi mynde in alle þe daies of þi lijf, for whanne þe word of god is out of þi mynde it is voyde fro vertu. (MS Harley 2322, ff. 85r–v)

It is at once obvious that the version contained in MS Harley 2322 has far fewer otiose repetitions of phrases than the other version quoted, which is standard in most other manuscripts of the tract. For ease of reference, I have emboldened two passages in the above quotations which may be easily compared. In both cases MS Harley 2322 not only preserves a more compact reading, but usually gives better sense, although MS BN F.Fr preserves a text closer to the source in Deuteronomy 11. So, for instance, the injunction to govern all one's thoughts and public and private members of one's household according to the bidding of God is rendered in the first version as an injunction to govern all one's private and public thoughts, words, and deeds according to the bidding of God, with the phrases 'with inne hous and wiþ oute' and 'in ech place' serving merely as qualifiers.

These examples are not unique: indeed, in the case of most differences between the B_2L_1 version and the other manuscripts it is possible to see the former as preserving better sense. It seems not impossible, then, that even from within this group of early Lollard manuscripts, B_2L_1 might preserve something akin to, for want of a better term, an original reading. Further evidence of the close relationship of these two manuscripts is to be seen in contents they preserve in common. MS Harley 2322 has a peculiar arrangement of the *Pore Caitif* tracts, beginning with the *Pater noster*, following with an interpolated tract on the *Ave Maria*, then the tracts on the creed and the commandments, a further interpolated Wycliffite tract ('Answeris to hem that seien We schulden not speke of holy writte'), and then the remaining tracts of the *Pore Caitif*. MS Add. B.66 is an incomplete volume, but in its extant prose contents it follows MS Harley 2322 exactly, breaking off partway through to the Wycliffite tract in defence of translation. The prose tracts in the volume are preceded by some folios of pious verses. It is quite clear that these texts had a pattern of circulating together, for a third copy of the *Ave* tract is to be found also in Oxford Bodleian Library MS Bodley 938, thus accounting for three of four copies.

At this point it is worth examining further the commandments tract in the *Pore Caitif* for signs of Wycliffite ideas or sympathies. The exposition of the commandments in the *Pore Caitif* conforms to certain patterns identified by A. L. Kellogg and E. W. Talbert as characteristically Wycliffite in their study of Middle English versions of the ten commandments. Extending this study, C. A. Martin later posited several rhetorical devices around which expositions of the ten commandments are frequently organised.[29] According to Martin's analysis, these treatises are to be found in three versions: rhetorical, discursive and mixed. In the rhetorical version, the statement of the commandment is usually followed by a list of breakers, sometimes structured around such a question as 'Who breaks this commandment?' This compactness is lost in the other versions where emphasis on the trinities of breakers is replaced by a more diffuse exposition of other points.[30]

Yet, the relationship between these different versions is fairly clear, as is the relationship of the ten commandments tract in the *Pore Caitif* with this general tradition of commentaries on the Decalogue. As an illustration, the discussion of the first command-ment in the Rylands treatise[31] (John Rylands Library, Eng MS 85) may be compared with the corresponding section of the *Pore Caitif* text. The particular similarities are highlighted in bold type.

> Who brekiþ þe first comaundement / proude men. Worldly men. And fleshly men // Whi proude men : for þei maken þe deuel her god. As Iob seiþ / **þe deuel is king vpon alle þe sones of pride** // Whi worldly men : for þei maken worldly goodis her god . as **Poul seiþ / an auarous man is a seruaunt of mawmetis** . . . Whi fleshly men: for þei **maken her wombe her god**. (Rylands Treatise)

> þus whanne man eiþir womman forsakiþ mekenes þat ihesu crist comaundiþ and heueþ him to hihenes and pride, makiþ þe feend his god **for he is king ouer alle proude folk**, as it is writen in þe book of Ioob. And so . . . þe couetous man and womman maken her god þese wordli goodis, for couetise is þe roote of alle yuelis and **seruise to mawmetis as to false goddis, as seint poul seiþ**. Glotouns and drunkelew folk **maken her wombe her god.** (Paris, BN MS Fonds anglais 41, f. 28r)

These similarities have also been noted by Judith Jefferson, who has studied the composition of these several commentaries on the Decalogue as part of her edition of some versions of het-erodox commentaries. Jefferson elaborates on Martin's categories by giving sub-types of each version: the commandments tract in the *Pore Caitif* is her Discursive Version VI (DVI).[32] Even in its orthodox version the *Pore Caitif* tract preserves numerous instances of verbatim parallels with the heterodox commentaries in Harley 2398 and Dublin, Trinity College MS 245 (Jefferson's B and T versions respectively). To take one instance, all three make use of an extract, ascribed to a 'grete clerke', from Wyclif's *De mandatis divinis* in their discussion of lechery in the sixth com-mandment, where the Christian man is enjoined to be Christ's coward in the face of this sin.[33] One further pertinent comparison may be made between the final section of the *Pore Caitif* tract, 'The Charge of the Heestis' discussed above, and the conclusion of another Wycliffite commentary on the commandments. The verbal correspondences between these two texts would suggest more than mere coincidence: rather, I am led to conclude that the commandments tract in the *Pore Caitif* has close affinities with other Wycliffite commentaries on the Decalogue. A part of the concluding section of 'The Charge of the Heestis', dealing with God's wrath on the breaker of the commandments, is reproduced here, first from MS Harley 2322, then the standard version from Paris MS BN 41, and finally the corresponding part of the Wycliffite commentary in MS Bodley 789.[34]

> if þou kepist not myn heestis, þou schalt be cursid in citee. Þou schalt be cursid in feeld. And cursid schal þi berne be and þin oþir relikis, cursid schal be þe fruit of þi body and þe fruit of þi lond þe droues of þin oxen, and þe flockis of þan scheep. Þou schalt be cursid goinge in and goinge out and god schal distrie þee, for þou hast forsaken hym for he schal smyte þee wiþ pestilence wiþ nedinesse wiþ feuere wiþ cold, with hete, wiþ corupt eir, and ᵇpursue ᵃschal ᶜþee til þat þou perische. (MS Harley 2322, f. 86v)

> if þou schalt not heere þe vois of þi lord god, þat þou kepe and do in deede his comaundementis, alle þese cursyngis schulen come on þee and take 'þee'. Þou schalt be cursid in citee, þou schalt be cursid in feeld, curside schal þi bern be and alle þin oþire relikis, cursid schal be þe fruyt of þi bodi and þe fruyt of þi lond, þe droues of þin oxen and þe flockis of þi scheep, cursid schalt þou be goinge in and 'cursid' goinge out. God schal bringe in upon þee hungir and blame in to alle þe werkis þat þou schalt do til to he distrie þee . . . And he schal smyte þee with nedynes with feuer, with coold, with heete, with corrupt eir, and he schal pursue þee til to þat þou peresche. (Paris, BN MS Fonds anglais 41, ff. 65v–66r)

> And hif þou kepist not þe comaundementis of God, as I have seide bifore to þe, cursid þou schalt be in feelde and in toun; cursyd be þi bernys, and cursid be þe fruyt of þi wombe, and þe fruyt of þin erþe, and of alle þi bestis, ingoynge and out-goynge. And þe Lorde schal sende upon þe hunger and blamynge in to alle þei werkis . . . And þou schalt have pestilence and fevere, cold, and brennynge hete, and corrupt aier.[35]

This passage comes from the earlier mentioned *Augustinus ad Iulianum comitem*, and is of some significance since this is where both this Wycliffite commentary and the B_2L_1 text of the commandments end. The reading of the standard version is once again prolix (so, for instance, the opening clauses: 'if þou schalt not heere þe vois of þi lord god : þat þou kepe *and* do in deede his comaundementis'), whereas the more compact B_2L_1 version preserves a text closer to that of the Wycliffite commentary. This pseudo-Augustinian text was popular in Wycliffite circles, and this correspondence may be read as further evidence in support of the theory that the compact B_2L_1 version may represent the earliest form of this tract in the *Pore Caitif*. In any case, what is obvious is that the compiler of the *Pore Caitif* had in front of him the same or a very similar translation of the pseudo-Agustinian text as the compiler of the Wycliffite commentary on the commandments.

It is possible to find other instances of the compiler of the *Pore Caitif* showing particular concern for matters dear to the heart of Wyclif's supporters. So, for instance, colourful rhetoric in the fifth commandment derived from Grosseteste inveighs against ill-gotten gains that deprive the poor of sustenance:

> and so he þat weeldiþ bi violence . . . haþ hondis defoulid with þe blood of pore men. And þilke þat eten and drinken of siche possessioun and cloþiþ him silf and bildiþ housis and wallis of sich possessioun etiþ and drinkiþ þe blood of pore men and is cloþid in þe blood of pore men and makiþ foundementis of his bilding in þe blood of pore men. (Paris, BN MS Fonds anglais 41, f. 48v)

Similarly, in the exposition of the seventh commandment, the warning against withholding the workman's wages is amplified in these manuscripts by the use of biblical references derived from the *Floretum*.

One could reasonably argue against the notion of the *Pore Caitif* as a Wycliffite text on a number of grounds. The sources, for example, are among the few available to the compiler in pre-*Constitutions* England, and would therefore have been used by the compiler regardless of affiliation. Yet, I find the evidence compelling enough to suggest that the *Pore Caitif* has its genesis in the early Wycliffite activity discussed earlier. A fruitful method of inquiry would be linguistic analysis of the early *Pore Caitif* manuscripts, which have generally not been analysed, and which might help in tying the text down to some regional Wycliffite activity. Certainly, the later manuscript tradition of extracts is too fragmented to provide any valuable information on these grounds; as early as 1400 we have evidence of the circulation of the treatise, probably in its constituent tracts, but within the Lollard group there is some evidence of a stemmatic relationship. The fragmentary nature of the later tradition might well arise from some attempt to conceal the contentious origins of the treatise, or from the circumstances of lay use.

Unlike manuscripts of the Wycliffite sermon cycles, those of the *Pore Caitif* were accessible to and often intended for the use of lay persons, thus increasing the incidence of extraction and fragmentation.[36] However, these early heterodox manuscripts do betray a concern with replicating closely the contents and presentation of the text, and militate strongly against any theory of random interpolations. This is not to suggest that they were produced in a Wycliffite scriptorium, although that possibility cannot be discounted, but rather that the origins of the *Pore Caitif* are closely associated with early Wycliffite activity.

The implications of this theory are many, and because of the nature and the popularity of the *Pore Caitif*, they reach far beyond the textual history of one religious manual. While these implications cannot be dealt with within the scope of this chapter, I will touch upon some of these issues by means of conclusion. Primarily, this theory complicates the debate about the circulation of religious material in English and what it means to write in the vernacular where the rigidities of orthodoxy and heterodoxy are difficult to maintain. Jefferson, for instance, counts the *Pore Caitif* tract among the sources for her mixed Discursive/Rhetorical Version I (DRI), although I think there is some room for debate about whether or not a version of the *Pore Caitif* commentary might predate her B and T versions.[37] The important issue here is the nexus between vernacular heresy and censorship, which has been the topic of much critical debate. The cleaned-up *Pore Caitif* seems not to have suffered much during the fifteenth century, and owners of Lollard manuscripts have even boldly written their names in their books. On the other hand, Simon Hunt, for instance, contends that 'an unhappy side-effect [of Arundel's legislations] is the high degree of reluctance shown by fifteenth-century owners [of contentious vernacular books] to put their names to the manuscripts'.[38] In this case, Thomas Roberts, the fifteenth-century owner of MS Harley 2322, was definitely begging to be burned, for he puts his name not only in bad Latin couplets at the end of the volume, but also at the top of the folio where each new tract begins. If Thomas Roberts was a Lollard sympathiser, then he was a confused one, for at the front of the volume is a crude image of Christ on the cross, very probably from his pen. The evidence of these early, heterodox manuscripts of the *Pore Caitif* must, then, make us reconsider any facile narrative of the issue of censorship in late fourteenth- and early fifteenth-century England.

Secondly, this study has also revealed interesting patterns of circulation for some other orthodox texts. For instance, fifteen manuscripts with all or part of the *Pore Caitif* also contain the *Mirror for Sinners* or the *Three Arrows of Doomsday* or both. Of the eight complete or substantially complete copies of the *Pore Caitif* among these fifteen, six are manuscripts studied here. In her analysis of the manuscripts of the *Mirror* and the *Three Arrows*, Jill Havens describes the close textual connections between the versions of those texts as found in the heterodox manuscript group of the *Pore Caitif*.[39] It stands to reason, then, that towards the end of the fifteenth century exemplars of the 'interpolated' *Pore Caitif* and the *Mirror* and the *Three Arrows* are circulating together. While I am not suggesting that the latter two texts are also Wycliffite in origin, can we posit Wycliffite interest in these on the grounds of their association with the *Pore Caitif*? It is probably this association that prompts the later addition of a booklet containing the *Mirror* and the *Three Arrows* to Cambridge, Trinity College MS B.14.53 in the fifteenth century. There is also the case of MS Bodley 938, which includes an orthodox *Pore Caitif* in an otherwise Wycliffite collection, with six Lollard tracts placed between the creed and the commandments. Is this because the text is recognised as being originally Wycliffite? It has been suggested that the scribe is aware that these tracts are apocryphal to the *Pore Caitif*, yet it is my belief that the rubrics which point this out are a later addition, rather in the manner of William Cotson's repeated rubric, *cave*, against the Lollard sentiments in CUL MS Ff.vi.55.[40] The scribe of Bodley 938 is also known to have copied an orthodox section in CUL MS Ff.vi.31, one of the 'comon profyt' books, among which is also found a copy of the *Pore Caitif*.

Derrick Pitard is undoubtedly correct when he states that manuscripts like Bodley 938 and CUL Ff.vi.31 help encourage vernacular literacy and interpretation precisely because of their mixture of Lollard and orthodox items. If the motive is an interest in education then the *Pore Caitif* evinces this quite well, straddling as it does the realms of both orthodoxy and heterodoxy. For instance, Lambeth Palace MS 541, an orthodox text, was owned by Thomas Eborall (d. 1471) a London cleric, who is mentioned in a note in Manchester, John Rylands MS Eng. 77, a later Wycliffite version of the New Testament, as having certified the book free of error.[41] The point I am trying to make by stacking up these examples is that our current perception of the divisions between orthodoxy and heterodoxy is top-heavy; these narratives are constructed from the perspective of Lollard trials and Arundel's and parliamentary legislation. The evidence of manuscripts, however, reveals a much more complicated, and at times confused picture. Indeed, as Cole notes, 'the major ecclesiastical and secular initiatives against Wycliffism did not succeed as planned', encouraging instead, in many instances, a great interest in vernacularity and 'experimentation in theology and literary form'.[42]

To conclude, I would like to return to the title of this paper as well as the prologue to the *Pore Caitif*. In the passage below, the compiler is very keen to stress the relevance of the Old Testament and the commandments to the plan of salvation and castigates those who would have it otherwise:

> ech man mai vndirstonde þat þer is noon oþir wey to heuene but bi kepinge of þese heestis. And . . . dispise he alle sofyms and argumentis of **false** flaterers and **heretikis**, þat boþe in werk and in word dispisen þese heestis [. . .] So þese men confusid in inwit, aheinstonden **trewe teching** þoru þe which goddis peple schulde be delyuerid. (Paris, BN MS Fonds anglais 41, f. 24r–v)

These sentiments are not far removed from those of Wyclif in the following passages.

> *Cum autem sint viginti duo libri veteris testamenti, quos eciam Hebrii cum Cristianis accipiunt, quid moveret sophistam contendere quod illi libri non sunt scriptura sacra?* (*De veritate sacre scripture*, I, 218/4–6)

> *Cristus enim non dat pictaciam legi reprobe quante autem Cristus approbat legem veterem, patet Matth. quinto.* (*De veritate sacre scripture*, I, 221/6–8)

> *Ad primum suppono ex fide quod Christus instituit unam legem, que est Vetus et Novum Testamentum ad ecclesiam catholicam regulandum.* (*De civili dominio*, 118/27–9)[43]

From the evidence presented here, it would seem that the *Pore Caitif* is connected with the literary activities of the early Wycliffite movement, from a time before Wyclif's ideas were subsumed into the invention of Lollardy by ecclesiastical authorities. Studies of Wycliffite literary activity have illuminated much of the modes and significance of the biblical scholarship, theology and politics of the movement; we still do not know much, however, about the devotional practices of the Wycliffites. Surely, their theology, which comprises the desire to communicate with a lay, English-speaking audience, would have necessitated covering material from the Peckhamite syllabus, expounded with references to authorities they held dear; this is precisely the nature of the *Pore Caitif*, whose early manuscripts, as we have seen, are in the format of priests' books. This compendium must grow from the exigencies of such Wycliffite activity, and it is to be hoped that further research into the early textual history of the *Pore Caitif* and other texts related to it will help to establish these matters more clearly. Wyclif's political and theological failure did not come until after his publication of *De Eucharistia* after 1379, in circumstances described by Wilks as a combination of 'indescribable folly and . . . appalling bad luck'.[44] If indeed the *Pore Caitif* was composed in part or whole before this time in the circumstances I have been outlining, its author need have feared no censure, nor would he have felt an overwhelming urge to define his positions with any degree of niceness.

Notes

Several people have read drafts of this chapter, thanks to which it is greatly improved. I must record my particular gratitude to Andrew Cole, with whom I have discussed these topics in great detail, and whose many suggestions have proved invaluable in the writing of this essay.

1　These and other papers can be found in *Lollards and their Books* (London: Hambledon Press, 1985).

2　Anne Hudson, 'Some problems of identity and identification in Wycliffite writings', in *Middle English Prose: Essays on Bibliographical Problems*, ed. A. S. G. Edwards and D. Pearsall (London: Garland, 1981), pp. 81–90 (81).

3　Michael Wilks, 'Misleading manuscripts: Wyclif and the non-Wycliffite Bible', in *The Materials, Sources, and Methods of Ecclesiastical History*, ed. Derek Baker, *Studies in Church History*, *Subsidia* 11 (1975), 147–61.

4　Hudson, 'Some problems of identity', p. 81.

5　See, for instance, the numerous entries in the Harley catalogues of the British Museum or the Quarto catalogues of the Bodleian Library that ascribe the *Pore Caitif* to Wyclif, and the plethora of texts ascribed to Rolle by Horstmann. The first printed version of this treatise, for instance, was produced in 1831 by the Religious Tracts Society as part of an edition of the works of John Wyclif.

6　Sr. M. T. Brady, 'The Lollard sources of the *Pore Caitif*', *Traditio* 44 (1988), 389–419 (389, n. 1).

7　Brady, 'Lollard sources', 389 n.1. and '*The Pore Caitif*: an introductory study', *Traditio* 10 (1954), 529–48. As this material has been dealt with by Sr. Brady elsewhere it is not of value to dwell upon it in this chapter. Where I have any additions or refinements to make they are included with the appropriate argument.

8 For more details, see Brady, 'Lollard sources', *passim*.

9 To term these manuscripts 'Lollard' is obviously problematic. 'Manuscripts containing some unorthodox material' is probably the most accurate descriptor; for the purposes of brevity and clarity, however, the following manuscripts, which are the object of this study, are usually referred to as 'Lollard' manuscripts: Oxford, Bodleian Library, MS Bodley 3 (B); Oxford, Bodleian Library, MS Bodley 938 (B_1); Oxford, Bodleian Library, MS Additional B. 66 (B_2); Cambridge, Trinity College, MS B.14.53 (C); Cambridge, University Library, MS Ff.vi.55 (C_1); London, British Library, MS Add. 30897 (L); London, British Library, MS Harley 2322 (L_1); London, Lambeth Palace, MS 484 (La); Glasgow, Hunterian Museum MS 496 (G_1); Glasgow, Hunterian Museum MS 520 (G_2); New York, Public Library, MS De Ricci 68 (N). There are two manuscripts containing unorthodox material that I have not considered for this paper: viz., London, Westminster School MS 3 and Colchester and the Essex Museum MS. Manchester, John Rylands Library MS Eng. 85 is only touched upon incidentally. The rationale behind this has been to investigate in the first instance volumes which contain either complete texts or substantially complete texts including the major tracts on the creed, the ten commandments and the *Pater Noster*, as much of the debatable material occurs in the earlier part of the treatise, or manuscripts which are fairly early in date. A manuscript that is not usually associated with this unorthodox tradition, Oxford, Bodleian Library, MS Lyell 29 (B_3), is, however, included here as it offers some interesting evidence. Corresponding evidence from an orthodox version of the treatise is usually supplied from London, British Library MS Harley 2336 (the base text of Sr. Brady's edition), or Paris, BN MS Fonds anglais 41. The *sigla* supplied here are not generally used in this essay except in the section dealing with some textual comparisons where the discussion would be encumbered otherwise. I have particular occasion to refer to the group B_2L_1, made up of MSS BL Harley 2322 and Bodleian Library Add. B.66, which offers some important evidence.

10 On this see Trivedi, '*Lectio* through *Compilatio*: some manuscripts of the *Pore Caitif*', in *Framing the Text: Reading Tradition and Image in Medieval Europe*, ed. K. L. Boardman, C. Emerson and A.P. Tudor, *Mediaevalia* 20 (2001), 127–50. The definitive order established by Sr. Brady consists of fourteen tracts, excluding the prologue, in the following order: The Creed, The Prologue on the Commandments, The Commandments, The Prologue on the *Pater Noster*, The *Pater Noster*, The Counsel of Christ, Of Virtuous Patience, Of Temptation, the Charter of Heaven, Of Ghostly Battle, The Name of Jesus, The Love of Jesus, Of Meekness, The Effect of Will, Active and Contemplative Life, The Mirror of Chastity. This order is represented by, among others, Cambridge, Trinity College, MS B.14.53, a heterodox copy.

M. T. Brady, '*The Pore Caitif*, edited from MS Harley 2336 with introduction and notes', unpub. PhD thesis, Fordham University, 1954, xlvi–xlvii.

11 These and other instances are detailed by Sr. Brady, 'Lollard interpolations and omissions in manuscripts of *The Pore Caitif*', in *De Cella in Seculum: Religious and Secular Life in Late Medieval England*, ed. M. Sargent (Cambridge: D. S. Brewer, 1989), pp. 183–203.

12 Anne Hudson, 'Lollard book-production', in *Book Production and Publishing in Britain, 1375–1475*, ed. Jeremy Griffiths and Derek Pearsall (Cambridge: Cambridge University Press, 1989), pp. 125–42 (136).

13 Anne Hudson, *The Premature Reformation: Wycliffite Texts and Lollard History* (Oxford: Clarendon Press, 1988), p. 119.

14 Hudson, *Premature Reformation*, p. 394.

15 See, for instance, Hudson, *Premature Reformation*, p. 2: 'Whatever the origin of the term . . . its first recorded use in England . . . occurred in 1382'; see also Ralph Hanna, 'Emendation to a 1993 "Vita de Ne'erdowel"', *Yearbook of Langland Studies* 14 (2000), 185–98: '[the word's] prominence within religious discourse is datable from late Spring 1382, when an Oxford don was censured for insulting some of his fellows as *Lollardi*' (190). The entry in the *Fasciculi Zizaniorum* mentioning Crumpe is dated between 1393 and 1399 (see James Crompton, '*Fasciculi Zizaniorum* I & II', *Journal of Ecclesiastical History* 12 (1964), 35–45, 155–6 (163–4)).

16 Kantik Ghosh, *The Wycliffite Heresy: Authority and the Interpretation of Texts*, Cambridge Studies in Medieval Literature 45 (Cambridge: Cambridge University Press, 2002); Rita Copeland, *Pedagogy, Intellectuals, and Dissent in the Later Middle Ages: Lollardy and Ideas of Learning*, Cambridge Studies in Medieval Literature 44 (Cambridge: Cambridge University Press, 2001). Ghosh, for instance, does not speak of 'Lollards' when opposing a known Wycliffite to a known orthodox figure (as in chs 1 and 2), but by the time he discusses Nicholas Love (ch. 5), he now speaks of an undifferentiated mass of 'Lollard' heretics. See also the grouping together of 'Wyclif and the Lollards' in the introduction (p. 5).

17 Andrew Cole, *Literature and Heresy in the Age of Chaucer*, Cambridge Studies in Medieval Literature 71 (Cambridge: Cambridge University Press, 2008), p. 31; see also his 'William Langland and the invention of Lollardy', in *Lollards and their Influence in Late-Medieval England*, ed. Fiona Somerset, Jill C. Havens and Derrick Pitard (Cambridge: D. S. Brewer, 2003), pp. 37–58 (43).

18 Ghosh, *The Wycliffite Heresy*; Cole, *Literature and Heresy*; Fiona Somerset, *Clerical Discourse and Lay Audience in Late Medieval England*, Cambridge Studies in Medieval Literature 37 (Cambridge: Cambridge University Press, 1998).

19 Brady, 'Lollard sources', 409–11.

20 S. L. Fristedt, *The Wycliffe Bible*, 2 vols. (Stockholm: Almqvist & Wiksell, 1953–70) 2: xlviii–xlix, lxiii–lxiv; David C. Fowler, 'John Trevisa and the English Bible', *Modern Philology* 58 (1996), 81–98; J. Forshall and F. Madden, *The Holy Bible, Containing the Old and New Testaments . . . Made from the Latin Vulgate by John Wycliffe and His Followers*, 4 vols. (Oxford: Oxford University Press, 1850), 1: xvi–xvii; Hudson, *The Premature Reformation*, p. 247. Ian R. Johnson states that 'work on [the Wycliffite Bible] probably began in Oxford during the 1380s' and dates the *General Prologue* to the 1390s, which is commonly held to have been composed after the completion of the *Late Version*. See '*The General Prologue to the Wycliffite Bible*: chapter 12 (extract)', in *The Idea of the Vernacular: An Anthology of Middle English Literary Theory, 1280–1520*, ed. Jocelyn Wogan-Browne, Nicholas Watson, Andrew Taylor and Ruth Evans (Exeter: University of Exeter Press, 1999), pp. 91–5 (91). Wilks goes so far as to suggest that a version of even the New Testament was available by 1382; 'misleading manuscripts', 154–5.

21 Anne Hudson, 'A Lollard compilation and the dissemination of Wycliffite thought', *Journal of Theological Studies* n.s. 23 (1972), 65–81 (73, 75); *Selections from English Wycliffite Writings* (Cambridge: Cambridge University Press, 1978), pp. 167–8; *The Premature Reformation*, pp. 14, 16.

22 Wilks, 'Misleading manuscripts', p. 160.

23 The English text of the commandments is underlined in red and the rubrics, presented in bold text here, are copied in red. The punctuation and capitalisation have been modernised and standard abbreviations are expanded silently in all quotations from manuscripts.

24 The orthodox manuscripts too are coherent in their own way, textually, but incoherent codicologically.

25 The case of this 'interpolation' and several others is discussed in Brady, 'Lollard interpolations and omissions', pp. 183–203. I do not discuss the actual passages here, but am interested only in how different manuscripts of this group agree or disagree in their readings.

26 Oxford, Bodleian Library MS Ashmole 1286, f. 45vᵃ.

27 See Brady, 'The apostles and the creed in manuscripts of *The Pore Caitif*', *Speculum* 32 (1957), 323–5.

28 Paris, BN MS Fonds anglais 41, f. 64r; f. 67r; f. 70r.

29 A. L. Kellogg and E. W. Talbert, 'The Wycliffite *Pater Noster* and *Ten Commandments* with special reference to English MSS 85 and 90 in the John Rylands Library', *Bulletin of the John Rylands Library* 42 (1960), 345–77; C. A. Martin, 'The Middle English versions of *The Ten Commandments*, with special reference to Rylands English MS 85', *Bulletin of the John Rylands Library* 64 (1981–2), 191–217.

30 Martin, 'The Middle English versions', 202–11.

31 All quotations from the edition in Kellogg and Talbert, 'The Wycliffite *Pater Noster* and *Ten Commandments*'; I preserve their punctuation.

32 Judith Anne Jefferson, 'An edition of the Ten Commandments Commentary in BL Harley 2398 and the related version in Trinity College Dublin, 245, York Minster XVI.L.12, and Harvard English 738 together with discussion of related commentaries', unpub. PhD thesis, University of Bristol, 1995, pp. cxxx–cxciii (clxxix–clxxxi).

33 'and þerfor seiþ a greet clerk, þat in þis synne, a man moste speciali be goddis coward and fle fro occasioun þat moueþ to þis synne and triste not to strenkþe, to witt, ne to wisdom. For what man was strengir þan Sampson? Who was wittier þan Dauiþ and who was wiser þan Salamon his sone? And þese þre weren brennyd wiþ þe fier of leccherie. And þerfore who þat wole be goddis clene child fle he as goddis coward alle occasiouns and cumpanyes þat mouen to þis synne' (Paris BN MS 41, f. 51v; *cf.*, Jefferson, T117/1–118/6 and B11712–118/8).

34 This is printed in *Select English Works of John Wyclif*, ed. Thomas Arnold, vol. 3, *Miscellaneous Works* (Oxford: Clarendon Press, 1871), pp. 82–92. All quotations are from this edition.

35 Arnold, *Select English Works*, 3: 91.

36 For a detailed analysis of some instances of lay use, see Trivedi, '*Lectio* through *compilatio*', 136–42.

37 See Jefferson, 'An edition of the Ten Commandments Commentary', cxciii, clxxix–clxxxi.

38 Simon Hunt, 'An edition of tracts in favour of scriptural translation and of some texts connected with Lollard vernacular biblical scholarship', unpub. PhD thesis, University of Oxford, 1994, p. 39.

39 Jill Havens, 'Instruction, devotion, meditation, sermon: a critical edition of selected English religious texts in Oxford, University College 97, with a codicological examination of some related manuscripts', unpub. PhD thesis, University of Oxford, 1995, pp. 317–19 and 440–5.

40 The rubrics in this part of Bodley 938 are either filled in black ink and underlined in red or the space is left empty. The rubrics noting the disorder in the *Pore Caitif* tracts are the only ones to be copied in red, besides which there are certain differences in script. It is therefore, in my opinion, the work of either a corrector or a later owner. I presented a fuller examination of this manuscript at Kalamazoo 2002 and I hope to publish the findings in the near future.

41 On Eborall, see A. B. Emden, *A Biographical Register of the University of Oxford to AD 1500*, vol. 1 (Oxford: Clarendon Press, 1957), pp. 622–3. The note is printed by N. R. Ker, *Medieval Manuscripts in British Libraries*, vol. 3 (Oxford: Oxford University Press, 1969–83), p. 404.

42 Cole, *Literature and Heresy*, p. xvi.

43 R. Buddensieg, (ed.) *De veritate Sacrae Scripturae*, 3 vols. (London: Trübner for the Wyclif Society, 1905–7); R. L. Poole (ed.), *Iohannis Wycliffe Tractatus de Civili Dominio*, 4 vols. (London: Wyclif Society, 1884).

44 Michael Wilks, '*Reformatio Regni*: Wycliff and Hus as leaders of religious protest movements', *Studies in Church History* 9 (1972), 109–30 (110).

9

A life's work: John Anderson and the *Gawain*-poet

Ralph Elliott

On 11 July 1979 John Anderson wrote to me from Manchester: 'I think you are absolutely right that there is something distinctive in the *Gawain*-poet's evocation of the world of nature, particularly in his landscapes.' John was right, but as he has clearly demonstrated in his editions and in his splendid, comprehensive volume, *Language and imagination in the* Gawain-*poems*,[1] there is a good deal more that is distinctive in the four poems that have happily survived in London, British Library, MS Cotton Nero A.x. This is not the place to enter into a critical appreciation of Anderson's contribution to our understanding of the *Gawain*-poems. Other scholars have done so and will continue to do so. If I confine myself to the poet's evocation of the world of nature, especially his landscapes, it is because Anderson himself, in the letter quoted above, recognised my own long-lasting preoccupation with these particular aspects of the four *Gawain*-poems.

It all began quite a few years earlier when Anderson arrived at the University of Adelaide in the early 1960s to undertake postgraduate studies under my supervision, which led to an edition of the shortest of the four poems in Cotton Nero A.x, *Patience*. He came from his native New Zealand where his own appreciation of the natural environment had no doubt been nurtured by the varied beauties of that country's islands. I have myself lasting memories of the bright green pastures full of playful lambs in the North Island as well as the enthralling grandeur of the mountains and waters of Milford Sound in the South Island. When Anderson joined me in Adelaide I had not yet visited New Zealand, but the bond which thenceforth united us was our shared interest in the *Gawain*-poet and his four remarkable poems.

My own interest in these poems and in the poet's evocation of the world of nature owed much to my teacher and and later colleague at the University of St Andrews, James Parker Oakden, whose two massive volumes of *Alliterative Poetry in Middle English*, published respectively in 1930 and 1935, dealt with 'The Dialectal and Metrical Survey' and with 'A Survey of the Traditions'. Both were rightly hailed as 'most important contributions to Middle English scholars', and it was at Oakden's instigation that my own first venture into Middle English scholarship was published in 1951.[2] That this article focused on *Pearl*, the first of the four poems in Cotton Nero A.x, and on the poem's natural settings, was an unexpected anticipation of my future interest in these aspects of the poet's work. The fact that Dr Oakden was born near Leek, the little town in the north Staffordshire countryside which future research would associate with the *Gawain*-poet, added an almost prophetic touch to our scholarly relationship.

The last sentence in Anderson's introduction to his own first venture into the *Gawain*-poems, the brief but helpful discussion of dialect in his edition of *Patience*, provided an early indication of the region to be associated with the poet: 'Such evidence as has been considered suggests the area of South-East Lancashire, East Cheshire, North Staffordshire, and West Derbyshire, and is fully in accord with the conclusion of A. McIntosh that *Sir Gawain* is to be assigned to South-East Cheshire or North-East Staffordshire'.[3]

Patience, the third poem in the manuscript, is the shortest of the four but it nevertheless exhibits a few indications of the poet's interest in nature and environment. Admittedly, the inside of the whale where Jonah finds himself was not an environment familiar to the poet, but as the whale is about to swallow 'Jonas þe jwe', it swings and sweeps to the bottom, 'Bi mony rokkeȝ ful roȝe and rydelande strondes', a glimpse of the natural environment in the biblical story which resonates strikingly with depictions in the other three poems (245, 254).

Anderson's next tribute to the *Gawain*-poet is his excellent edition of the second of the poems, *Cleanness*, published in 1977, by which time Anderson was well established in the English Department of the University of Manchester.[4] This poem had also been edited as a doctoral dissertation many years earlier by Robert J. Menner, published by Yale University Press in 1920 under the title *Purity*, and reprinted in an unaltered and unabridged edition by Archon Books in 1970. There were other editions as well as the facsimile of the manuscript which Anderson acknowledged in his preface, adding, 'at the same time I have tried to look at every problem afresh'. And so he did.

Whereas *Patience* offers only a glimpse or two at the natural environment of Jonah, *Cleanness* revels in the absorbing detail of the impact of the biblical flood on the natural environment of the world. Here, perhaps for the first time in his work, the *Gawain*-poet enjoys free rein to describe the world in all its manifestations. In the manuscript *Pearl* precedes *Cleanness*, but in *Pearl* the opening garden is deliberately sketched only briefly, while the stream and the heavenly city are visions endowed with dreamlike adornment, a far cry from the natural world facing destruction by the waters of the flood in *Cleanness*. Here the poet's vocabulary revels in descriptive words anticipating the richness and diversity of his vocabulary in the descriptions of Sir Gawain's journey and his host's hunting exploits in *Sir Gawain and the Green Knight*. Even hares and harts and bucks and badgers receive a brief mention in *Cleanness* (391–2), a foretaste of the hunt at Hautdesert.

The garden in the opening stanzas of *Pearl* is a solemn place, appropriately given the speaker's loss, but it is rich in spices, notably the gillyflower and ginger as well as the peonies scattered among them, while gromylyoun attracted bees and bees meant honey. One is reminded of monastery gardens, such as the poet may well have been familiar with. Could this be another pointer to the *Gawain*-poet's identity? It does confirm Anderson's suggestion of 'something distinctive' in the poet's natural settings. That this applies particularly to the landscapes in *Sir Gawain and the Green Knight* seems incontrovertible. Here we are led to actual places, as Sir Gawain travels from north Wales across the Dee into the Wirral and thence into the nearest hilly country, where the knight finds himself 'not two myle henne' from the Green Chapel which he is seeking.

That such a place exists and is closely associated with the crossing of the Dee suggests the poet's own familiarity with the countryside he describes. This is especially evident in the lively pictures of the landscapes of the three hunts in the poem, as well as the approach to the Green Chapel. The topographical words used in the other three poems now recur in abundance: 'the depe slades', 'bonkkes' and 'klyffes' seen in the deer hunt; the 'ker syde', 'the rocherez', 'a flosche in that fryth and a foo cragge', 'the knarre and the knot' in the boar hunt; 'a holt syde / [where] Rocheres roungen bi rys', 'a strothe rande', 'the wode', 'the clamberande clyffes', 'the mountes' in the fox hunt. Rocky hills and valleys, fields and hedges, streams and marshes: it is a wild, varied landscape where to this day words the poet uses survive in place names, like the Roaches, Knotbury, Knar Farm, Flash, Wildboarclough, all within the hilly countryside where the counties of Staffordshire, Cheshire and Derbyshire meet at the Three Shire Head.

That the 'two myle' from castle Hautdesert to the Green Chapel can also be travelled today suggests 'something distinctive' in the poet's evocation of the natural world to which Anderson referred. It is just two miles from the site of the grange of the Cistercian abbey of Dieulacres, which began life at the river Dee, and in more recent times became the manor of Swythamley Park, to what Sir Gawain aptly describes as 'the corsedest kyrk that ever I com inne', the strange, huge rock fissure of Ludchurch, a refuge for Lollards in the poet's own time. Having travelled in the footsteps of Sir Gawain, I can testify to the poet's remarkable ability to describe the world of nature, especially the landscapes which figure so memorably in his poetry.[5]

But more important than personal searches is the realisation that towards the end of the fourteenth century, the century dominated by one of England's foremost poets, Geoffrey Chaucer, there was another poet writing in the English north-west midlands in the old alliterative tradition, who continues to attract our study and our admiration. John Anderson's lifelong study of this poet's works deserves our admiration and our thanks. 'Hony soyt qui mal pence', as it says at the end of *Sir Gawain in the Green Knight* in the Cotton manuscript. So be it.

Notes

1 J. J. Anderson, *Language and imagination in the* Gawain–*poems*, Manchester: Manchester University Press, 2005. In 1976 Anderson wrote to me: 'I have long had in mind a critical book on the poems of the Gawain-group. I'm particularly interested in the complex of religious ideas which I think lies behind all four poems.'

2 R. W. V. Elliott, 'Pearl and the medieval garden: convention or originality?', *Les Langues modernes* 45 (1951), 84–98.

3 J. J. Anderson (ed.), *Patience* (Manchester: Manchester University Press, 1969), p. 23.

4 J. J. Anderson (ed.), *Cleanness* (Manchester: Manchester University Press, 1977).

5 See R. W. V. Elliott, 'Searching for the Green Chapel', in Jan Lloyd-Jones and Julian Lamb (eds.), *Art and Authenticity* (Melbourne: Australian Scholarly Publishing, 2009).

John Julian Anderson: colleague and friend

Alan Shelston

My friend and colleague, John Anderson, was one of a number of antipodean scholars who came to Britain in the post-war period. Many of them were classicists or, like John, scholars of early English. John was also a good Latinist who had in fact begun his university studies in the field of law, before transferring to English. His precision of mind in the field he finally adopted reflected these earlier interests.

Born in Dunedin in 1938, John graduated in 1960 from the University of Otago, where he was Walter Scott Scholar in English. He then left New Zealand to take up a tutorship at the University of Adelaide, taking his PhD there in 1966 with an edition of *Patience*, published in 1969 by Manchester University Press. It was a text to which he was to return at various times in his academic career. After teaching in the universities of both Adelaide and Sydney, he came to England in 1968 for a sabbatical period as the beneficiary of an Eleanor Sophia Wood Travelling Fellowship and he remained here for the rest of his career. John worked at the University of Leeds with Professor A. C. Cawley, described by John as 'my mentor and friend', on the revision of Cawley's 1962 edition of *Pearl* and *Sir Gawain and the Green Knight* for the Everyman's Library series. To this edition, John added *Cleanness* and *Patience*, thus making available the complete corpus of the *Gawain*-poems in one volume. The work was published in 1976 and would be completely revised some twenty years later.

John was appointed as Lecturer in English Language at the University of Manchester in September 1968. In those days at Manchester lecturers on what was called 'the language side' were expected to teach the language and literature of the Anglo-Saxon, Middle English and Early English periods and while John's work became centred in the later periods he retained his interests in Anglo-Saxon, and notably in *Beowulf*. His research took him increasingly towards early English drama and he became UK development officer and a member of the editorial advisory board for the Records of Early English Drama series (REED), a major international project initiated in Toronto under the leadership of Dr (now Professor) Alexandra Johnston. This wide-ranging project, still ongoing, aimed at a comprehensive printing of all records of early English (and Welsh) dramatic texts and performance up to the closing of the theatres in 1642. John's contribution, devoted to the records of Newcastle-upon-Tyne, was the fourth volume to appear, after the volumes dealing with the great cycles of York, Chester and Coventry. It was important for the very fact that it was not concerned with one of the major cycle towns; it was the first investigation of a little-known collection of material, which centred on the existence of a Corpus Christi play represented by a single pageant, the Newcastle *Noah*, surviving only in a scrappy eighteenth-century copy. It was thus a formative element in the development of the series, suggesting for later volumes problems that might arise and possible solutions, and revealing more out-of-the-way dramatic manifestations. The series now numbers thirty-one volumes and includes the records of counties as well as towns and cities; a record of success which is at least in part due to the remarkable base created by the early volumes. John's interest in the drama was extensive; he was a familiar figure at conferences and in 1971 he published a substantial article on *Love's Labour's Lost* in *Shakespeare Survey*. Many more articles and conference papers on the history of early drama were to follow.

John was not one to see research as exclusively an activity for tenured academics. In 1986 he was instrumental in setting up an interdisciplinary Faculty of Arts MA in Medieval Literature at Manchester. In 1997, together with his colleague Carole Weinberg, he instigated a specialist MA in Middle English Studies, one of the first of its kind in Britain, making use of the extensive collection of Middle English manuscripts in the John Rylands University Library of Manchester. Such was the success of this course that papers by four of the first intake of students were published in the *Bulletin of the John Rylands Library* (vol. 74, 2000). Later, some of John's PhD students were to gain academic appointments in universities in Britain and overseas. Another of his effective initiatives resulted in the Manchester Middle English Seminar, which brought together students and staff, with input from distinguished visiting speakers; again the presence of students was a stepping stone for them towards projects of their own, and they were able to develop a sense of research as a corporate activity in the best sense of the word. John was also heavily involved in conferences and events at other universities, while in his own university he played an important role, with Professor Donald Scragg, in the various G. L. Brook symposia, instituted for the support of Early English studies.

Without prejudice to his enthusiasm for the drama, John moved back towards poetry in his later work, and in particular to the challenging subject of the long poem, with conference papers and articles on the works of the *Gawain*-poet, on Chaucer and on Langland. His revision of the Everyman edition of the poems of the *Gawain*-poet, updating the scholarship, was published in 1996. With John's usual generosity it carried a tribute to his Middle English colleagues, amongst them Ray Barron and Gale Owen-Crocker but especially Joy Anderson, his wife, herself a long-standing contributor to a very strong Manchester Middle English team. All this led the way towards John's comprehensive study, *Language and imagination in the* Gawain-*poems* (Manchester, 2005). This major critical work initiated the Manchester Medieval Literature series of which, with Gail Ashton, John was the joint series editor: it is thus absolutely appropriate that the present volume should be dedicated to his memory. John had long planned a book on Langland, a poet whose complexity fascinated him, but sadly it remained incomplete at the time of his death. At the point of retirement he was still devising courses to engage with the new mindset, but if his 'Monstrosity' MA course was perhaps planned to appeal to a new generation, it still began with *Beowulf*.

John was, as I have suggested, a committed teacher and colleague, and as an external examiner he was much in demand. As a teacher he operated at all levels from first-year undergraduate to PhD and he brought to all his classes equal thoroughness of input, stimulating the interests of generations of students in medieval studies. It was not at all unusual to call at his office at lunchtime, only to find that a long queue of students had got there before you. His students learnt the rewards of enquiry; they learnt also the patience that was necessary for enquiry to be successful.

In the first paragraph of the preface to his initiating volume of the Manchester Medieval Literature series John wrote, 'I have made reader-friendliness a high priority and so where possible have avoided critical jargon and technical language'. At the conclusion of the introduction he insists of the poet that 'the reader who does *not* read him closely, down to the individual word, must miss important meaning'. Both statements are typical of John, and their implications extended beyond his literary work. John served on a number of faculty and department committees where his approach was always meticulous; he could be very firm when something that mattered to him was at stake. I often felt that the New Zealand Presbyterian conscience lay behind much of what John said and did; throughout his years in England he remained in close contact with his home country. At Manchester, as elsewhere in the university world, John had many long-standing friends and colleagues. It is our cause for regret that he left us when he still had so much to do, and when we might have had time and space to enjoy his company – and his learning – all the more.

Index

In Memory of J. J. Anderson

Christopher Abbott
David Alderson, University of Manchester
Julia Boffey, Queen Mary, University of London
Tom Burton, University of Adelaide
John V. Fleming, Princeton University
John M. Ganim, University of California
Alfred Hiatt, Queen Mary University of London
Chris McCully, Rijksuniversiteit Groningen
Jenna Mead, University of Western Australia
Carol M. Meale, University of Bristol
Ad Putter, University of Bristol
Susan Rastetter-Gies, Hochschule Aschaffenburg/University of
Applied Sciences, Aschaffenburg
Margaret Rogerson, University of Sydney
Sarah Salih, King's College London
Don Scragg, University of Manchester
Leah Scragg, University of Manchester
Allen Shoaf, University of Florida
Toshiyuki Takamiya, Keio University
Ronald Waldron, King's College London
Lawrence Warner, University of Sydney